THE
THINKING
HEART

OTHER ESSAYS FROM QUARRY PRESS

Quiet Voices: Diverse Essays & Stories from The Whig-Standard Magazine
Edited by ROGER BAINBRIDGE

In Defence of Art: Critical Essays & Reviews
by LOUIS DUDEK

The Crowded Darkness
by DOUGLAS FETHERLING

Letters from Managua: Meditations on Politics & Art
by GARY GEDDES

Powers of Observation
by GEORGE WOODCOCK

THE THINKING HEART

Best Canadian Essays

EDITED BY
George Galt

Quarry Press

The publisher acknowledges the financial assistance of The Canada Council and the Ontario Arts Council.

Canadian Cataloguing in Publication Data

Main entry under title:
The Thinking heart

(Best Canadian essays)
ISBN 1-55082-033-8

1. Canadian essays (English). I. Galt, George, 1938-
II. Series: Best Canadian essays (Kingston, Ont.).

PS8373.T44 1991 C814'.54 C91-090438-3
PR9197.7.T44 1991

Cover art by Jack Shadbolt entitled "Northern Elegy" reproduced by permission of the artist.
Design by Keith Abraham.
Type imaging by Queen's University Imagesetting Services.
Printed and bound in Canada by Hignell Printing, Winnipeg, Manitoba.

Published by **Quarry Press, Inc.,** P.O. Box 1061, Kingston, Ontario K7L 4Y5 and P.O. Box 348, Clayton, New York 13624.

CONTENTS

Introduction by George Galt

1. Margaret Atwood
    IF YOU CAN'T SAY SOMETHING NICE,
    DON'T SAY ANYTHING AT ALL 13

2. Peter Behrens
    REFUGEE DREAMS 25

3. Clark Blaise
    THE BORDER AS FICTION 31

4. Rose Borris with Paulette Jiles
    AT A LOSS FOR WORDS 43

5. Sharon Butala
    FIELD OF BROKEN DREAMS 57

6. Dalton Camp
    THE PLOT TO KILL CANADA 69

7. Denise Chong
    THE CONCUBINE'S CHILDREN 87

8. Ann Diamond
    ZEN IN AMERICA 105

9. Moira Farr
    WOMEN AND WANDERLUST 117

10. Don Gillmor
    CLUES 125

11. Hugh Graham
    LIFE AND DEATH IN ONTARIO COUNTY 131

12. Ernest Hillen
    BACK ON JAVA 139

13. Michael Ignatieff
    AUGUST IN MY FATHER'S HOUSE 149

14. Marni Jackson
    GALS AND DOLLS: THE MORAL VALUE OF BAD TOYS 161

15. M.T. Kelly
    THE LAND BEFORE TIME 165

16. Myrna Kostash
    PENS OF MANY COLORS 175

17. David Macfarlane
    LOVE AND DEATH 181

18. Joyce Marshall
    REMEMBERING GABRIELLE ROY 189

19. Joyce Nelson
    THE SAGA OF SPACE DORKS:
    TECHNOPHILIC FLYING BOYS FROM PLANET EARTH 199

20. David Olive
    CONRAD BLACK WRIT LARGE 205

21. Stephen Phelps
    BE STILL, MY TEENY-BOPPER HEART 213

22. Jane Rule
    DECEPTION IN THE SEARCH FOR TRUTH 219

23. Rick Salutin
    BRIAN AND THE BOYS 223

24. Audrey Thomas
    PERIL BY THE LAKE 235

25. William Thorsell
    LET US COMPARE MYTHOLOGIES 243

Notes on the Authors

Acknowledgements

INTRODUCTION

Intelligent and troubling, an illumination and a goad, the well wrought essay can inform, console, provoke, demystify, and entertain. Why, then, was it in eclipse not so long ago, overshadowed by what we called in North America "the new journalism"? Perhaps because for so many adult readers the idea of an essay — *any* essay — could call up a particular childhood dread and its associated escape fantasies. In the 1950s and 1960s, when I was in school, an essay meant a chore. It was either some dense chunk of antiquarian literature written by a long-dead Englishman which you had to read, annotate, and paraphrase in your own piece of "English composition"; or it was an assignment that could, and very often did, cloud your weekend: the little piece of prose of your own making that had to be handed in, letter perfect, on Monday morning. Mention the word "essay," and many of us instinctively wanted to reach for a comic book, just to spite Charles Lamb and William Hazlitt who haunted our classrooms with their boring, windbag treatises.

Much later, I came to understand the virtues of Lamb and Hazlitt, Addison and Steele, Carlyle and Arnold. But it wasn't a resurgence of interest in the literary old masters that revived the essay. You don't have to blow the dust off the old books to find eloquent, insightful pieces of non-fiction. Artful essays now appear in many good magazines in Canada, Great Britain, and the United States, and the best Canadian non-fiction periodical writers create literature as important for our time and place as was the work of the old English and American essayists for theirs.

Thoughtful Canadian magazines — *Saturday Night, This Magazine, The Idler, The Canadian Forum*, among others — also publish reportage, usually delivered in the package that we call an "article." It's not articles, however well written, that I'm aiming to collect in this book. The writer of an article serves as a catcher and selector of information — in short, as a reporter. A good magazine reporter, after extensive research, tells you what he or she thinks you need to know about a subject. There's usually an attempt to be fair and accurate. And reporters also interpret facts. But they seldom indulge in personal confessions associated with the subject at hand, nor do they canter along the margins of the topic for a paragraph or a page chasing some obsession that may seem frivolous to their more fact-bound readers. Essayists do these things, and the good ones ensure that each literary feint and flourish, and any conspicuous personal obsessions loop back like hungry horses to the main barn and help the reader give shape and volume to whatever interior the essay is trying to explore.

A strong element of the personal, then, is what separates most contemporary essays from their cousin, the article. Personalized prose is not, however, a good definition for the form. In this collection most of the pieces do draw in some openly acknowledged way on the writer's own experiences, but a few don't, and they are no less essays because of it. David Olive's piece on Conrad Black's penchant for libel litigation, for example, is a sharp analysis of why a writer should think twice about suing another writer for defamation. On one level this is simply a timely newspaper article about a public-affairs issue that has been much talked about in the early 1990s. But it reaches beyond the transience of daily news, partly because the questions of slander and libel, unfairness and distortion, and pride and reputation are eternal; and partly because Olive has invested the writing with carefully crafted wit and a strongly felt commitment to his subject. Style and commitment distinguish this piece, elevate it above the daily din of newspaperese, and stamp it as an essay.

To my mind style and passion, even if that passion has been sublimated into irony and wit, are the defining characteristics of the good essay. Articles are crafted by literary carpenters. There's a world of difference between excellent carpenters and mediocre ones, but they're all aiming for the same result at the end of the day: cost efficiency and solid work that won't wobble under pressure. Essays are fashioned by cabinetmakers who pay more attention to the detail they are carving than to the clock. And essays are less likely to be assigned by an editor, more likely to spring from a writer's own intellectual agenda. For these reasons, essays more than articles are infused with the writer's personality. Many people write in both capacities — as reporters and essayists — and often the distinction is blurred. But it's almost always true that their essays outlive their other journalism, and that when they've mobilized their hearts and souls as well as their intellects at their desks, they are writing an essay, not an article.

Some of the writers in this collection don't work as reporters at all. Margaret Atwood, Peter Behrens, Clark Blaise, Sharon Butala, Ann Diamond, M.T. Kelly, Joyce Marshall, Jane Rule, and Audrey Thomas are all admired authors of fiction who only occasionally write short non-fiction pieces. Others in these pages — Dalton Camp, Don Gillmor, Ernest Hillen, Michael Ignatieff, Marni

Jackson, Myrna Kostash, David Macfarlane, Joyce Nelson, and Rick Salutin — are respected writers who have been and in some cases still are regular contributors to newspapers and magazines. David Olive and William Thorsell are the only full-time journalists collected here. Olive is the editor of *The Globe & Mail*'s *Report on Business* magazine. Thorsell is the newspaper's editor. Rose Borris, Denise Chong, Moira Farr, Hugh Graham, and Stephen Phelps may be less well known, but if they continue to write as well as they do in the essays here, it won't be long before their names are familiar.

Whether they come from the minds of journalists, novelists, or those literary chameleons who inhabit the ground in between, what all the pieces in this collection have in common is an alert intelligence and some degree of palpable emotion. I've called this book *The Thinking Heart* because, as I've suggested, reason and passion marshalled together make the most engaging prose. Old-school purists may disagree that all my selections are essays in the classic sense. They may feel that an essay should be more rigorously analytical than some of these pieces. But genres evolve, definitions shift, and I don't mind edging the essay away from the kind of dry, cerebral performance that helped to give the form a reputation for worthiness at the expense of enjoyment.

This book is an attempt to gather together some of the most lively and thoughtful non-fiction prose written by Canadians in the past few years. It's also an attempt to reflect what's on our minds as we move into the 1990s. In the pieces that touch on public issues I don't endorse every point of view these writers represent, but I do admire the honesty, clarity, and conviction with which they make their cases, whether it's Margaret Atwood on feminist politics, or Sharon Butala on the problems of prairie ranchers, or Rick Salutin on the collusion he perceives between *The Globe & Mail* and the CBC , or William Thorsell on what he believes ails Canada. These and some of the other essays here are advancing complaints about and solutions to cultural and political ills that have been identified by some of our most intrepid and perceptive minds. The country has been in a querulous mood of late, and this book certainly touches on that mood, but it also, I hope, makes conspicuous one of the reasons we should count ourselves lucky: there's a richness of active talent among Canadians equal to that of any national population of comparable size anywhere.

This book pays homage to that talent.

George Galt

1
Margaret Atwood

IF YOU CAN'T SAY SOMETHING NICE, DON'T SAY ANYTHING AT ALL

1   Long ago, in the land of small metal curlers, of respectable white cotton garter-belts and panty-girdles with rubbery-smelling snap crotches, of stockings with seams, where condoms could not legally be displayed on pharmacy shelves, where we read Kotex ads to learn how to behave at proms and always wore our gloves when we went out, where cars had fins like fish and there was only one brand of tampon, women were told many things.

We were told: a happy marriage is the wife's responsibility.

We were told: learn to be a good listener.

We were told: don't neck on the first date or the boy will not respect you. Home may be the man's castle but the fluff-balls under the bed are the woman's fault. Real women are bad at math. To be fulfilled you have to have a baby. If you lead them on you'll get what you deserve.

We were told: if you can't say something nice, don't say anything at all.

Things that were not openly discussed: Abortion. Incest. Lesbians. Masturbation. Female orgasm. Menopause. Impotence. Anger.

Things we'd never heard of: Anorexia. Male-determined. Battered women.

Metonymy. Housework is work. Bulemia. Herpes. Ecology. Equal pay. P.M.S. Surrogate motherhood. Faking it. Sisterhood is powerful. Dioxins. AIDS. The personal is political. A fish and a bicycle. Trashing.

Things we heard from men: Put a paper bag over their heads and they're all the same. She's just mad because she's a woman. Nothing wrong with her that a good screw won't fix. Bun in the oven. Up the stump. Frustrated old maid. Cock-teaser. Raving bitch.

We were told that there were certain 'right,' 'normal' ways to be women, and other ways that were wrong. The right ways were limited in number. The wrong ways were endless.

We spent a lot of time wondering if we were 'normal.' Some of us decided we weren't. Ready-to-wear did not quite fit us. Neither did language.

2 Technology changed first. Big rollers. Home hair dryers. Pantyhose. The Pill.

Some of us made it through the mine-field of high school to the mine-field of university.

We read things. We read many things. We read *Paradise Lost*, about Eve's Sin, which seemed to consist partly in having curly hair. We read the glorified rape scenes in *Peyton Place* and *The Fountainhead*, which proposed sexual assault as a kind of therapy. (For the woman. Leaves you with that radiant after-glow.) We read D.H. Lawrence and his nasty bloodsucking old spiderwomen, and his young girls melting like gelatin at the sight, thought or touch of a good man's nicknamed appendage. We read Norman Mailer, who detailed the orgasmic thrill of strangling a bitchy wife. We read Ernest Hemingway, who preferred fishing. We read *Playboy*, and its promises of eternal babyhood for boys, in the playpen with the bunnies — well away from the washer-dryer in the suburbs and the gold-digging wife and her (not his) screaming kids. We read Kerouac, the Beat version of much the same thing. We read Robert Graves, in which man did and Woman Was. Passivity was at an all-time high.

We read sex manuals that said a man should learn to play a woman like a violin. Nobody said a word about a woman learning to play a man like a flute.

We did some investigations of our own, and concluded that virgins were at a premium not because they were pure but because they were stupid. They made men feel smart by comparison. We realized we'd been well-groomed in the art of making men feel smart. We were disappointed that this was an art and not something inherent in nature: if men really were that smart, it shouldn't take so much work.

3 Some of us wanted to be writers. If we were in Academia we concealed this. Respectable academics did not 'write,' acceptable writers were safely dead. We did not want to be thought presumptuous. We were keeping our presumption for later.

We read writing by women. Our interest was not so much in technique or style or form or symbol or even content, although these were the things we wrote papers about. It was in something much more basic: we were curious about the *lives* of these women. How had they managed it? We knew about the problems; we wanted to know there were solutions. For instance, could you be a woman writer and happily married, with children, as well? It did not seem likely. (Emily Dickinson, recluse. George Eliot, childless. The Brontës, dead early. Jane Austen, spinster. Christina Rosetti, her wormholes, her shroud.)

It seemed likely that the husband's demands and those of the art would clash. As a woman writer you would have to be a sort of nun, with the vocation and dedication but without the chastity, because of course you would have to Experience Life. You would have to Suffer. We read Sylvia Plath and Anne Sexton, suicides both. Novel writing was safer. You could do that and live.

Even so, combining marriage and art was a risky business. You could not be an empty vessel for two. The instructions were clear: one genie per bottle.

Then there was the Canadian complication. Could you be female, a writer, be good at it, get published, not commit suicide, and be Canadian too? Here the news was a little better. Canadian writers were for the most part not at all well-known, but if you dug around you could find them, and many of the best ones were women. Of these, none had committed suicide.

Around this time, I was reading: P.K. Page, Margaret Avison, Dorothy Roberts, Jay Macpherson, Elizabeth Brewster, Gwen MacEwen, Anne Hébert, Marie-Claire Blais, Gabrielle Roy, Margaret Laurence, Ethel Wilson, Jane Rule, Miriam Waddington, Anne Wilkinson, Phyllis Webb, Colleen Thibideau, Sheila Watson, Dorothy Livesay, and Phyllis Gottlieb. (Alice Munro, Marian Engel and Audrey Thomas had not yet published books, and Mavis Gallant was unknown — to me, and to most — as a Canadian.)

It was comforting as well as exciting to read these writers. I was not thinking, however, about a special, female *kind* of writing. It was more like a laying on of hands, a feeling that you too could do it because, look, it could be done.

Still, it was taken for granted then that you had to work harder and be better to be a woman anything, so why not a woman writer? I felt that I was writing in the teeth of the odds; as all writers do, to be sure, but for women there were extra handicaps. I was writing *anyway*, I was writing *nevertheless*, I was writing *despite*.

4 Things that were said about writing by women:

— that it was weak, vapid and pastel, as in strong, 'masculine' rhymes and weak 'feminine' ones;

— that it was too subjective, solipsistic, narcissistic, autobiographical and confessional;

— that women lacked imagination and the power of invention and could only copy from their own (unimportant) lives and their own (limited, subjective) reality. They lacked the power to speak in other voices, or to make things up;

— that their writing was therefore limited in scope, petty, domestic and trivial;

— that good female writers transcended their gender; that bad ones embodied it;

— that writing was anyway a male preserve, and that women who invaded it felt guilty or wanted to be men;

— that men created because they couldn't have babies; that it was unfair of women to do both; that they should just have the babies, thus confining themselves to their proper sphere of creativity.

The double bind: if women said nice things, they were being female, therefore weak, and therefore bad writers. If they didn't say nice things they weren't proper women. Much better not to say anything at all.

Any woman who began writing when I did, and managed to continue, did so by ignoring, as a writer, all her socialization about pleasing other people by being nice, and every theory then available about how she wrote or ought to write. The alternative was silence.

5 It was the mid-sixties. We began to

read subversive books. We knew they were subversive because we read them in the bathroom with the door closed and did not admit to it. There were two of them: Betty Friedan's *The Feminine Mystique* and Simone de Beauvoir's *The Second Sex*. They weren't about our generation, exactly, or about our country; still, some things fit. We didn't know quite why we wished to conceal our knowledge of them, except that the implications were very disturbing. If you thought too much about them you got angry. Something might blow up.

I first became aware of the constellation of attitudes or wave of energy loosely known as 'The Women's Movement' in 1969, when I was living in Edmonton, Alberta. A friend of mine in New York sent me a copy of the now-famous 'Housework Is Work' piece. There were no feminist groups in my immediate vicinity that I could see. Not there, not then. After that I went to England: similarly none.

I've said from time to time that I pre-dated the women's movement, didn't create it, and didn't even participate in its early stages. I feel that this was a modest — and accurate — attempt not to take credit where credit wasn't due, but this has been interpreted by some as a kind of denial or repudiation. Why this pressure to lie about your real experience, squash it into the Procrustean bed of some sacrosanct Party Line? It seems, unfortunately, to be a characteristic of Party Lines.

Similarly, I've been under pressure to say I was discriminated against by sexist male publishers. But I wasn't. However sexist they may have been in their private lives, in their professional behaviour towards me no male Canadian publishers were ever anything but encouraging, even when they didn't publish my books. (I'm quite prepared to believe that the experience of others has been different. But your own personal experience is supposed to count for something, and that was mine.) It's true that my first collection of poems and my first novel were rejected, but, although this was hard on me at the time, it was in retrospect a good thing. These books were 'promising,' but that's all they were.

In general, the Canadian publishers then were so desperate for any book they thought they could publish successfully that they wouldn't have cared if the author were a newt. 'Successfully' is the operative word. Success in a publisher's terms can be critical or financial, preferably both, which means an audience of some kind. This state of affairs mitigates — at the moment — against poetry, and against new, experimental and minority-group writing — writing that cannot promise to deliver an audience — which is also the reason why a great deal of such writing first sees the light through small presses and literary magazines. Many of these have been controlled by men with a distinct penchant for the buddy system, which in turn has led to the *de facto* exclusion of non-buddies, a good number of whom have been women. Or that's my theory.

Finding that they were too new, offbeat, or weird for what little 'mainstream' publishing there was, many writers of my generation started their own presses and magazines. This is hard work and drinks your blood, but for writers who feel excluded, it may be the only way to develop an audience. Sometimes the audience is already there and waiting, and the problem is to locate it, or enable it to locate you. Sometimes audience and writer will each other into being. But many, even those belonging to the supposedly automatically-privileged white male middle-class, never make it at all.

Being reviewed holds different perils. I'm quite happy to line up for a group spit on sexist reviewers, since over the years I've been on the receiving end of every bias in the book. *She writes like a man*, intended as a compliment. (I've always read it, 'She writes. Like a man.') *She writes like a housewife*. Witch, man-hater, man-freezing, Medusa, man-devouring monster. The Ice Goddess, the Snow Queen. One (woman) critic even did an analysis of my work based on my jacket photos: not enough smiles, in her opinion. Girls, like the peasants in eighteenth-century genre paintings, are supposed to smile a lot. And Lord help you if you step outside your 'proper' sphere as a woman writer and comment on boy stuff like, say, politics. You want to see the heavy artillery come out? Try Free Trade.

6 Looking back on the women's movement in the early and mid-seventies, I remember a grand fermentation of ideas, an exuberance in writing, a joy in uncovering taboos and in breaking them, a willingness to explore new channels of thought and feeling. I remember the setting-up of practical facilities such as Rape Crisis Centres and shelters for battered women. Doors were being opened. Language was being changed. Territory was being claimed. The unsaid was being said. Forms were fluid, genres were no longer locked boxes. There was a vitality, an urgency, in writing by women that surpassed anything men as a group were coming up with at the time. It was heady stuff.

Did all this affect my writing? How could it not? It affected everyone, in one way or another. It affected ways of looking, ways of feeling, ways of saying, the entire spectrum of assumption and perceived possibility.

But some people got hurt. Some men felt confused or excluded or despised, their roles questioned, their power base eroded. Some women felt excluded or despised or bullied or marginalized or trashed. When you've devoted much time and energy to bringing up your beloved children, frequently single-handedly, it didn't perk you up a lot to be called a dupe to men and a traitor to women. When you'd bucked the odds, worked your little fingers to the bone and achieved some form of success, it was not overjoying to be labelled a 'token woman.' It wasn't great to be told that your concern with race did not somehow fit into the women's movement. It wasn't any more fun being told you weren't a real woman because you weren't a lesbian than it had been for lesbians, earlier, to be squashed for their own sexual preferences.

But you weren't supposed to complain. It seemed that some emotions were okay to express — for instance, negative emotions about men. Others were not okay — for instance, negative emotions about Woman. Mothers were an exception. It was okay to trash your mother. That aside, if you couldn't say something nice *about Woman*, you weren't supposed to say anything at all. But even saying *that* is saying something *not nice*. Right? So sit down and shut up.

Women can domineer over and infantilize women just as well as men can. They know exactly where to stick the knife. Also, they do great ambushes. From men you're expecting it.

7 Writing and *isms* are two different things. Those who pledge their first loyalties to *isms* often hate and fear artists and their perverse loyalty to their art, because art is uncontrollable and has a habit of exploring the shadow side, the unspoken, the unthought. From the point of view of those who want a neatly ordered universe, writers are messy and undependable. They often see life as complex and mysterious, with ironies and loose ends, not as a tidy system of goodies and baddies usefully labelled. They frequently take the side of the underdog, that flea-blown house-pet so unpopular with regimes in power. Plato excluded poets from the ideal republic. Modern dictators shoot them. And as the germination stage of any *ism* ends and it divides into cliques and solidifies into orthodoxies, writers — seized upon initially for their ability to upset apple carts — become suspect to the guardians of the *ism* for that very reason. Prescription becomes the order of the day. If Rousseau had survived to witness the French Revolution, he

would have been guillotined.

I have supported women's efforts to improve their shoddy lot in this world which is, globally, dangerous for women, biased against them, and at the moment, in a state of reaction against their efforts. But you pay for your support. The demands placed on those seen as spokespersons, either for women or for any other group-under-pressure, are frequently crushing: for every demand you satisfy, ten more come forward, and when you reach the breakdown point and say you just can't do it, the demanders get angry. Women are socialized to please, to assuage pain, to give blood till they drop, to conciliate, to be selfless, to be helpful, to be Jesus Christ since men have given up on that role, *to be perfect*, and that load of luggage is still with us. This kind of insatiability is particularly damaging for women writers, who, like other writers, need private space and as women have a hard time getting any, and who are called by inner voices that may not coincide with the strictures of prevailing policy-formulators. I think of a poem by the young Maori poet Roma Potiki, addressed to her own constituency: 'Death Is Too High a Price to Pay for Your Approval.' Which about sums it up.

So — as a citizen, I do what I can while attempting to remain sane and functional, and if that sounds whiny and martyred it probably is. But as a writer — although it goes without saying that one's areas of concern informs one's work — I view with some alarm the attempts being made to dictate to women writers, on ideological grounds, various 'acceptable' modes of approach, style, form, language, subject or voice. Squeezing everyone into the same mould does not foster vitality, it merely discourages risks. In farming it would be monoculture. In fiction, those who write from the abstract theory on down instead of from the specific earth up all too often end by producing work that resembles a filled-in colouring book. Art created from a sense of obligation is likely to be static.

I think I am a writer, not a sort of *tabula rasa* for the Zeitgeist or a non-existent generator of 'texts.' I think the examination of 'language' is something every good writer is engaged in by virtue of vocation. I write about women because they interest me, not because I think I ought to. Art created from a sense of obligation is bound to be static. Women are not Woman. They come in all shapes, sizes, colours, classes, ages, and degrees of moral rectitude. They don't all behave, think or feel the same, any more than they all take Size Eight. All of them are real. Some of them are wonderful. Some of them are awful. To deny them this is to deny them their humanity and to restrict their area of moral choice to the size of a teacup. To define women as by nature better than men is to ape the Victorians: 'Woman' was given 'moral superiority' by them because all other forms of superiority had been taken away.

8 There's been a certain amount of talk lately about who has the right to write what, and about whom. Some have even claimed that a writer should not write about anyone other than herself, or someone so closely resembling her that it makes no nevermind. What was previously considered a weakness in women's writing — solipsism, narcissism, the autobiographical — is now being touted as a requirement. Just for fun, here are a few woman writers who have written in voices 'other' than 'their own' — those of other genders, nations, classes, ethnic groups, colours, other ages or stages of life, other times, and other life forms: Emily Brontë, George Eliot, Beatrix Potter, Virginia Woolf, Nadine Gordimer, Mary Shelley, Kay Boyle, Adele Wiseman, Bharati Mukherjee, Marie-Claire Blais, Jane Urquhart, Marge Piercey, Louise Erdrich, Daphne Marlatt, Carolyn Chute, Toni Morrison, Audrey Thomas, Alice Munro, Nicole Brossard, Gwendolyn MacEwen, Cynthia Ozick, Anne Hébert, Margaret Laurence, Mavis Gallant, Alice Walker, Anita Desai, Blanche D'Alpuget, Rita MacNeil, Sarah Sheard, Nayantara Sahgal, Katherine Govier, Nawal El Saadawi, Ruth Prawer Jhabvala, Susan Swan, Anonymous, almost all playwrights, many crime writers, and all science-fiction writers. That's just a few that spring to mind. There are lots more.

Having said all this, I'll say that if you do choose to write from the point of view of an 'other' group, you'd better pay very close attention, because you'll be subject to extra scrutinies and resentments. I'll add that in my opinion the best writing about such a group is most likely to come from within that group — not because those outside it are more likely to vilify it, but because they are likely, these days and out of well-meaning liberalism, to simplify and sentimentalize it, or to get the textures and vocabulary and symbolism wrong. (For what it's worth, I think it's easier to write from a different-gender point of view within your own group than from a same-gender point of view from a different group.) Also, writers from outside a group are less likely to be able to do the tough, unpleasant, complex bits without attracting charges of racism, sexism, and so forth. Picture Toni Morrison's *Beloved* written by a white person and you'll see what I mean.

But to make such a judgement *in advance*, to make it on the basis of the race, sex, age, nationality, class or jacket photo *of the writer* instead of on the quality of the writing itself, is to be guilty of prejudice in the original meaning of the word, which is *pre-judgement.* This is why, when I judge writing contests of any kind, I prefer to do it blind. Recently I gave first prize in a short-story-collection contest to Reginald McKnight, a writer of great verve and energy, who turned out to be Black, male, and American. One of the stories was written from the point of view of a bigoted white Southern male. Should this have disqualified my writer — that he was not writing with 'his own' voice?

To lend support to an emerging literature does not mean you have to silence yourself. Being a good listener is not the same as not talking. The best thing you can do for a writer from a group in the process of finding its voices is to form part of a receptive climate. That is, *buy the work and read it,* as intelligently and sensitively as you can. If there's something new and valuable to be learned about form, symbol, or belief system, learn it. But don't condescend. And never call anyone from such a group a token. For a writer, that's a big insult; it implies she can't really write.

Surely in the final analysis critical evaluation should be based on performance. I didn't give first prize to Reginald McKnight's *Moustapha's Eclipse* because the author was Black, but because it was the best.

9 For me, the dangers of dictatorship by *ism* are largely metaphorical: I don't have a job, so no one has the power to fire me. But for some members of what I now geriatrically refer to as the younger generation, things are otherwise. When younger women writers come to me, at parties or under cover of night, to whisper stories about how they've been worked over — critically, professionally, or personally - by women in positions of power, because they haven't toed some stylistic or ideological line or other, I deduct the mandatory fifteen points for writerly paranoia. Then I get mad.

Over the years I've built up a good deal of resistance to such manipulations; in any case, those likely to be doing them probably think of me as the Goodyear Blimp, floating around up there in an overinflated and irrelevant way — just the Establishment, you know, like, who cares? But other, younger woman writers, especially those with academic jobs, are not so lucky. An accusation of Thoughtcrime, for them, can have damaging practical consequences.

If the women's movement is not an open door but a closed book, reserved for some right-thinking elite, then I've been misled. Are we being told yet once again that there are certain 'right' ways of being a woman writer, and that all other ways are wrong?

Sorry, but that's where I came in. Women of my generation were told not to fly or run, only to hobble, with our high heels and our panty-girdles on. We were told endlessly: *thou shalt not*. We don't need to hear it again, and especially not from women. Feminism has done many good things for women writers, but surely the most important has been the permission to say the unsaid, to encourage women to claim their full humanity, which means acknowledging the shadows as well as the lights.

Any knife can cut two ways. Theory is a positive force when it vitalizes and enables, but a negative one when it is used to amputate and repress, to create a batch of self-righteous rules and regulations, to foster nail-biting self-consciousness to the point of total block. Women are particulary subject to such squeeze-plays, because they are (still) heavily socialized to please. It's easy to make them feel guilty, about almost anything.

The fear that dares not speak its name, for some women these days, is a fear of other women. But you aren't supposed to talk about that: if you can't say something nice, don't say anything at all.

There are many strong voices; there are many *kinds* of strong voices. Surely there should be room for all.

Does it make sense to silence women in the name of Woman?

We can't afford this silencing, or this fear.

2
Peter Behrens
REFUGEE DREAMS

No TWO places on the continent are less alike than Montreal, where I grew up, and Santa Barbara, where I live. Montreal is big and dirty, with the worst weather of almost any city on the continent, Winnipeg the possible exception. Hockey has been a civic passion since the 1850s, long before Wayne Gretzky tied on a skate. Local history means the struggle between French and English. There's a Notre Dame de Grâce Kosher Meat Market, a museum operated by French-speaking midgets, a Portuguese/Central American neighborhood called St-Louis de Mile End. Taxi drivers are Haitian and almost all pizza places are owned by Greeks, some of whom emigrated from Egypt. French-Canadian politicians have names like Johnson, Ryan, O'Neill.

In Santa Barbara almost everyone is either Hispanic or white/Anglo. There's perfect weather and zero interest in hockey. I don't know who drives the taxis because I've never taken one; who takes taxis in southern California? It makes sense to own a convertible. Rents are two to three times more expensive than in Montreal; gas, booze, and cigarettes much cheaper. Winter, a short, brisk season, makes everyone feel especially healthy. There's plenty of local history, but, except for the destruction of the native American Chumash culture, it's history done in soft pastels. Chapters that can't be peddled to tourists are readily forgotten.

After two years I'm starting to think of myself as settled in Santa Barbara, but most of my fiction is stuck in Montreal. I'm restless in either town these days. Only on a jet between the two of them do I feel at peace, suspended, neutral.

Flying the cheap route means making three connections, a long, numbing jour-ney, one I've been doing a lot since last winter, when my father was diagnosed with cancer.

Flights from California to Canada pass over desert, red canyons, wheat fields, lakes, and then the northern wilderness. Waiting for a connection at Chicago-O'Hare, I try not to think about what I'm leaving or what I'm heading into. I feel alert and vulnerable, sitting in the post-modern United terminal, concen-trating on a book. At such times I feel free.

Airports remind me of my father in his heyday: business-suited, briefcased, fedora'd, flying in from sales trips, shareholders' meetings, conferences. My sisters and I would wait by the baggage carousels, sometimes sneaking onto the shining, whirring belts and riding in circles, always keeping a careful eye out for him — so crisply dressed, so glad to see us, so tired.

My father was born on the Isle of Wight in 1910. Life was sunny until the First World War, when my grandfather, a German national, was interned. From 1914 to 1918, my father and grandmother saw him only on once-a-week visits to the internment camp in north London. After the war, the family went to Ger-many and my father was sent to school in Frankfurt, without knowing any Ger-man at first. He was a tall, skinny adolescent who wore English clothes, collect-ed overseas stamps, read Kipling and Conrad. With a British passport, an Irish mother, and a Catholic father who'd remained resolutely Anglophile in the face of four lost years, he wasn't exactly certain where he belonged. When he grad-uated in 1929 he took a job with a chemical company. After his apprenticeship, the company decided to send him to Shanghai, but plans shifted when the Japanese invaded Manchuria, and he was posted to Canada instead.

Going through his desk last week I found postcards from his mother, dated 1934, warning him to dress warmly for the Canadian winter. He skied the Lau-rentians, camped in the Gaspé, learned to sail on Lac St-Louis. He bought his first car in 1936, a five-year-old Oldsmobile that he held on to for a decade.

In 1939 he returned to Germany and tried to persuade his parents to leave. My grandfather had been reported by a neighborhood butcher for declining to return a Nazi salute. My grandmother, who spoke German badly, had kept her British passport, but my grandfather worried that if they went to England or Canada he'd be interned again.

Unable to persuade them, my father squeezed aboard the last train to Rotter-dam the day war was declared. He didn't hear from his parents for six years.

I feel welcome in Santa Barbara, though not necessarily at home. We harvest avocados and oranges from trees in our back yard, and in winter the grass grows greener with January rain. There are palms in the park across the street. Trees flower in November, pungent blossoms dripping purple berries that stain my car's sun-bleached finish.

I haven't lived in Montreal for eight years, and when I return to it the city feels old, complicated, and mysterious. Maybe writers' hometowns always feel that way. My French has gotten rusty. These days, it's when I fly into Santa Barbara, witness the last pink light on the Santa Ynez Mountains, that I sometimes feel I'm coming home. On the freeway coming in from the airport I'm reassured by the familiarity of flowering shrubs, the smell of the Pacific, the polished thirty-year-old Chevys and chopped-down, chrome-wheeled VWs rumbling towards State Street. Three generations in my family have been born in different countries: Germany, England, and Canada. My son or daughter might be born here.

My father was a tall man with white hair and big, beautifully shaped hands. When he came to Santa Barbara two years ago he insisted on wading out into the surf. While my mother anxiously watched from the beach, I stood behind him with my arms around his chest, supporting him when the waves threatened to knock him over. He had a big, handsome body, but ancient skiing accidents had nearly crippled him, and he carried the scars from a lifetime of car accidents, kidney- and gall-stone operations, heart attacks, torn ligaments, slipped discs.

He had studied enough maps so that he knew his way around town better than I did. He liked the yachts in the harbor and the windsurfers off Jalama Beach, but often he seemed sad, tired, and grouchy, not as thrilled with paradise as I had wanted him to be.

After ten days we drove my parents to San Francisco, where they boarded a plane to Montreal. My wife and I headed south on the Bayshore Freeway. Trucks were shouldering through traffic to San Jose, everything looked decrepit, and somewhere around Redwood City I admitted that I thought my father was dying. It felt like treason to say it out loud. At that point he hadn't even visited the heart man, the specialist in internal medicine, the oncologist.

The cancer was diagnosed in January. He had a colostomy operation two days later. It was 70 degrees the morning I left Santa Barbara; in Montreal it was snowing. My father insisted on walking down the hospital corridor, holding a tight grip on my arm. We sat in the patients' lounge and talked, not without difficulty. He was forty-two when he married, forty-four when I was born, more than a single generation separating us. He said he was taking things one day at a time, but that he felt he had a pretty good chance of getting better.

Walking back to bed exhausted him and he wasn't on his feet again for a week.

When I visited him in March he was home, adapting to the colostomy and being treated with chemotherapy. He invited me to lunch at his club. I shined my shoes and dug out an old tweed jacket from the closet. We had Prince Edward Island oysters, Czech beer, and an argument about Quebec politics — everything according to ritual. Outside, it was nearly spring. The black humps of snow were shrinking. Mansfield Street was sloppy with slush. My father, in shiny black rubbers, cashmere overcoat, and a hat he'd purchased in Milan twenty years earlier, seemed relaxed, dapper, undefeated. Things were looking up.

Later, when the snow disappeared and the weather got warm, there were good days and not-so-good days. My parents travelled to Boston for my younger sister's college graduation. Later in the month, my father's appetite weakened. Chemotherapy had not tamed the cancer, and the doctors were starting him on radiation therapy. The strain of the illness had etched into my mother's voice, and one day early in the summer she began sounding old.

In early August the pain began, dimly, in my father's chest. He swallowed furtive doses of aspirin but it only got worse. There were three sudden ambulance trips in the middle of the night. Heart trouble, they thought, then the pain was diagnosed as metastasized bone cancer. Now he's *really* dying, my sister told me over the phone.

Santa Barbara was hot and dusty when I left in September. Fall colors were breaking over Montreal, and my father was having restless refugee dreams, trying to climb out of bed. When he recognized me, he told me anxiously that he had to catch a train for Vienna before the Austro-Hungarian frontier closed. The train was leaving the station in a few minutes and he had to gather up everything and get aboard.

I knew the dream, the hallucination, was welling from his own displaced history: the obscure Isle of Wight, the "enemy alien" father, the Irish mother, the 1919 exile to Germany, the Weimar collapse, the Nazi street gangs, the lost dreams of China, the crowded train to Rotterdam. When my father returned to Montreal in 1939 he attempted to join the Royal Canadian Navy. He was turned down at first because of his German name, then because of his bad knees. He didn't hear from his parents until a friend serving in the Canadian Army located them, half-starved but luckier than millions, in the Frankfurt rubble of 1945.

I walked to the window and pointed out the lights of downtown Montreal. I picked up my father's watch from his bedside table and made him read the hour and the date. I felt depressed and frightened. I'd never pitied him before.

At that point we didn't know how long he was going to live, so later in the week I flew back to Santa Barbara. After ten days in California, the call to come home again came. This time my wife flew with me. My father was alive when we got there, but he died four days later.

It was a bitter, colorful day. Scarlet leaves were still hanging on the maples and a north wind was piling up the clouds. I wasn't in the room when he died. My wife and I were walking in the neighborhood where I grew up. I heard the news when I called home from a pay phone on Sherbrooke Street. My sister and my mother had been with him; my sister had held his hand and afterwards shut his eyes.

People keep asking how I feel, but it's hard to give a meaningful answer. My father and I were too close in temperament ever to get along easily, though we had many things in common. I dedicated my first book of stories to him. Some of the stories were obviously about him, and I know he read them all, but we never talked about them or about how lives get mixed up with fiction. Being a writer's parent isn't a very gratifying role. Fathers, strong or weak, don't usually get off easily in their sons' first books.

My father loved reading and took on *Ulysses* the summer he was seventy-four. I don't think he liked it but I'm sure he finished it: he was a very conscientious man. Among other things, he believed in honor and mercy, in London tailors, in paying his taxes, in Pierre Elliott Trudeau, and in being scrupulously honest with insurance claims. He distrusted flag-wavers, Mexican food, long-distance telephone calls, George Bush, and travelling anywhere without reservations. I learned from him how to see the world, but I sometimes used to wish I'd been his grandson instead of his son.

On that last trip we never got a chance to talk, but I held his hands the night before he died and stroked his arms, which were swollen and bruised from intravenous needles. The next day my wife and I drove north of Montreal along the Ottawa River and into the Laurentian hills. There was cold rain mixed with sunshine and a blustering wind out of Labrador. It was so much the landscape of my youth that I knew I could drive through it and not even look at it, yet see it and feel it and be reassured by it.

Back in September, when everyone had known my father was dying but not how long it would take, we'd been able to say goodbye, which is all you can ask, really. That night, leaving the hospital, I sat in the car and wept. He still had some weeks to live, but I knew I'd never speak to him again. I tried to hold back the sobs but they insisted on tearing themselves free, like sons, like dying fathers.

3
Clark Blaise
THE BORDER AS FICTION

How do you get eighteen French Canadians into a Volkswagen?
"Tell them you're going to Plattsburgh." — old joke

IN THE last days of 1987, during our latest move, while unpacking boxes of books that had lain in storage for over two years, I uncovered a slim, discolored volume entitled *The Borderland and Other Poems*, by a certain Roger Quin, poet and Bohemian (born 1850). The book is updated (but is circa 1910), and is published by A. Walker and Son of Galashiels. That, I take it, is in Scotland. The discoloring comes from smoke, a reminder of our house fire in Montreal in 1973. Books purchased before that fire, and preserved through two dozen moves since, are signs of a certain naive commitment. I had probably purchased Quin's book at a church rummage sale in rural Quebec in the mid-sixties.

Anything to do with borders speaks to me personally. I am animated by the very thought of border; crossing the border is like ripping the continent, tearing its invisible casing. I look upon borders as zones of grace, fifty miles wide on either side, where dualities of spirit are commonplace.

The Scots, of course, first cultivated border consciousness to a bardic art. That invisible, near-mythical Scottish border is a primeval literary marker, and the prototype for the border that obsesses me, the Canadian-American. I'm not Scottish, and have never set foot in Scotland, but at one time in my life the thought of such a border appealed to me, as it would to many Canadians. Now, as though to prove that no written word is ever lost, I put Roger Quin ("the tramp poet") at the head of an essay, a piper to his lost, disparate clan.

In a preface to a book of nineteenth-century Scottish short stories, the editor, Douglas Gifford, writes of the conflicts in the characteristic Scottish story: "Disorder, romance, imagination and feeling" are set against "rational Order." Sir Walter Scott's novels are "seen as extended metaphors for the dissociation in Scotland of thought and feeling, materialism and imagination, repression and sensitivity." Later Gifford notes that "two major forces shape the major fiction; protestantism and profit."

These divisions have their echoes in Canada, certainly in my own family and in my sense of what Canada and the United States represent, and of the purpose of the border that lies between them. In an autobiographical essay, the late Quebec (actually Franco Manitoban) novelist, Gabrielle Roy, speaking of her own family, wrote, "with which side should I identify myself especially? With the Roys, troubled people, strict, Jansenists according to what I have been told, but also idealists and dreamers? Or with the Landrys, vivacious, impulsive, gracious and smiling? Where should I turn to learn from where I came?" The borders in Quebec do not require a checkpoint.

This dissociation, or at least conflict, between Protestantism and profit, secularism and the Church, seems to me a useful point of departure for discussing Canadian visions of the United States. Surely the United States has embodied to Canadians a promise of wealth and self-assertion, and a threat to stability, while the border — increasingly mythical, one might add, as free trade and modern communications erode its ancient protections — affords only a tattered shelter. Canada's initial mission on this continent was the extension of parliamentary civilization — anti-republican, and anti-individualist — and there are substantial segments of Canadian society, and deep responses in the collective Canadian cortex, that resist the anarchic, litigious sprawl of American life, even when attracted, or pulled, to the American marketplace. This tension is the transparent casing that supports the border; it is central to the reading of the Canadian character and, not incidentally, to its literature.

Wouldn't most Canadian thinkers, and writers, agree with the proposition, drawn from the Scottish example, that adherence to Canada (an ideal of Canada that is every bit as operative as the stars-and-stripes ideal of America) implies a certain material sacrifice? One clings to Canada out of inertia, yes, but faintly from virtue as well. One gives up Canada — the conclusion is inevitable — for the same reasons a Glaswegian treks to London: guilt and greed.

Look again at the self-awareness in that little joke (a Québécois joke, actually, told in French) that heads this essay. See the disparity between a Quebecker's image of Plattsburgh, and an American's sense of the same, dreary, air-base town. In the United States, Plattsburgh is seen as the last outpost; from Canada, it is the shopping mall of milk and honey.

Our move this year is deeper into Manhattan; last year was Queens. In the past eight years we have lived in Iowa City, British Columbia, Atlanta, Saratoga Springs, Toronto, and Montreal. From a lifetime of crossing borders, I have developed a border consciousness. Borders mean metamorphosis, personal transformation. They offer the opportunity to be and not be simultaneously, or to be two opposing things without deception. I suspect I am not alone in sensing the pull of alien gravities, yet I've often felt lonely, wondering if anyone else out there on our continent of rootless adventurers ever felt as I did.

For me, growing up in a map-strewn apartment in central Florida, countries were like bodies, and borders were their skin. I attributed personalities to shapes, and learned to recognize and respond to outlines of states, countries, and even counties the way salesmen do to faces. I projected personalities on barren outlines.

I fantasized the embrace of Vermont and New Hampshire; they share their diagonal slice of a rocky rectangle like lovers. I approved the tentacular, border-state handshake of West Virginia and Maryland, snaking over Virginia and sliding under Pennsylvania. I detected disloyalty, however, in West Virginia's dagger thrust into the latitudes of Ohio and Pennsylvania. (The suspicion was borne out years later, in the late fifties, when I used to drive between my Pittsburgh home and my Ohio college, crossing that West Virginia panhandle at Wheeling. Between two abolitionist states stood the stark "colored-white" motel signs.) I thought of Tennessee and North Carolina as a sliced earthworm — two separate bodies from a single diagonal cut. I inferred hostility between Mississippi and Alabama as they turn their backs on each other, just like Arizona and New Mexico. I saw Arkansas as a chipped flowerpot, Louisiana as an overstuffed armchair, Minnesota as an enveloping protoplasm about to ingest Wisconsin. I liked broad, smiling Iowa, with its bulging cheek. I wondered about the twinning of inanimate objects — why Missouri and Georgia took on similar shapes, even to tiny nipples at their lower right. Alberta and British Columbia were bloated and blunted versions of Nevada and California. The Yukon mimicked Idaho, and Montana played the American version of the Northwest Territories. Canada leaned its Western provinces vertically, while the Western states were boxes, cut square for stacking.

Later, watching television weather forecasts, I wondered how the Americans could cut off their borders at North Dakota and complain of "Canadian cold" emanating from sheer blankness to the north. Books as well seemed to end at the border. I loved Faulkner's sense of Canada, the use of Shreve McCannon, Quentin Compson's Harvard roommate, as the implied audience to the greatest of all American novels, *Absalom, Absalom!* It's Shreve who asks the major question in the book and in Faulkner's writing — "Why do you hate the South?" — and it's to Shreve, a Canadian, that Quentin cries his response: *"I dont."* (At one time, I made something of that formulation: the Southerner and the Canadian, back-to-back brothers with the belt of individualist, ahistorical Yankeeland in between.) The only other American author with a consistently continental sense of origins was Ross Macdonald, and he, of course, was an old Canadian.

There is, I think, a border mentality, just as there is a small-country mentality (as recently expounded by Milan Kundera), or an exile mentality, a ghetto mentality, an imperialist mentality, an island mentality. The border mentality is alert to differences, to calculating loss and advantage. It watches for tinctures of change as one demographic landscape blends into another.

And there is a border mentality that can take liberty with borders as they are drawn, and that seeks to arrange things more coherently. I've written in the past of my own helpless fascination with the observed facts of the atlas, my attempts to memorize everything on the face of the globe, until finally those facts were not enough and I embarked on a childhood reinvention of the world, of countries, cities, continents, on a movement from history and from memoir into fiction. I was inspired to read, in a *Paris Review* interview, of Carlos Fuentes's literary reinvention of the world. There is, for Fuentes, a Caribbean literature, subversive of history and language, a multilingual literature of history's castaways: "There is a culture of the Caribbean ... that includes Faulkner, Carpentier, García Márquez, Derek Walcott, and Aimé Césaire, a trilingual culture in and around the whirlpool of the baroque which is the Caribbean, the Gulf of Mexico." The point is, there are many more borders in the world than those we traditionally honor. In the process of growing up, we writers reinvent borders in the same way politicians and businessmen rediscover constituencies and markets.

The two borders of the United States offer interesting contrasts. The Rio Grande appears as a giant bug zapper, a lure behind a grid. The attraction is greater than the risk, and risk is a physical calculation compounded of jail time, humiliation, and possible death. Presumably few of the millions of Mexicans and Latin Americans who attempt to breach the Mexican-American border annually are much concerned with possible loss of culture and identity, or with the new political and psychological landscape they'll be asked to inhabit. The same cannot be said of those who cross the forty-ninth parallel and its New England equivalent. Because the Canadian identity is consciously maintained, the border is as much a psychological as a physical one. Each Canadian emigrant must come to America prepared to die a subtle, psychic death.

Some borders are cages; others are mirrors. Some purely political borders rasp on our consciousnesses — the various Koreas, Germanies, Irelands, Lebanons, "Bantustans," and West Banks. They seem to defy the common meaning of *border*, which is to define differences — these are borders that separate likenesses. Traditional borders, such as those in Europe, are natural reminders of where ancient armies ran out of steam, where languages and religions died, where empires faltered. European countries, so far as European consciousnesses are concerned, are separate but equal. (It would be hard to imagine a Danish joke using the nearest German city, Flensburg, in the same way the Quebecker uses Plattsburgh.) A few borders are aesthetic or cultural, such as that of Scotland, or the Mason-Dixon Line, or hundreds of others with poetic and psychological potency — the various *Gaeltaecht* regions of Ireland, the Breton, Welsh, Basque, Kurdish borders that don't really exist except as maintained fictions. There are borders made of the thinnest membrane, such as that between Canada and the United States, which is undefended because the two sides have reached a mental stasis. (To call the border "undefended" is an absurdity; Canadian defensiveness is a standing army of twenty-five million. We stand on guard for thee.) And there are the new, economic supraborders: the postcolonials, and those dividing east and west, north and south, industrialized and developing countries, and free and communist ones. Increasingly, they are the borders with which our children will be dealing — my obsession with minute shapes and whimsical curlicues will be seen as a harmless hobby akin to stalking stamps with a magnifying glass.

I trust, however, there will always be ambiguous borders like the Canadian-American — not exactly a fiction, yet clearly special. As a child, I thought of borders, or at least the ones that I knew well, as force fields. I was powerless to move. I could see across them into a pure Canada or America, but those places were not for me. Borders threw back a likeness that partook of parody and distortion. The images were like us, but just a little strange. The border seemed to move with me, hanging overhead like a cloud.

I would say now that borders are fictions. Within a given territory's boundaries, and determined by the nature of those boundaries, exists a collective character: the European confidence, the Japanese insularity, the American naive openness, the African touchiness, the Canadian desire for identity. Africa suffers a surplus of borders, none of which speak to the consciousness of the people. Africans live, simultaneously, within three or four sets of borders (tribal, religious, racial, linguistic). Canada has only one external border, which is a protection against assimilation (like Scotland's), and a host of regional and linguistic barriers that are internal variants of the same thing. To be Canadian is to state a preference, and to maintain that preference every day in a series of symbolic acts. By their borders ye shall know them.

My Canadian parents, fleeing the war, dipped into North Dakota in 1940 to have me. And so I carry a mythical birthplace around for life — Fargo — a place we left within the year. And then we hit the road, my French-speaking father and my aristocratic mother: Cincinnati, Pittsburgh, Atlanta, a dozen stops in Florida, New York, Cleveland, Chicago, Winnipeg, Springfield (Missouri), Cincinnati, Montreal, and Pittsburgh again. All of this before I was twelve. In stories and novels I've treated my suitcase-and-Greyhound life as an uncommon existence and I'm sure it is, but it's not unknown. Many children of feckless parents travelled as much or more — but not all developed a border consciousness. I was overdetermined, but I'm not sure where it came from. If I had to guess, I would say that my parents were so profoundly different from one another, that I grew up loving and fearing a border consciousness every day of my life.

A border means that certain things are more likely to occur on this side, *here*, than *there*. Certain other things are probably impossible. There is comfort in knowing that in Canada chances are you won't be gunned down by a random psychopath. You probably are safe from serial murderers. You will not be beggared by medical bills and education costs. The part of the country from which you come will determine your outlook, you will be regionally determined. (A Canadian friend, now married to an American novelist, remarked to me this winter, "I've been here two years and only now am I learning not to ask 'where do you come from?' as a first question.") It means, if you're a writer in Canada, writing about high school, you're more likely to sympathize with the teacher over the student (with Laurence's *Jest of God* and Metcalf's *Going Down Slow* over Knowles's *Separate Peace* and Salinger's *Catcher in the Rye*.) If you're writing about small towns, you are not necessarily advocating the use of an incendiary device to obliterate them. Members of Parliament, policemen, clergymen, will not be seen, necessarily, as fools, thugs, or hypocrites.

I was a passionately Southern boy in the segregated Deep South of the late forties, and I was a fervent Canadian singing "O Canada" and "God Save the King," and I was a child of the Ozarks, and a member of the Reds' Knothole Club in old Crosley Field, and I passed out of my boyhood in the post-Kiner, Clemente era of Pittsburgh. Especially Pittsburgh, my home for seven years, American city I know best.

I suffered for all the rebukes that clung to grim, sooty Pittsburgh and so I memorized — it always helps to have a hungry memory — lists of Pittsburgh's accomplishments. (Why, I wonder now? Native-born Pittsburghers could be merciless about the city's patent ghastliness. I never had the confidence to ridicule. The city was me. Everyplace I've ever been has been me; I've expanded myself right out to everyone's borders.) Pittsburgh's great fortunes were my benefactors, its institutions were mine for the taking. Loving Pittsburgh wasn't easy — except as a lover of losing efforts, a true Scotsman, or perhaps Southerner, Canadian, or one of Fuentes's Caribbeans — back when the Pirates, Steelers, and Pitt Panters were all at the bottom of their respective leagues. We had Duquesne basketball to cheer, and the rest was civic endowment: the Carnegie Library and Museum, Buhl Planetarium, the Civic Light Opera, the Pittsburgh Symphony, the Art Students League, and the astronomy clubs and archaeology clubs that worked out of the basements of those gray-granite institutions. I belonged to all of them, they developed my talents, they gave me friends who were nerdy, just like me. They carried me through high school, as proud of my city as any New Yorker or Parisian is of his.

Which is, of course, the point. By the age of fourteen I had manufactured myself half a dozen times into a native of a place. Border crossing could have made me feel alien, and deep down it probably did; overtly, however, I responded only with a puppylike loyalty. Seeking always to blend in, I did so by memorizing the box scores and the trolley grid, and tracing out the city maps at night and poring over the regional maps so I could picture each outlying town and suburb as it surfaced in the news. Oh, the satisfaction gained from those Friday night high-school football scores, and knowing, after a few months, where each of those schools were located! Thirty years later, as I drive the continent at night and KDKA (Pittsburgh's fifty thousand watts) weaves the airwaves, I realize I *still* remember. But I'm not a native of anywhere, and I still fear the inevitable question: "Where are you from?" Fargo, North Dakota?

Or Montreal, the city where my parents had met and married, and from which they'd emigrated, and which is still the place I feel most attached to, and have lived in longest? Or the Deep South, which I remember with a special ferocity, a place whose smells and visions still assault me? Or Manitoba, the only repository of my family, where my maternal grandparents and cousins and aunts and uncles lived, and the family had its farm, and I was sent most every summer? My mother is buried in Winnipeg, in the family plot, with her parents and sisters. (My father is buried in Manchester, New Hampshire, next to his last wife's first husband.)

Or perhaps, in the hungriest leap of all, Europe, where my mother spent the most exciting years of her life, studying art and design in Germany from 1929 until the closing of her school in 1933? Crossing the border into Denmark in 1935, she told me, and seeing a smiling porter sweeping the platforms, had made her cry with gratitude. She hadn't realized, until leaving Germany, the strain that she and everyone else had been under inside those Nazi borders. Her stories had made a vanished Europe, or a pre-World War I Saskatchewan winter, more real to me than anything in my experience.

I wanted to be anything but what I was, and to come from anyplace but where I had. The real me was always somewhere else, but I never found it. Which is the other side of saying, with Roger Quin (poet and Bohemian), that "my errant Muse" lives only here, "in the ruins of Lincluden, Torthorwald, Caerlaverock" (or Montreal, Pittsburgh, Europe, Winnipeg, and the Deep South, with stopovers in India, due to my exotic marriage).

Until my recently married Canadian friend mentioned it, I hadn't thought of intense regionalism as a national trait of Canadians — it was always so much an urgent aspect of my personality — but of course she's right. Canadians ask where you're from, because where you're from reveals relatively more about you if you're a Canadian than it does if you're an American. Being from Saskatchewan or Nova Scotia, at a Toronto cocktail party, probably accounts for sharper self-definition than being from Kansas or Maryland does in New York.

That is, I *think* it does. One feature of a psychologically maintained border, a subjectively felt border, is its porosity, the fact that it blends differences but does not eliminate them. Border mystique exists in Scotland, where differences must be internalized and perpetuated, formed into symbols, and rehearsed as

works of art. But some people, alas, are not good actors. Historical borders —
solid, traditional, European-style borders where fifty meters on the other side of
a striped kiosk people speak a different language and practice a different religion, share a different history, and even *look* a little different — do not require
symbols or rehearsals. Those borders served only to define territory and protect
against invasion. *Maintained* borders, such as Canada's with the United States,
protect against assimilation. Presumably, a group of young Italians would not
identify a group of German tourists on a camping trip as anything but German
(nor would it occur to them to question the Germans' identity), but in Margaret
Atwood's *Surfacing*, the narrator discovers — with a shock and with depression
— that some typically loud and vulgar American campers and fishermen,
despoilers of a pristine Canadian nature, turn out to be Canadian (that is, they
may be *from* Canada, but that fact is not contiguous, in the self-conscious Canadian psyche, with *being* Canadian). If Canadians do not suffer continuing identity crises, then they are contaminated with the American virus of total, blank,
unselfconsciousness.

There are, conversely, many Americans who hold classically Canadian opin-
ions of the United States and think of themselves as "belonging" to a different
culture (Canada being an alternate of choice). Such people, I feel, act from sen-
timent. They feel Canada embodies an innocence or purity lacking in America,
that its border is somehow an ecological and social time tunnel. A clean, progressive place to fish and ski and swim. "Toronto's like New York was thirty
years ago," say wonder-struck friends, reflecting New Yorkers' contemporary
anxiety over dirt and violence. For most Canadians and Europeans, to visit New
York City is also to engage in time travel; the city poses many of the shocking
confrontations of a preindustrial age.

Psychological borders are, by their nature, unequally felt. The English don't
feel oppressed by the Scottish border. If they think about what it means to cross
that border at all, their thoughts are probably folkloric, full of stags at eve and
Highland flings. Such a border crossing involves rugged, ecological time travel.
Americans don't feel cramped by the Canadian helmet tight on their heads. The
fugitive virtues of Plattsburgh are differently weighted in the two cultures. For
Canadians, however (especially for those who would strenuously deny it) the
American border is a central, imaginative fact of life. Proportionally, I suspect
there are many more Canadians who feel themselves to be "basically American," and do not weight the cultural and psychological costs of free trade (for
example) with the same scales as they do the economic costs. My father, who

gave up the French language and Catholicism, was such a person. For all of his American life he lied about his background, his names, and his origins. He claimed, like me, to be a native of anyplace he lived. My mother, who went along with all the moves, never claimed to be anything but a Canadian, from "the West," Wawanesa born and North Battleford and Winnipeg educated — these places were truly the frontier West when she was a child.

Borders are a supreme fiction. For the once colonial, newly liberated, borders are a deformity. They do not define, they do not protect, they do not express a collective will. Borders, in fact, exacerbate instability. Borders are madness, they separate natural brothers, they enclose natural enemies.

It took a psychic insurrection for V.S. Naipaul to realize he was not defined by the accidental quadrant of his birth, the island of Trinidad, but that paradoxically, his accidental, colonially determined birth as an uprooted Hindu in a Caribbean barracoon made him a citizen of the colonial master, Britain, as well as of the rest of the postcolonial world. So, too, the India-born residents of the United States, Vikram Seth and Bharati Mukherjee. Guyana-born Wilson Harris sails the world in his imagination, as does the nominally Pakistani, Brazil-anointed American resident Zulfikar Ghosh. Small wonder that in the works of all these writers madness lurks at the edges. They have seen too much, twisted themselves into too many shapes. They are extensions of Fuentes's super-Caribbean — new border crossers, new mapmakers, citizens of a new world literary order.

For Europeans, borders are definitions, especially perhaps for the British and Scandinavians, who fortify their ancient identities with islandlike isolation (that's why the few of them who travel do so in such an entertaining manner). Authors such as Bruce Chatwin and Jonathan Raban are not travelling to discover new selves — they know what they are. They travel without the edge of danger, the risk of character loss; travel, if anything, enhances their confidence.

For Canadians, borders are a protection against assault, which always happens elsewhere. When they travel, it is to try on possible new identities; what they often encounter is a mirror of themselves they can't accept. In Alice Munro's story "Miles City, Montana," the narrator and her young husband and two daughters drive from British Columbia to Ontario. To reduce the story rather brutally to a portion of its plot, something happens when they enter the United States. In their car game of "Who Am I?" (yes, of course, one thinks), the older daughter identifies herself as "somebody dead, and an American, and a girl." (She turns out to be a shot doe, seen slung on a pickup truck that morning.) They want to swim in a pool, but it is closed between noon and two o'clock. The young lifeguard, however, is accommodating, if somewhat distracted by her boyfriend; she lets the girls use the pool. The parents stay in the car. The mother eventually gets out to stretch her legs, then has a sudden jolt of recognition — "Where are the children?" Of course, she intervenes just before the younger girl drowns. The lifeguard was inattentive; her boyfriend smiles and turns down the radio. The family drives off, and eventually rejoins the Trans-Canada north of North Dakota.

In Munro's story, death and recognition are averted, but not forever. The grace of good fortune *this time* becomes a moral wariness, a realization of vulnerability. The mother sees an equivalence between the heedless young Americans and herself and her husband, as they seek approval from his Ontario parents, wanting to prove themselves as grown-up and responsible.

In Atwood's *Bodily Harm* and *The Handmaid's Tale*, the assault is not avoided. Canada is an incubator of innocence for the protagonist of *Bodily Harm*, whose sanitized Toronto trendiness offers no protection from, and no warning of, the impending violence on a tiny Caribbean island. In *The Handmaid's Tale*, Canada exists as an unaffected bystander to American fundamentalist violence, a place to which fugitive women, the runaway slaves of the late-twentieth century, may escape. In the work of Michael Ondaatje (Ondaatje, like Atwood, is a poet and novelist), violence is also animating, embraced as a consciousness' dark companion. In Ondaatje's *Coming through Slaughter* and *The Collected Works of Billy the Kid*, violence as an art form arises south of the border.

The worst that can be said of Canadians is that they are frequently silly, tasteless, indecisive, or vulgar — for confirmation see the collected satires of John Metcalf or Mordecai Richler. The best that can be said is that they are rational, sober, decent, humble — see the New Age cycle of novelist Hugh Hood. Or — because of their peculiarly passive position on this continent, torn between the American beast and the European ideal, acted upon but essentially powerless — Canada and the Canadian psyche becomes the proper testing ground for the anima/animus formulations of Robertson Davies.

Space has run out, but the border lingers in my mind. I want to speak of borders and margins, borders and frontiers, borders and mimicry, borders and subversion. I want to say my childhood perceptions were entirely backwards: I was not imposing character on the maps I studied and tried to memorize — the map I was born with had imposed its character on me.

4

Rose Borris

with

Paulette Jiles

AT A LOSS FOR WORDS

ONE of my sisters, she used to pretend that she knew how to read. I didn't pretend. I said, "There's nothing I can do. I don't know how and that's it!" This was common in my parents' time, that people couldn't read or write. My father never went to school and my mother only went for a bit. My father could sign his name, but it took him ten minutes. My mother knew a little bit more. But to them, it wasn't important. My mother said she wanted the house clean, she didn't like paper lying around. That's how it was. Your life was in the bush and when my father went there to work my mother took all the kids along. There were fourteen of us altogether. Only five ever learned to read.

I was born in 1932 in a little place called Maltais, New Brunswick. My grandmother always told me I looked like a bear when I was born, I had hair all over me. And she said to my mother, "Caroline, you didn't have a kid, you just had a bear." My grandmother had a baby herself, a month after. She came to help my mother, and then my mother went to help her. This is the way it is with big families.

In Maltais the school was our neighbor. Just a one-room school. But sometimes the people couldn't pay their taxes so there was no teacher. And then somebody burned the school down so they would have some work building it again. I was five maybe, my brother and I saw a man go to the school at night with a can of gas. I remember our dog, Siffleur, barked and barked. Nobody reported the man, people were tired of the tax. Everybody was cousins anyway.

Before I was eight years old, we didn't have any money. But we had enough to eat, because of relief. It was the same with everybody in Maltais. You had a paper to go to the store and now and then people would come to your home and check your supplies to see if you had anything left over. If you did, then they would cut you off. My mother would hide the stuff we had under a rock out in the field — beans, brown sugar — and she would trade it to other people for the things she needed.

We had a little bit to eat from our farm — my father had a horse, a cow, and a few pigs and chickens. Every summer, we used to pick blueberries by the Northwest river. I once saw seven bears in the blueberry patch. We stayed in a black tar-paper thing, like a tent, and everybody slept on spruce boughs. I took care of the younger kids.

When I was eight I went to school, but in February I had an abscess on my knee and I couldn't go back. Anyway I didn't like it, I didn't have nice clothes and the kids would laugh. And if I hit somebody, my mother would beat me for it. The trouble was, I didn't speak very well. We had to read out loud, and I couldn't pronounce words and I was afraid and I forgot everything. Boy, I hated school. I was happy when we left for the bush.

I don't even remember the first time my family went into the bush. We would stay there five or six months, the whole winter. The camp buildings were made with logs so we had to chink them again every winter. There were always porcupine quills stuck in the bark. The buildings had only tar-paper roofs with dirt on top. My mother always had a little baby two or three months old, and sometimes the snow fell in our faces. All the children helped. We carried water and helped to cook for the men and washed dishes and put them out again, the plates upside down. We finished our work about ten o'clock at night.

When I was ten, an Englishman took a big contract for a hundred men to cut wood and work in the forest at Upsalquitch. He talked to my mother and we never came home to the farm again. This camp was big, a place where my father could make more money. But we had to work much harder.

We had three stoves, big ones. We made soup and meat and beans every day, and sometimes a roast with gravy in a big iron pot. We cooked the bread at night. Breakfast was beans and hot biscuits and bread. We made lunch for the men too — cold meat, bread, butter-molasses cookies, molasses cake, and white cake. We also had to make all the beds in the morning when the men weren't there. But it was the first time we kids had a room of our own to sleep in, even if I never had my own bed.

We never had time to play. But we talked a lot and we fought a lot, we made jokes and laughed — I miss this. I love people around me all the time. You smell food cooking, you wash the floor, and the wood smells so good, your stove is always red — this is life.

This was wartime, too. My father's cousin Emile Maltais went to war. His mother cried so much. He later said he fought and killed people. Awful thing, to kill people with a gun! And telegrams came saying people were dead, so if somebody went to be a soldier people thought he would never come back.

My uncle listened to the radio, but he didn't understand it too well. He would say: "And now the Germans are going to take that place there! Now they're going to take this place!" The way people talked, I thought the war was just behind home, maybe five miles from Maltais.

Our neighbor didn't want to be a soldier, so he hid in the bush and every day a girl went to feed him. They never caught him. In a little place like Maltais, everyone was his friend. It rained sometimes so the girl couldn't go, and once he went two days without food. He fell in love with that girl, they got married and had a big family after the war. You know, he *had* to marry her. But that's what happens when you take food to a guy in the bush, eh?

At the camps you didn't have to work so hard in the spring, and always some old people would sit down and tell stories. There's never one that's the same. Old Ouellet was a very good storyteller and he never read in his life. Sometimes a story would last two, three nights. And it was so nice when they'd say, "We ain't going to finish tonight." All the kids would listen, we loved this so much, and sometimes the small ones fell asleep. But I don't think I ever fell asleep. This was how I learned to tell stories. They'd say, "Tell us a story, Rose!" and everyone would come to listen.

There were lots of stories about Ti-Jean. He was a little man, maybe he comes from the moon. These stories have kings in them and dragons and princesses. A story like this would come over from France a long time ago, and people would repeat it and change it all the time. So beautiful!

And then there were also stories about local people. *Le vieux Joseph*, my father said, had eyes so shining that he knew when the moon was changing to full. Then this man would turn himself into the werewolf, the *loup garou*. He walk into the bush and push his knife into a log. It was a magic could touch it or he would die. Then *le vieux Joseph* would walk ds and kill people in the dark.

We lived at Upsalquitch for two years. On the Upsalquitch River there were big timber rafts, and we would stand and watch them pass. The family moved when there was no more wood to cut. We moved many times, that's the way it was.

It was when we were living at Upsalquitch that my sister Stella and I took First Communion. I was eleven and we had to get on the bus, and go to the church at Kedgwick. We stayed with my grandmother Maltais. You can never get married if you are unable to pass your First Communion.

We had to learn the catechism. I had trouble because I couldn't read and my mother was not the kind of person to teach us at home. After a week of going to church I thought it was all finished. But I didn't go to confession and I didn't know I needed to. On Sunday, the first thing I know, all the people got up and went to Communion. When I saw the little kids, five, six years, going up, I said to Stella, "It's time we go. If we don't go, we're not going to pass." Some of the women knew that you had to go to confession before you can take Communion, but they didn't stop me. And the priest didn't know and he gave us Communion.

These women told the priest after Mass. And the priest was so mad, he made us get on our knees in front of everybody and stay there for an hour. He said that God was going to come and get us, and we were never going to be saved. We were so afraid we were shaking.

He asked us, "What kind of a mother do you have? What kind of a father do you have?" The priest didn't know we were in the bush all wintertime. He said, "We never saw people like this in our lives!" I never believed a priest again.

After my brother Léo was born, my mother met some people who had visited Montreal. They said there was a convent where the nuns had a school for girls six to fourteen years old. The people said Stella and I could go there, and work for room and board and learn to read and write. We would get twelve dollars a month. That was good money in 1945. I was thirteen, Stella was twelve. I thought about this and finally I said yes.

My mother and father put us on the train. You know, I was afraid. On the train we met a sailor, he was drinking liquor and he tried to catch us. I got mad and I told the conductor, but after he found us a room with a bed that opened up the conductor came in and tried to lift our blankets. After that we were so afraid we didn't sleep all night.

I had heard so many people say, "It's a very big place, Montreal!" You see, my father's cousin used to buy horses in Montreal to take them back to New Brunswick. When the train stopped, I never saw any horses so I never thought we were in Montreal. We waited a long time. The train started to move and the conductor came to find us. He said, "This is Montreal!"

I said, "What? Montreal!" I thought it was some other city, I was waiting for the horses.

The conductor told us to go up the escalator. It was the first time I was on one and I was scared. Two sisters were waiting at the top for us, they were always in pairs. They took us to the convent on a streetcar.

The convent was a big place, very beautiful. There was a curtain to close off your room, and a washroom, and water — you could take a bath. But I said to Stella, "You know, I don't like this too much." When you come from a big family, you feel so lonesome in such a place.

We had to work hard. I had to take care of seven tables in the dining room. When the kids wanted something, I had to go and get it. When they finished eating, I had to wash all the dishes and dust the tables and set them again. I also had to clean the hall and wash and wax the floor all the time. Every day I had to clean each washroom.

I learned many things there that I never knew before. Cut the sandwiches fancy, place the plates and forks very fancy. I learned how to run those huge laundry machines, and we ironed and pressed the clothes with the big ironing machines. I started to like the laundry because there was a nun there who was very nice. She wasn't yelling at me all the time, you know?

But the nuns wanted us to read and write. And I was ashamed. The way I spoke, it wasn't good French like they spoke. The little girls there, eight or nine years old, they knew how to read and write. I used to pass by the classrooms and think, "There's no way we can learn this. They're smart." Later when you're grown-up, you think: "They're smart, but they've got their problems too."

We were not allowed to talk to the kids. The only time we played outside was when the kids weren't out there. We could play outside for an hour, and after that we had to go to the chapel. We had to pray every morning and every night.

Seven months I stayed there, and the first thing I found out was who could write. You see, I had to make some of the kids write for us. I had learned to spell my name when I was smaller but I never used it, so I forgot. When you never have a book at home, you even forget how to sign your name. If a letter came, the nuns didn't read it to us right away, they had to know what was in the letter first. I was not allowed to touch it. Oh, how I hated this! My own mail.

Then the kids started leaving school for the summer and I had to do more and more. I worried about getting the rooms clean and waxing the floors. The first thing I knew, I was sick for two days and I didn't even eat. Then the eczema started. I had it for two years, I think. I was poisoned from the floor wax so I borrowed six dollars from Stella to go home on the train.

After I arrived home from the convent, we moved to a place called Squaw Cap. We had a store there. In the store, I found every box was a different color or there was something different about it so I could tell what it was. I couldn't read the labels. I don't know why, but "tomato" I could read. I guess it was because I loved tomato soup. What I hated was when they started to put the salt in bags like the sugar.

My mother was expecting another baby that fall, and my father said if she left to go in the bush with him everything was going to freeze up at the store. He said, "Rose, if you come instead, you'll be head cook at the bush camp. Five dollars a day, good money."

I wanted to bring my brother Normand with me to carry water. He was eight years old. We had to wait till the river froze, then we took all our stuff and moved in. I had to get up at four in the morning and peel seventy-five pounds of potatoes, cook beans, make bread and pies and cakes all morning, and then make all the lunches. I cooked for forty-nine men. Nobody helped me, only Normand.

Now I was fourteen when I started to fall in love with a man. His name was Edmond, he was eighteen. He used to come to our house every night. When he went out with me, I just talked to him. When he tried to kiss me one time, I hit him in the face.

I had my fifteenth birthday when I was in the bush. I never wanted to turn fifteen. I wanted to stay fourteen forever. I guess I was afraid that at fifteen you had to get married.

Then I went to work in Campbellton. I lived in a boarding house with five other girls and I washed dishes in a restaurant. I enjoyed the job — it was hard work, but I was used to that. Campbellton was English, but I couldn't be a waitress because I couldn't read the menu anyway. You also had to buy your dinner at the restaurant. I had learned how to say "pork chops" from my brother so I ordered pork chops all the time. Sometimes I wanted something else, but what can you do?

One night a circus came to town and Edmond's cousin Albert Borris came to take me. He was a mechanic, but he used to chop wood when he was a boy for twenty-five cents a day. I won a doll there — I wanted one so bad. It was just a porcelain head, without any hair, but it was the first doll I'd ever had.

And then Albert asked me to meet his family. They were nice, a big family like mine. He was a good mechanic, I trusted him to have money in his pocket. Maybe that's why I kept going out with him: I cared for him, he respected me. I was afraid of the men who worked in the bush.

But Stella started to bug me about going to the convent again. She made my mother write to the nuns. They wrote back and said, "We don't need any girls to work but we know another convent where they can go." I made up my mind and said yes. Albert was coming around all the time but I wanted to be free. I was young, eh?

This time the convent was a little bit outside Montreal, on the St. Lawrence River. It was a beautiful place. But the first thing the nuns told us was, "You have to take all your clothes out of your trunk. We want to see everything you have there."

I said, "What do you mean, you? This is *our* stuff."

She said, "This is the rule."

I had a cigarette pack in there. "You're not going to make me take my stuff out!"

I got mad and cut the cord around my trunk and opened it. Then I took my cigarettes and kept them in my hand and threw everything else out. She didn't see that. I had time to put the cigarettes under the mattress.

That night I went to bed and I cried. I slept for maybe two hours. I felt like I was in prison. The walls were so high and I knew the place was strict from the way they talked.

In the morning I got up and they showed me everything. I had the same job as in the other place. All those tables to take care of, the windows to wash and the stairs and the floors — and the same wax again.

I didn't mind the work. But every night we had to go to church. And they wanted me to put my hat on, and I didn't want to put it on. And this nun I hated, Sister Vachon from the kitchen, she didn't want us to wear lipstick. The nun took a Kleenex and grabbed Stella and wiped the lipstick off. She was a big nun, almost two hundred pounds.

The nuns didn't trust anyone, they only trusted themselves. I couldn't live where there's no trust. My mother trusted us, but here there was none at all. I wanted to write my mother. I tried to make a little orphan girl of eleven years write for me, and the nuns found out and punished the little girl.

Then Stella said, "We're going to say yes for the nun to write. But we're going to make all kinds of lies and we're going to laugh at them and enjoy ourselves."

That night the old nun began a letter for us. She said, "You want me to say how much you love it here?"

I said, "No, say 'I hate this place so much, if I don't get out of here I think I'm going to kill somebody. Hurry and send me money because I want to go home.'"

She wrote, "Your little girl, she likes it here very much and she's a good girl and works very hard...."

Then Stella started. Stella had a boyfriend too.

"Tell him I miss him so much I don't know what I'm going to do."

The nun said, "Who is this?"

Stella said, "It's my brother."

She knew we came from a big family so she said, "Oh, your brother."

I told her, "Say hi to Albert. Tell him I miss him a little bit."

"Who is this Albert?"

"It's my brother, he's a baby, he's only seven months old."

She liked this. But later, we got a letter from my mother.

"Albert is fine, he still drives his truck and he stops by here and asks how you feel and misses you so much."

And with Stella it was the same. Our letter stayed in the office two days, I saw it there, but there was no way I could take it. And the nun, she was so mad.

I was in that place three months. I wanted to go home right away. No way I can phone, no way I can write. To be in a jail and I couldn't even do anything!

Anyway, the nuns had to let me go. And before I left, they made me a cake. A fruitcake, they are very expensive. "We know you want to get married soon, and this is your present." The nuns felt sorry for me because they thought I was going to get married soon.

They brought me to the train and they gave me a rosary and told me, "Sit by yourself. Make sure you don't talk to anybody. Promise us this: think about God." And they waited until the train started.

I threw the rosary away as soon as I could.

Everyone was at home and I was so happy to see all the family again. But after a while my mother went to the bush camp and I had to make the food and look after the store. The baby, Aline, was fifteen months old and there were four other children to take care of too.

At Christmas Albert bought me a watch. My father said, "He loves you very much, that man."

I was only fifteen. But around there, everybody got married at that time.

Albert came to see me. He said, "You're going to have to listen. I have something to say." It took him four hours, and he finished by asking me to marry him. I had to say yes. You know, when you get married, you always marry a stranger. You never know how it's going to work.

I got married in a big church close to Campbellton. I remember I didn't sign the marriage certificate — the priest said, "Make a cross." And my father made a cross too. Albert could sign his name, he had been to school a little bit, he knew enough to fill out a paper. But he's not fast and he hates to read.

We had a big dinner and a party, and we went back to sleep at Mrs. Borris's at Val-d'Amour, we had a room there. Albert wanted to leave at eleven o'clock. I didn't want to go, I loved to dance. If it were today I'd tell him, "Go by yourself!" He wanted to go before his parents came, to be first in the house. We went into the bedroom and I started to look at the presents, I was so embarrassed I didn't know what to do. I went to another room and put on my nightgown over my brassiere.

Then Albert's brother came home. Albert said, "Hurry up!" And he caught me and we fell to the bed.

What I found hard was to get up in the morning. Mr. Borris was there and he said, "And how did you pass the night, Rose?" If I got married again I would never stay in the same house as my in-laws.

Ten years later I had five kids: Clayton, Garry, Betty-Ann who is deaf, Shirley Ann who died as a baby, and Jerry. But one of my brothers had moved to Toronto and he said it was beautiful. Then my father got a job in construction and my parents moved to Toronto. I missed my family.

Then Albert asked me to move. When he found a job at Master Buildup we moved to Cabbagetown. I loved Toronto. It was the best of all the places that I have lived. I said, "This is where I want my life, not in a camp. In a house where you have water, hot water."

At first we stayed at my brother's place. I was twenty-seven and Jerry was only fifteen months. Albert said, "At first, Rose, it's going to be hard in the city because we're not going to make enough money." But I saw some of my relatives had rooming houses and I wanted one too. One of my cousins, he was a bootlegger on Carlton Street. He got caught and had to sell his home. I said to my mother, "I'm going to go get this." Albert was afraid. But I borrowed the money from my mother to rent the house and buy the furniture and pay my cousin's fine.

Now I had everything. A big house, ten rooms, with my own bedroom and my own kitchen. Pretty soon my brother had two houses, then more of the family did the same, and first thing I know there were eleven rooming houses around me.

I was never afraid when my boarders drank — it made me mad. When they fought too much I'd just go and yell at them to shut up. If they didn't do that, I would hit them. Sometimes people would come in with no money. But I found I would get my way. I always have.

I didn't speak good English but I was learning it all the time. Every time I got mad, I learned some new words. I had to learn English because Betty-Ann was already in English school, the school for the deaf in Belleville, and I only knew French. Betty-Ann didn't understand French at all. I said to myself, "The time will come when she's going to be able to talk to me, I've got to be able to understand her." It was hard. We had to go up to Belleville every week. She was so lonesome, she was like me at that convent I hated so much.

It is hard to make people believe that you can't read and write. In Toronto, it's awful. You go into an office and they give you a paper to fill out and they say, "This is easy."

"All right, it's easy for you!"

"You're *sure* you don't know how to read? It's not hard."

And I say, "Well, do you speak French then?"

And they say, "Oh, but we don't know how to speak French."

"But I don't know how to read and write! Don't you understand this?"

And they say, "Oh, we're very sorry. We didn't believe you couldn't read."

When I was first in Toronto, my son Clayton wasn't old enough to fill out a cheque. I would buy a money order, and use it to pay the gas and telephone bills. The woman at the post office put on the address. And my mother, she knew all the rules for a rooming house. She said, the first thing you do is put up a sign, NO LIQUOR ALLOWED IN THE HOUSE. There's always somebody in the house who can read and write.

It's not hard to get around in the city and not be able to read. With the streetcar, I knew where I was going and you can see if it's stopping at the place where you live. But the subway, I hate this. I was afraid to go underground. The trains go so fast and I find it's not fair — they should have somebody to call out the names of the stations. If I wanted to go to a place where I've never been before, I would take a taxi. Then the second time I'd know where to go.

When Albert and I would go to a restaurant, we always asked for the special. You ask for the special and they tell you what it is. If you like it, you get it. People used to ask me, "How do you know a washroom when you stop in a restaurant?" This isn't hard — you look around and see a woman get up and leave, then you go where she goes.

I know numbers, so I always knew where to find an address. We had to learn numbers as children, my father and mother were very good on this. But when I would go in a building where they have names, I hated it. I had to ask people where to go.

I enjoyed my job. But if I had known how to read and write, you think I would have had a rooming house? No, I would have had a big restaurant on Yonge Street. The kids used to show me their report cards and they had to make sure they passed — this was very important to me. I made them so scared of not passing, they would shake.

I think when you get older, you don't like yourself as much as before. Some people hate themselves because they're getting old, or they hate the job they do, but there's no way you can stop. They're too chicken to change their lives. Then other people, they want to stay the same — and there's no way you can do this. Everybody has to change.

I was thinking about my family. My sister Aline hanged herself, and my brother Ted drowned. I was at my doctor's many times. I was dizzy when I got up or when I moved. He told me it was my nerves. I didn't believe him at first. But later, I said, "I'm going to do something for myself. I'm not going to wait to have a breakdown. I'm going to make myself a road."

Now I had lots of reasons to learn how to read and write. My kids had started to leave home and I was thinking: "If I'm left on my own, what am I going to do?" I'm independent, but I knew it would be hard. Even if I wanted to phone someone, I had to wait for somebody to look up the name in the book.

When I was younger, I didn't have a phone. And in New Brunswick, when I wanted to order something from the catalogue, I would walk to my girlfriend's and she would do it for me. But now every weekend, at our cottage north of Belleville, people would come to visit and sit around on the beach, or underneath a tree, and read. And others would walk in with a newspaper. This killed me.

People would ask, "Did you read this? You know what happened here?" Oh boy, that made me mad. I would listen to the news on the radio but it was never like the paper. I said to my son Clayton: "It sure must be nice to know how to read and write."

Betty-Ann sent me a card and her little girl, Roxanne, made an X. She was only two years old. It was all that I had learned since I was small, because when somebody wrote a letter to Betty-Ann for me I always used to make many Xs, many kisses. The first thing I know, Roxanne would know how to read and write. If she can learn, what's wrong with me? But I didn't know how to start.

Just before Christmas, 1977, I went up to the cottage for three months with Albert. He had a bad leg and I was stuck there, so stuck. I had to wait for somebody else just to come and read my Christmas cards. Albert wanted me to stay, he didn't want me to learn how to read. We moved back to Toronto in February and I started to watch "Sesame Street." But all the letters went by so fast. I'd try this and I'd try that but later I'd forget.

Then it was Clayton's birthday, the 31st of March. Clayton's the one who has made the movies about our family. He did *Paper Boy* and *Alligator Shoes* and *One Hand Clapping*, and he made *Rose's House* about my boarding house in Cabbagetown. Now he's making movies in Hollywood. I said to my son Jerry, "I want you to write, 'Happy Birthday Clayton, it's going to be a beautiful party.'" He wrote it and it took me over half an hour to copy the message down on the card. I would look at the letters and then forget what they looked like. It's hard, you know. They were not very nice letters.

Clayton found this beautiful that I wanted to read and write. He went and put my name down at Jones Avenue School in Toronto. I started there in October, 1978.

It's hard to get out of home when the man doesn't want you to do this. You're lucky if you can get out the door. That's why I didn't start in September — I had to fight with Albert all the time because he wanted me at home. He said I was never going to learn. Maybe he was afraid. But one day he said, "It's no use, Rose, I can see what you want. I can't stop you."

I said, "No, you can't stop me."

But when I was first at school, I was so depressed. After two months I phoned my mother. I was crying and I said, "I made a mistake, I should never have said, 'Rose is going to school.' I was crazy to think I could learn."

And she said, "Rose, you got nothing to lose. You did the best thing."

I was forty-six years old. I had always helped other people, but now I had to ask for help. This was hard to do.

At first I hated all the teachers. I didn't understand how they could go so fast, and I was just a little thing in the corner. But then I understood why I hated them. It's because I was thinking about the nuns in Montreal. You couldn't trust those people.

I went to school five days a week, for three years. Once I started to trust people, I was okay. It was strange, I had always bought school supplies for the children, and now I had to buy them for myself. The other people in the class were from all over the place — China, Vietnam, Quebec. It was so hard! I remember sitting in the library, trying to read a book for an hour and I understood six words. Maybe it would have been easier if I'd been learning in French. But I don't speak French the way they do in books.

I didn't understand so many things. *That apple is red — that apple is not red* — it's funny when you're not used to it. "Why do you say it's red when I know it's red? If it's red, then why do you say it's not red? Why do you change your mind?" I thought that probably my eyes were different. It's hard on the eyes. The first thing you know, I had to change my glasses.

But I kept on going to school. And after I was there seven months, I wrote a letter to my principal. This is what I wrote:

Jones School, Tuesday, June 12, 1979.

The first day I came at school, I was lost and nervous. I saw all around. The principal gave me a paper. I forgot the room and my names for one week. I was always thinking about my house and I felt stupid and crazy. I hated the teacher, the principal, and myself so much. Not now. I was thirty years at home. It was strange, when my teacher Susan talked to me I jumped. Here it is nice, because we have a private teacher every day in the library. Today I'm happy because I didn't stop my school. I read and I write today, I like my two teachers very much.

Rose Maltais Borris

And at the bottom of my letter, the principal wrote: "This is an excellent piece of work."

Albert used to say to me: "You're crazy!" But now, I read in front of him. And the first thing I know, he was trying to read too, a Bible. I laughed at this: he's trying to find out what happened to his wife and he hasn't found out yet and he's probably never going to find out. Not in there!

5
Sharon Butala
FIELD OF
BROKEN DREAMS

LAST summer as Saskatchewan farmers ate their noon meal (still called "dinner" out here on the land), their radios tuned to CBC's "The Noon Edition," they heard about a film shown on Soviet television commending farming Saskatchewan-style. Here on the Butala ranch, in the heart of Palliser Triangle wheat country, our response was a silence, followed by laughter. But apparently, if *perestroika* is to be a success, the Soviet government wants its farmers to consider family farming a possibility. If we — our situation being what it is — saw this as something of a joke on ourselves, Bernard Lavigne of the University of Regina's Film and Video school, the man who is now co-producing a second documentary with the Soviets, didn't. He assured me that, although we tend to focus on the problems, in places like China, India, and the Soviet Bloc our Prairie agriculture is seen as highly productive and successful.

This impression might surprise the farmers of the province, most of whom had watched Premier Grant Devine on television in March when he told us, "For the first time since 1933, the forecast is for a realized net farm income of minus $9 million." In other words, again this year, most of us will find ourselves spending more to seed, grow, and harvest our crops than their sale will bring us, further eroding what capital we still might have. What we see here is a pretty grim picture by anybody's standards and one that, if Soviet farmers knew about it, would surely give them second thoughts about giving up the security of their collective farms — however inefficient they might seem — for some version of family farming.

Soviet farmers have never had to worry about selling their wheat (they are net importers), nor about the availability of markets. The fact that governments around the world had found it necessary to pay subsidies to their farmers to bring their incomes up to the cost of production, thus throwing world grain economies into confusion, didn't bother the Soviet farmer. As a state employee, he had, in a sense, a guaranteed income. But Canadian farmers are all too well aware that our markets are dwindling. The countries of the European Economic Community have started to export instead of import wheat as they move closer to self-sufficiency. Mexico, China, Brazil, and India, among others, are reducing imports as well. The future of the 20-million metric tonnes of wheat we export each year and the $2.5 billion it brings to the economy is in doubt. And unlike in the U.S.S.R., questions of competition for markets and the price of wheat have a direct and immediate impact on each family farmer. In 1956, 17 percent of the population of Canada was on farms; in 1986 only 3.5 percent was, and the percentage continues to drop.

The National Farmers Union did a study in 1989 and found that about 1.5 million acres (just the tip of the iceberg of debt secured by land), in the three Prairie provinces are already under direct title to financial creditors. Since farm bankruptcies in Saskatchewan (the province that produces 60 percent of the country's wheat) jumped by 32 percent in 1989, accounting for 45 percent of all farm bankruptcies across Canada, the loss of control of land by small farmers continues, and the failure rate throws into question claims of success.

And the cost to keep our farmers growing an export crop — 20-million of the 26-million tonnes grown annually — is tremendous. In 1989, governments poured $1.2 billion into the bottomless pit of Saskatchewan agriculture in the form of "program payments." In 1987, it was closer to $2 billion (roughly $30,000 per farm). About 25 percent of the income of the average Saskatchewan farmer in 1989 came from the government and not from farm sales — although, to be fair, a proportion of this money had been paid into some of these programs by the farmers themselves through various taxes and levies. Yet despite the gold-plated bandaids, the success of the Prairie family farm, as imagined by the Soviets, is an elusive beast. In 1931, there were 1,186,608 people living on farms; today, there are about a third that number. What kind of success is that?

Hanging in a place of honor on our kitchen wall is a Family Farm Heritage Award certificate that pays tribute to Peter's father, George Butala. It gives the date of his filing under the Homestead Act as 1923. (This was the Dominion Lands Act of 1872, under which, for a $10 registration fee, a settler obtained the rights to a quarter-section of land.) Actually, George and his brothers had been in the country for more than 10 years by then, working in the mines in British Columbia, which George soon gave up in favor of cowboying near Maple Creek, Saskatchewan, till he could save enough money to buy the cattle to start his own place. Eventually, though, all three brothers settled on adjacent quarters here in the extreme southwest corner of Saskatchewan and began to build up the ranch that Peter now runs. Unwittingly, they had chosen to settle in the area that is unofficially known as the Palliser Triangle, the driest area of the Prairies. In 1859, explorer John Palliser had defined an area of roughly 259,000 square metres as "a triangle having for its base the 49th parallel from longitude 100°" (roughly south of Brandon, Manitoba) "to 114°" (south and a little east of Calgary) "with its apex reaching to the 52nd parallel of latitude" (about at Kindersley, Saskatchewan), which he described as infertile and unfit for settlement because of its aridity. The area now contains the bulk of the wheat farms on the Prairies, where, paradoxically, some of the finest grain in the world is grown.

I try to imagine what southwest Saskatchewan must have looked like to those first Butala boys, fresh in from Slovakia. Treeless, rolling shortgrass — mostly grama and buffalo grasses, which grow only about 30 centimetres high, in contrast to tallgrass, which occurs where the soil is richer and there is more rainfall — it is ideal for grazing cattle, as American ranchers well knew, the horizon lost in a sea of hills in each direction, in the blazing heat of summer and the long, lovely falls, a pale yellow shading to cream and silver. This is a country of the sun, which cures the grass, making it rich in nutrients — ranchers here have always boasted of their healthy, grass-fed cattle — and, to these men coming from overcrowded and land-poor eastern Europe, the amazing limitless spread of sky and empty grazing land must have seemed paradise.

About the same time, Charles E. Saunders, a plant breeder on a Dominion experimental farm, later appointed Dominion cerealist, developed early-maturing, hardy Marquis wheat, vital for successful farming in the harsh prairie climate. The Butala brothers each ploughed up some of the grass on their homestead quarters to grow it. They primarily raised cattle, though, and, as they acquired more land, broke a minimal amount for grain crops, preferring the free-riding cattleman's life to the back-breaking drudgery of farming.

It was not an accident that these dry southern plains were settled by farmers and ranchers. The late Toronto-based historian Donald Creighton wrote, "The whole world seemed ready to hasten to the exploitation of the Canadian West." It had been evident early on that a transcontinental railway would be needed both to hold the new nation together and to make it possible to fill up the west with settlers in order to stave off American "Manifest Destiny" fever, which threatened to extend the U.S.A. northward. These were the aims of national policy; once the railway was completed in 1885, settlement became possible. Recruitment began in the British Isles and Europe, where agents succeeded in uprooting thousands of people from milder climates and densely populated countrysides, many of whom knew nothing about farming and were unprepared for the extreme isolation the government's system of subdividing land ensured. It was a "fill up the west and never mind the cost" policy.

In its eagerness, the government even ignored its own experts. Despite John Palliser's famous warning and, earlier, in 1857, Henry Hind's similar report that the southern Prairies were too dry and infertile for farming, most of the area had been opened for farming by the turn of the century. This is described by several historians as largely the result of the report of botanist John Macoun, who was inadvertently sent out in a wet year (1872), and who was so impressed by the growth he saw that he declared much of this area to be suitable for the plough. This was what the government had hoped to hear, and it used his report as proof that all the west might be opened for homesteading.

When Clifford Sifton became head of the Ministry of the Interior in 1896, he thought the hardy Slavic people would make ideal immigrants, and his army of recruiters swarmed over central and eastern Europe exaggerating conditions and often lying outright about the climate, soil fertility, and amenities available to the settlers. They came by the thousands, the Butala brothers among them, and the hardship that awaited them is a familiar story. The provincial archives at the University of Saskatchewan in Regina has, in its homestead documents, a cache of piteous letters written by settlers to government agents. They tell of whole families reduced in winter to a diet of potatoes, or wiped out by scarlet fever or diphtheria, of devastating poverty, and of insanity brought on by deprivation and loneliness.

Some hung on, and the west adopted the proud slogan "Breadbasket of the World," and the phrase "next year country" entered the language, not so much in bitterness as in a good-humored self-mockery that failed to hide the unquenchable hope behind it. The truth is there were good to wonderful crops in

1911, 1925-28, 1952, 1963, 1966, and 1969 (the 1940s had a mixed record), which were offset by failures from 1917 to 1921, all through the 1930s, in 1954, and in 1961.

The 1970s were mostly good to very good years. In the early part of the decade, when the farmer got about $8 a bushel for durum wheat, the still-standing record, all around us farmers were ploughing up any grassland they had left. Peter, who had an ingrained dislike of the monotony of farming, stuck to the course of action laid down by his rancher father. He had by that time roughly 20 sections of land, mostly leased from the government, some deeded, available to him for breaking, of which about 1,000 acres had been broken by various settlers. At that time, cattle prices were low, and the Saskatchewan government was subsidizing farmers to break their Crown-owned lease land, and the possibility of at last making some real money tempted some of our neighbors to go even further: they sold all their cattle, ploughed up all their land, then borrowed heavily to buy more land and the huge, expensive machinery necessary to get the farming done in the short Great Plains farming season. It seemed that in the Palliser Triangle bigger was better; that was the lesson taught by the first settlers, the ones who left behind a few broken acres in a sea of grass and a depression where their cellars had been before they were starved out. Because of the aridity, even small-scale ranching was out of the question.

It turned out that the prosperity of the 1970s was only another in the southern Prairies' repeated, short-lived farming booms, and Peter's resistance to the trend around him turned out to be right. The good years were rapidly ended by the severe droughts that began in 1984, a drop in world wheat prices, and extraordinarily high interest rates on all that money farmers had borrowed. At the same time, input costs — the price of machinery, fuel, insecticides and herbicides, and chemical fertilizers — were up to 300 percent higher than they had been at the beginning of the 1970s. This spring, those who are still on their farms — and with the help of another government subsidy — will probably be seeding much of that newly broken land back to grass. Here on the Butala ranch, we are talking about seeding back to grass even most of the land broken 60 to 70 years ago by Peter's father and his brothers.

We have been farming the Prairies for about 100 years; more in southern Manitoba, less in southern Saskatchewan and Alberta. All the Prairie — as can be readily seen from the air — was laid out in a vast checkerboard of 160-acre, quarter-section squares, some in summer fallow, some in crop, very little in native prairie, with one isolated family per quarter-section or, as farm size grew, one per section or more. The land where the buffalo roamed had been tamed and put to work in the service of farmers, each an entrepreneur, with a major capital valuation (in Saskatchewan, it averaged $500,000 in the mid-1980s) and often a debt load nearly as large, who had been encouraged by agricultural experts to think of themselves as businessmen first and of farming, which once evoked a picture of a hardy yeoman cheerfully tilling his small plot to feed his family, as agribusiness.

Most of the agricultural experts in the bureaucracy, farm-supply corpora-tions, and academia — people whose livelihood depends on preserving a strong front — will tell you that this approach has proven out. After all, Canada's share of the international wheat export market was roughly 22.5 percent in 1987-88, second only to the U.S.A., which had 41.3 percent. Farms directly employed 209,000 people in the three Prairie provinces alone. Canadians could feel they played a significant role in alleviating world hunger since our wheat went to China, the U.S.S.R., India, and to feed the people in the developing nations of Africa and South America. Although vagaries of weather and markets still affected everyone in agriculture, by and large, many would agree wholeheart-edly with filmmaker Bernard Lavigne that our agriculture was very successful in its encounter with an often inhospitable environment and a highly competi-tive marketplace.

Even in an undeniably rough patch like this one, there are farmers, thorough-ly knowledgeable about agriculture and the world grain trade, who refuse to abandon the businesslike approach. If anything, they want to take it further. George Fletcher, a farmer, former president of the Western Canadian Wheat Growers Association, and a member of Saskatchewan's Community Futures Board (whose purpose is to encourage innovation and diversification in rural Saskatchewan), points out that we have more than half of all the arable land in Canada here in the Prairies. "I don't know where on earth there is more oppor-tunity than right here," he told me. He sees the current difficulties in agriculture as a result of "the government controlling our marketing system [through the Canadian Wheat Board]." This system makes it, in effect, illegal for farmers to market their own wheat, and cushions them from the direct effect of the mar-ketplace (of course, farmers with smaller spreads than Fletcher's appreciate being cushioned, especially during the current trade wars). Consequently, they have failed to change the products they grow and the quantities of them as the demands of the marketplace have changed over the years, and this, he believes, is largely what has landed farmers in the predicament they are in today, and not anything inherent in farming methods themselves. This he sees as a remediable problem.

Future remedies notwithstanding, things look bleak for the family farm. Through the 1980s, sometimes farm incomes were good, but equally often they weren't, and at best most farm families were never more than moderately well off — and it had taken them three generations to get there. In 1986, when the average Canadian male was earning $23,855, Revenue Canada reported the average farmer's income was $15,748, ranking it twentieth, below even fishermen, in a list of incomes from 24 major Canadian occupations.

Lack of capital or access to it has become a major problem for farmers. American agricultural economist Marty Strange, co-founder and co-director of the Center for Rural Affairs, a Nebraska-based nonprofit organization, demonstrated that government granting systems favor big farmers, as does agricultural research. The same is true of the Canadian granting systems and research, and very large farm partnerships can often get loans when smaller family farms no longer can. And it is hardly news that capital is slowly being withdrawn from the family farmer. The hard-luck stories, every one of them moving, continue to be trotted out by the media, as they have been during every bad spell since the turn of the century. And the bankers are always the hissing villains. Recently there was a report on television that the Royal Bank is concentrating on lending money to the most secure farmers, but rumors have been rampant among farmers for months now that this would happen, based mostly on the reports of startled and desperate farmers coming empty-handed out of banks where they have always dealt, of farmers who haven't missed a payment having their loans called in.

Although calling in non-delinquent loans may seem like an extraordinary measure, in fact, from the bank's point of view, it makes good sense. Most farm loans are secured by using land as collateral. Around 1984, as the world grain surplus built and the droughts combined to hobble Prairie farmers' income, land values began to drop seriously (an average Saskatchewan quarter-section dropped from $66,000 in 1982 to $42,000 in 1988). Banks began to look instead at a farmer's cash flow to ensure he would be able to repay his loan, since his land was worth so much less than it had been in the past. If a farm no longer appeared on paper to be profitable — and with all the other factors in play since then many (if not most) farms in Saskatchewan no longer make money — then the banks called the loans in while the farmer still had some assets with which to repay them.

The current woes have their roots in the fact that the western farm economy is set up along business lines, with a moral carrot — that is, we are to grow not just a crop for the needs of Canada, but for a hungry world. For three generations now, and with each new crop year and every report of famine somewhere in the world, they have been reminded that their crops were needed to keep the world from starving. With world population increasing by about 75 million a year, while every 24 hours more than 35 thousand people die of starvation, this approach of farming all the even marginally arable land available seemed unarguably the right thing to do.

But experts like Susan George, a fellow of the Institute of Policy Studies, a liberal, nonprofit research organization, and Frances Moore Lappé, founder of the Institute for Food and Policy Studies and author of *Diet for a Small Planet*, among others, have argued that there is no food shortage, that hunger is instead the result of mismanagement of food and funds by the elite class in rich and poor countries. More food is produced than is consumed, these authors claim, and people starve, essentially, because they are poor, can't afford to buy it, and live in countries where unfettered capitalism keeps it from them.

While we are not in danger of appearing on television looking like the starving farm people of Ethiopia whose small plots of lands were seized by bigger landowners, the statistics do give pause. Last year alone, 23,000 people left Saskatchewan. Meanwhile, the average farm size in this province has gone from about 400 acres in 1926 to almost 1,000 acres in 1990, while the number of farms is less than a third of what it was. We haven't reached the era of the big, faceless corporate farm yet, partly because of laws in the Prairie provinces restricting farm ownership to residents, but the trend can be seen: in 1985, individual family farms accounted for only 59 percent of all agricultural sales, down from 65 percent in 1980, while farms operated as partnerships, many of them families who've decided to go big, increased their percentage of sales from 14 percent to 16 percent.

All this upheaval in agriculture has had a bad effect on rural life in general. As farms get bigger, inevitably small farmers are displaced — and when they sell out, they move away. With a smaller population on the land to feed the life of the small towns, businesses close, the town's tax base is eroded, and services begin to disappear one by one, which leads to a further loss of population. G.E. Gordon, a consulting urban planner in Calgary, has predicted that by 2003, 90 percent of the Prairie population will live in urban centers, with the remaining 10 percent living in "corridors" between them.

As well, on the southern plains the landscape itself has been changed by farming and especially by the trend to large-scale farming. It is inefficient for today's giant machines to go around obstacles like old buildings or bluffs of trees, or wet spots. A typical sight is a 16-kilometre stretch of road south of here where every single homestead building along it has been burned and buried and the few acres thus gained ploughed and seeded. Even the windbreaks and farmstead hedges are gone, bulldozed and hauled away to produce a monotonous, even ugly, landscape of nothing but summer fallow or crops. Sloughs where birds once nested have been drained and filled, and gradually high spots are lowered. Even road allowances, the last refuge of plains wildlife, go under the plough. The beauty of the Prairies is rapidly becoming only a memory.

Big farming, however, is just the latest twist to an old problem: farming, period. "Agriculture has changed the face of the land the world over," according to geneticist Wes Jackson, a proponent of developing wheat plants that are more like perennial prairie grasses, and founder of the Kansas Land Institute, a non-profit organization of iconoclastic academics who describe themselves as being dedicated to "sustainable alternatives in agriculture." An example is Iraq. In ancient times, it was Mesopotamia in the Fertile Crescent where the first farms in the world, between and beside the Tigris and Euphrates rivers, were each spring flooded and fed with fresh deposits of nutrient-rich alluvial soil. Without any of today's technology (and partly by using an extensive irrigation system), these farmers supported a population estimated at about 20 million. Today, only an eighth of the original farmland is arable; the rest is mostly desert. Throughout history and in many sites around the world from the Holy Land, once rich in forests and farms, to Greece, Mexico, and Peru, this story has been repeated.

One thing farmers know for sure about farming is that they can't continue to farm the same piece of ground, no matter how fertile, year after year, without eventually destroying its fertility, unless they handle it gently, and regularly return an adequate amount of nutrients and organic matter to it. Although big farmers try to do this, they are hampered by, among other things, the increased need for chemical fertilizer and the breaking down and consequent erosion of soil by the constant crush of huge machinery.

The 1930s taught farmers a lot of lessons about how to prevent soil erosion using techniques such as planting windbreaks, strip farming, leaving the cut stalks for mulch, and so on. Then, after a few decades of good moisture and with a new generation of farmers who never saw the Depression, much of this hard-earned wisdom was ignored. During the worst years of the 1980s drought, on more than one occasion soil drifting was so bad across some highways in Saskatchewan that visibility was nil and the Mounties had to close them to travellers till the wind went down.

The basic problems with farming, no different today than they were 6,000 years ago, have their roots in the pressure on farmers because of decreasing profit margins to produce more crops, sometimes on marginal or "exhausted" soil. It's ultimately a losing proposition. According to the Worldwatch Institute, a Washington, D.C.-based think-tank on sustainable development, topsoil on cropland around the world is being lost at an estimated 24 billion tonnes annually (most of which ends up in the oceans). In the Prairies, it is estimated that as a result of cultivation 30 to 35 percent of the original organic matter of the soil (i.e., the nutrients) has been depleted, and that roughly 10 percent of the Prairies' soil is affected by salinity. Bushel-per-acre productivity may have increased, but the machinery and chemicals that have created this dubious harvest are inexorably wearing out the land. In Saskatchewan alone, an average of 10 to 15 tonnes of soil per hectare is being lost annually to wind and water erosion. At that rate, the 15 centimetres of topsoil in that province will be gone in 100 years.

We appear to have reached a turning point in our history as agrarian people and in our relations with the soil that nurtures us. With the serious concerns about the effects on a population of soil degradation and erosion, the greenhouse effect threatening us, and the trend to a smaller number of very large farms gaining control of our food supply, it's time for drastic measures. Knowing that my modest proposal will shock many and horrify not a few — farmers in particular — I offer this suggestion anyway:

Surely it would make more sense, in view of all the problems involved in farming the dryland prairie, to invest that annual billion dollars or more in turning those farms back into the grassland from which they came — not every farm in the Prairie provinces, by any means, but many if not most in the Palliser Triangle and elsewhere in the Prairies where farming has always been marginal.

Instead of fighting a losing battle for markets, instead of risking topsoil and environment — life itself — it might be better to move out the farmers and close off these areas of marginal land, especially in southern Alberta and Saskatchewan (both sites of huge, planned irrigation projects, as if the calamities in the Fertile Crescent and elsewhere had never happened), to farming entirely. Perhaps it is finally time to admit that, in terms both of heartache and cash, the settling of farmers on the dry, southern plains was an experiment that failed.

Much of that land, in a slow and gradual process, might be turned into a national park. Some farmers, loving the places where they have spent their lives, will be determined to stay even in the face of poverty, and those who want to might be set to raising antelope and buffalo, animals native to the region that, if allowed to run in relative freedom, don't do the damage to the land that cattle and sheep do.

Where soil and weather conditions make it feasible — parts of central Alberta, Saskatchewan, and southern Manitoba — sustainable agriculture geared to producing the six million tonnes of wheat for Canadian needs could be encouraged. Sustainable agriculture implies small farms and appropriate technology in terms of size and techniques, and it also implies a reverence for the soil, which is the source and end of all life. While it is not practicable in much, if not all, of the Palliser Triangle because of the aridity, it is feasible for farms in the fertile belt mostly north of the triangle.

Those who will be losing their livelihood sooner (rather than inevitably, as would be the case if we just let things go on) would be retrained in other fields — perhaps tourism and oil and gas development, both industries the Saskatchewan government is promoting. I believe that the vast expanses of regenerated prairie grassland, with rejuvenated wildlife stocks, could be successfully marketed internationally as a last-of-its-kind tourist attraction.

For all those who choose to remain on the newly seeded grasslands, some form of an income guarantee would be necessary until the new ways of making a living are established. But in time all of us would have back the majestic grassland to act as inspiration and balm and to remind us of who we are and the great mystery from which we came. It would be the end, too, of tragic stories we've heard repeated over and over again through the years of farm families in despair having seen a lifetime's work destroyed in droughts, as a result of market fluctuations, or both. It would mean that our grandchildren would have a prairie to run through, rather than desert. And for me, that is important.

In the Eastend cemetery, high above the town Wallace Stegner immortalized in *Wolf Willow*, is George Butala's red granite tombstone. It says simply, "Rancher." It represents a whole generation of immigrants and their dreams who are gone now, and I can't help but think that if there isn't some shift in our direction towards megafarms, that headstone will mark not only the death of one man who cherished the grasslands, and of the grasslands themselves, but worse: the death of the heart of a nation, its agrarian people.

6
Dalton Camp
THE PLOT TO KILL CANADA

Fᴏʀ a veteran Canadian, a unilingual Maritime wᴀsᴘ of Loyalist patrimony, a missionary-for-life in the tribal politics of his country, visiting Quebec City has always been a profoundly personal experience. This may have something to do with an inability to speak the language of Quebec; becoming functionally mute does concentrate the senses and creates in oneself a novel state of alert, a sensitivity to sights and sounds which need not lead to feelings of apprehension but simply confirms the existence of cosmic differences.

In the voluminous memoirs of Charles de Gaulle there is a single mention of Quebec. Visiting the city in 1944, near the end of the war, he wrote of his reception there: "I felt as if I were being inundated by a tide of French pride mingled with an inconsolable affliction, both sentiments flowing from history's backwaters." Despite the somewhat turgid metaphor, there's truth in it. René Lévesque used to say Quebec was "fed up with being seen as a museum." But in Quebec — the city — it is hard to step around all the museum pieces; history permeates the walls, is underfoot, in the penetrating chill of the wind blowing off the river, fills the eye as it crowds the mind. Could there be a museum without a history?

Just outside the tearoom of my hotel there is a statue of Samuel de Champlain. He is one hell of a pile of stone, Lévesque might have thought, standing there with empty eyes on distant horizons. "The Aeneas of a destined people and in his ship lay the embryo life of Canada," an American historian wrote of the great mariner's voyage up the St Lawrence. On the other side of the hotel, in the small park only a few steps from the American consulate, there is another museum piece. Not nearly so massive as the bulk of Champlain standing against the sky, instead a modest pile of stone, an obelisk; an understatement, one imagines. One side of the base, in gold leaf, reads "Montcalm," the opposite side reads "Wolfe." On the side facing the river, a plaque offers a carved inscription. Apart from the names of Wolfe and Montcalm and of George ɪᴠ, everything else is in Latin. A reader too long out of school could make no sense of it; perhaps this is what the donor intended.

The museum piece is useful as metaphor: history recalled to visitors to the museum in a dead language. It keeps the secret, as it has for centuries, not of The Conquest, but of the miracle, as Arthur Lower put it, of *survivance*. One cannot read the history of Quebec without discovering the miracle. Perhaps Canadians have not read enough of it, which may explain why, when they read *Je me souviens* on the plates of Quebec vehicles, some think it a coded message. Others write letters to the editor, complaining of ingratitude.

John Diefenbaker once said to me, during a futile argument about the flag issue, "The French, you see, have too much." (He thought the flag had been designed for Quebec.) It was a joke, not the knee-slapper you could dine out on, or retail in the company cafeteria, but almost thirty years later, looking out my window from the Château Frontenac at the Canadian flag flying against the winds blowing out of the north from Nouveau Québec, I was reminded Diefenbaker really did believe the French had too much; that's only half the joke. The other half is, he was right. They have a whole history, a triumphant and unassailable culture, an impregnable language, and they have a choice.

It *is* too much. And should the choice go the other way — the fire next time — what would become of the rest of us? A raggedy-assed collage of factions, a man-made disaster of epic achievement — who would take us in? Is there a world market for failed nations? Should there be a garage sale of the provinces? (What if three, four, or five were left on the table at the close of business? Would the Americans be interested in a greatly reduced Manitoba when they already have North Dakota?)

Not that this denouement would be without instant revelation. The morning after the cancellation of The Conquest, the sun would also rise on the nation of Diefenbaker's dreams, and of those legions of lesser statesmen who have walked in his train: One Canada, at last! Speaking of inconsolable affliction! Of historic backwaters!

My meeting with Jacques Parizeau had been set for 11:30 Monday morning, then moved to five o'clock. The change suggested more time for us to talk, and fewer interruptions. I had no plans for an interview between an *éminence*, the politician, and your enquiring reporter — none of that. I just wanted another, second, look at him, maybe walk around in his head. Someone had told me Parizeau was a charismatic personality. If so, he would be the first I'd encountered since Lord Beaverbrook; somehow, I couldn't conjure up a charismatic economist. But you never know.

The National Assembly building is itself a museum item, spectral presences afoot — Premiers L.A. Taschereau, Maurice Duplessis, the much-mourned Paul Sauvé (who many said was Canada's last, best chance), Jean Lesage, Dan Johnson, René Lévesque; all but Lesage died either in office or shortly thereafter. Since Quebec has hoarded its history, leaving next to nothing forgotten, each of its leaders leaves a legacy carefully preserved so that the flow towards its destiny may be almost exactly measured in the nudging progress of each successive regime. Incrementalism, like an incense, permeates the air.

For Quebec, politics has been the dutiful provider of continuity. In Maurice Duplessis and Robert Bourassa, who are as different as Lévis and Paris, there is a root connection. Doubtless this thesis would repel any historian worthy of the title. Even so, as *Visiteur 274* to the *Assemblée nationale*, being guided along the polished corridors through this hushed, cavernous, and empty pile of history (which reminds me of Versailles, with the furniture removed), it occurs to me how much political leaders in Quebec are unlike the others. (Joey Smallwood used to complain about Duplessis always being addressed as "Prime Minister" during federal-provincial conferences — something gained in the translation — as if premiers were a lower form in the pecking order of politics.) In Quebec, they are always prime ministers, and while leaders of the opposition are barely tolerated elsewhere, they are widely considered de facto members of the Quebec elite; after all, most of them will become prime minister.

The premises of the leader of the opposition are suitable for a politician who holds both office and turf. The Harlem Globe Trotters could practise here; conversational groupings of furniture are dispersed throughout the room, which is anchored by an executive desk so perfect in its tidiness as to suggest it is still awaiting the arrival of its first tenant.

Parizeau beckons me to a chair before his desk, thinks better of it, and we settle around a coffee table. An aide — his press secretary — brings coffee. She also brings a tape recorder.

The first time I saw, heard, encountered Jacques Parizeau — we both recalled — was at one of those eternal conferences on Canadian-American relations, which had been held at the Johnson Foundation (endowed with wax money), somewhere in Wisconsin. Parizeau had been advertised to the conferees as a "mystery guest" and after-dinner speaker by Mason Wade, the conference major-domo. (Wade, a New York-born historian, wrote extensively on Quebec and "French-English" relations.) This had taken place some twenty-two years ago — we guessed — and Parizeau, a mystery guest then fully deserving the description, had delivered essentially the same speech he was to make in New York twenty-two years later, about the inevitability of Quebec's independence. Then and now, Rimmer de Vries, managing director of Morgan Guaranty Trust, wasn't the only one to leave "the speech" asking, "Who is this guy?"

The academic credentials are impeccable: Ecole des hautes études commerciales (Montreal); l'Institut d'études politiques de Paris; the London School of Economics, where he received his doctorate. Returning to Montreal, to the Ecole des hautes études commerciales, he would teach for a decade before being drawn into the inner circles of the Quiet Revolution. Eight years later, having served three provincial administrations as consultant, adviser, commissioner, and all-round intellectual goad, Parizeau departed, leaving behind his own monuments — the Caisse de dépôt, Quebec's pension fund; and a public-sector union, the Common Front. Once again he resumed his teaching career, now an economic theorist with practical experience; he also became an activist in the Parti Québécois. After Lévesque came to power, Parizeau held, at one time or another, the portfolios of treasury board, revenue, financial institutions, economic development, and — of course — finance.

Already, this would be a public career worthy of *The Guinness Book of Records*. Has there been anyone else who has been so busily engaged from both sides of the ministerial desk? When the PQ government fell, in 1984, after eight years of power but without the consummation of its central idea, the party became a spiritless halfway house to separatism. After losing another election, the party turned to Parizeau, himself become something of an inevitability.

There cannot be much left for him to do, other than lead his province out of Confederation. This was once believed a job for a firebrand; Parizeau looks more like a banker, one of those with offices above the ground floor, overlooking the city. His father owned a Montreal insurance company — Parizeau & Parizeau — which bespeaks an early life of comfort and an apprenticeship in actuarial reckonings. The thing to remember about Parizeau is that he has lived all of his life in the company of money.

Second impressions may be no better than the first; the second one of Parizeau is the same. The voice is even — today's crises and tomorrow's weather reported from a detached, dispassionate observer, from someone who has seldom been surprised. His conversion to the cause, which to him is not a cause but a historic inevitability, took place on a train in 1969.

"My road to Damascus was the CPR," he says. "I was very tired. I had been working quite hard and I had a function to prepare for — a seminar in Banff — and I hadn't written the first line of the thing. So I boarded the train. I had a nice compartment and I started to write for three days and three nights. The paper started in a federalist fashion. It was the first three days where I had time to think about these matters...."

A collector of ironies interrupted with a question: "You became a separatist in Saskatchewan?"

"Probably between Regina and Calgary."

He had worked for Lesage, Johnson, and Bourassa — always in a senior role, usefully and importantly engaged, but finding "less and less to do." He had only recently finished off the report of the committee of inquiry into Quebec's financial institutions.

"I was chairman of the commission and I handed over my report to the government in September of '69. By October, I had turned to the Parti Québécois."

Obviously, there would have been other episodes, other stations to the cause, than the linear trip by train that carried him to the Saskatchewan Conversion. All along, perhaps, had he been packing his bags for a journey to his certain destination?

At Banff, the convert rattled the seminarians with his heretical conclusions. Redrafting the constitution while continuing a process of ad hoc improvisation wouldn't work, he said. Instead, it would be "more fruitful to find first an empirical equilibrium between governments, and then draft it into a legal text."

When I quoted the words to Parizeau, saying I had been struck by the phrase "empirical equilibrium" and what did it mean? — he could not remember writing it. Was it, he asked, "before or after I became a separatist?" In fact, the day after, but it was important to me only because it was, even if something said a generation ago, just about where the country was today — trying to work a legal text out of a near perfect disequilibrium, with no idea of where to begin.

To Parizeau, dismantling federalism into its present unworkable parts had been a joint federal-provincial project. "I think we had to go through the exercise, during the sixties, of divesting Canada of a great deal of its fiscal and budgetary muscle. And we did one hell of a job. We were all federalists. You know Lesage was obviously a federalist and Daniel Johnson, in spite of his demands for 'equality or independence' was at heart a federalist. We were all federalists. But for anyone of us who had any knowledge at all about economic and budgetary policy, we knew very well we were bringing the country into a state where, it was well known, it would be very difficult to govern. We had to be realistic about this."

Lévesque used to make the same point, sometimes quoting Parizeau. But this was, was it not, what Ottawa called "cooperative federalism"?

For Parizeau, these were "just words" covering a growing underground conspiracy. "For several years, we had opened up very dangerous inroads for ourselves in the federal system. For a time, the other provinces had a hard time understanding what on earth we were trying to do. Suddenly they realized that what we were doing was offering for some of them all kinds of possibilities. [When] we reached the crisis over the Canada Pension Plan, what Quebec had been doing had developed all kinds of appetites among other provinces."

Cooperative federalism reached its apogee in 1964, the scene of its ascendance a federal-provincial conference held in — Quebec City. The conference marked a turning point at which it would become clear that the more the new era of cooperation accomplished, the less it succeeded.

"Opting out" would be a feature of the new arrangements for which Ottawa, reflecting its usual insistence on an orderly withdrawal from the old federalism proposed two categories. Quebec alone exercised all its options in category one, involving hospital insurance, old-age assistance and disabled allowances, operating costs for technical education, welfare assistance, and health grants; in the second category, Quebec opted out of federal forestry programs, taking the equivalent cash for its own needs. All this amounted to more than twenty equalized points of personal income tax; more was to come.

The proposals put forward by Prime Minister Pearson for the Canada Pension Plan met serious disagreement. As Walter Gordon remembered it in his memoirs, Lesage reacted to the proposals "almost with contempt." Pearson had in mind a "pay-as-you-go" pension scheme, Lesage a funded one. Regardless, Quebec intended to proceed on its own and to collect more in contributions than was required for a pay-as-you-go plan in order to provide immediate capital funds for provincial investment.

What followed the confrontation was a spasm of shuttle diplomacy between Ottawa and Quebec City ending in a Pearsonian "compromise." The Canada

Pension Plan would become funded in the case of Quebec — and pay-as-you-go in the rest of the country, the latter scheme to be expressed forever after in red ink in Ottawa. Further, extended federal family-allowance payments for six-teen- and seventeen-year-olds, along with student-aid programs, would no longer be paid by Ottawa to Quebec residents but by the provincial government which would receive the equivalent amounts from the feds. The rout of cooper-ative federalism was on.

By 1967, "the assault on the federal government" was being conducted in broad daylight. Out of the smoke of chaos, federal finance minister Mitchell Sharp emerged, white flag in hand. When I asked Parizeau if he could identify the moment in time when federalism's dysfunction seemed to him to have become a terminal condition — this was the moment: "Mitchell Sharp threw in his hand and said, 'All right, from now on income tax can be very different from one province to the other. We will not any more share 100 points of a standard tax structure.' At that point, it was in a sense the last of an intelligible fiscal policy in Canada. Until then, all provinces — every once in a while — were trying to have the federal government, within that common tax structure for all Canada, abandon a few tax points. But the structure had remained the same. Our fault had been in not only driving these assaults but in developing such appetites among other provinces."

We are, all along here, drinking coffee and smoking up a storm. Parizeau stands and refills the cups.

"At that point, you know, I was very troubled," he says. "I was wondering where the whole bloody thing was going. I just didn't believe in that kind of exercise. I knew if the real game was being played with taxes and expenditures, there was the opportunity for each government to go its own way."

That same year — 1967 — Parizeau went his own way in other directions, among them trying to negotiate, as the premier's adviser, a communications system for Quebec that would involve a jointly made French-Quebec satellite and Russian boosters. This went on "while Canada was going along its road with the United States, Britain, and Japan. Within the same country, for God's sake." His independent negotiations for a provincial satellite system "didn't come to anything," although the effort was instructive.

He had been with Lesage then for four years, during the heady days of the Quiet Revolution. Eric Kierans, who served as the provincial minister of revenue, remembers Lesage coming to him early on to ask about Parizeau: "Can we get him?" Kierans thought they should try.

When George Marler heard about it, he protested to Lesage: "Don't touch him. He's a nationalist." Marler, an elder statesman in Liberal ranks, with both provincial and federal experience, knew the enemy. He lobbied Kierans, telling him Parizeau had once made a speech criticizing Kierans's appointment as president of the Montreal Stock Exchange. Kierans was unmoved. "All Parizeau said was it should have been a French Quebecker."

The economic whiz kid was not the only bright light in the firmament of Lesage's reconstructed bureaucracy: there were other future luminaries, such as Michel Bélanger, Robert Després, Claude Morin, Yves Pratte, and Arthur Tremblay. The result was an explosion of energy, more than enough for a quiet revolution, the likes of which has not been seen in Canada since the federal mandarinate assembled by Mackenzie King.

Parizeau says, "If you want to find a parallel with what happened here in the sixties — the small band of people involved — you really have to go to the construction of the civil service in Ottawa, starting [in 1939] with the war. One can't talk about social programs in Canada without going back to those people. The same thing happened in Quebec."

But the politicians?

"Some politicians were important. Lesage, obviously, raised us, all of us. He had the broad knowledge of public administration that he got from Ottawa. Then — Lévesque, Kierans, Gérin-Lajoie, and Laporte. You can't discuss the revolution in education with saying, 'Gérin-Lajoie,' but the man who built the system in Quebec was Arthur Tremblay — the Court of King Arthur we would say, speaking of the senior civil service. I have always said the Quiet Revolution was the job of five ministers and a dozen civil servants. But the fundamental characteristic of these so-called mandarins in Quebec was essentially the same as that of those in Ottawa in the forties and fifties. We were not partisan. We had nothing to do with partisan politics."

Are you partisan now?

"Of course I am. I have a hard time keeping my partisan reactions in range because of, shall we say, the constraints of my profession. Thank God I was an economist for so long."

Economists, even, can be forgiven their lapses into nostalgia. Kierans remembers drawing up the provincial budget "in Lesage's dining room." Four or five ministers and their deputies, Parizeau included, engulfed in cigar and cigarette smoke, sitting around the table in shirt-sleeves, a celebration of a rare egalitarianism.

"You couldn't tell who was who, or which was which," he remembers, "except the civil servants were younger."

They represented a good deal of cerebral thrust and, perhaps even more, sheer political muscle. After Quebec had pried twenty more points out of the federal income tax — moving the total up to forty-four, more than any province had ever had — Kierans, the revenue minister, set out printing Quebec's tax forms. But the new arrangements had not yet been tabled by the government in Ottawa. Pearson, the prime minister, feared not only public reaction to the newest development in cooperative federalism, but that of his own cabinet colleagues as well. While Kierans held up the presses, Walter Gordon, then federal finance minister, continued to stall.

Finally, Kierans called Gordon to advise him the Quebec tax forms were being printed. Shortly after, the government tabled its arrangements with Quebec late on a Friday afternoon, with most of the House absent. Ottawa's version of the old hidden-ball trick.

From 1962 through 1969, Parizeau remained in Quebec an eminent adviser and a professed federalist through three regimes. "The picture was so crazy that it was obvious to me we had to reorganize the system starting from the real source of evil, which was in trying to change the constitution by splitting hairs. By the time I became a separatist, I would often say that I agreed with Trudeau on just about everything except on where to put the capital city."

Between high school and college, Parizeau took the summer to hitchhike across Canada — at least from Montreal to Vancouver, and back. He remembers Revelstoke where "I had to jump a freight. No road traffic at all."

This was by way of responding to an observation made by a senior provincial civil servant who had watched, over the years, Parizeau's evolution, the progress of a born elitist, in which the man had seemed never to change, only his place at the table. He played each role to the hilt: senior adviser, senior bureaucrat, senior minister. Always comfortable in the company of power, self-assured to the edge of arrogance, and — most important — in the many delegations with which he travelled, the most French of the Quebeckers.

"When he became leader of the Parti Québécois," said the longtime observer, "I said to myself, 'Of course.'"

But Parizeau is not without experience in English Canada. A large part of his professional life was spent among economists, many of them Anglo-Canadian and most of them still his friends.

"I don't think that whatever I've been doing in politics might be influenced by the fact I've had very few relations with English Canada. On the contrary, I've always had them all my life."

He is not, he says, "closed-minded about what is going on in the rest of Canada." Of late, he is given a daily summary of press comments from the English newspapers, which he reads, although the impression is it is often a chore. Still, this view of him as the most French of the Québécois politicians? Would he rather go to Paris than New York?

"In that sense," he says, "culturally speaking, I'm very much French. I've travelled a great deal in my life, but as I get older, whenever I have a little time, I look at all the travel folders and the exotic destinations, and I say I will once more settle for Paris. My roots are there."

In the same way, I tell him, some of us end up in London. Kierans recalls Lévesque was a man who ended up in London. He was uncomfortable with Paris but loved to wake up in London, plunge into the newspapers, and delight in all the choices he would find — opera, ballet, theatre, even rock concerts. Where else in the world, he would say to Kierans, can you find so many choices?

It was difficult to get Parizeau to talk about Lévesque. They were, put simply, opposite personalities, from vastly different backgrounds, and while their politics converged on the same issue and nearly at the same point in time, Parizeau's conclusions were intellectual while Lévesque's seemed largely visceral. It would appear that although Parizeau really was not Lévesque's kind of guy, Lévesque was never quite Parizeau's kind of nationalist, and while they were comrades-in-arms, they remained at arm's length over method and strategies.

Even so, when he had been one of Lesage's ministers, and long after, Lévesque would often quote Parizeau to support his argument. Parizeau was his authority as to what Quebec could achieve as a nation, even a "nation unattended by sovereignty." Later on, as both were edging towards separatism, it seems clear Parizeau, a devout realist, was unwilling to take the lead. Looking back, it now appears the Quiet Revolution began a game of ideological leapfrog among the major players. By the end of the Lesage regime, one discovers Lévesque emerging at the head of a small army of the disenchanted, self-designated as the Souveraineté-Association movement, which Parizeau describes as a "sort of limbo, waiting for something to happen."

Something did, of course, happen. But before fixing on that, I asked Parizeau if there was not some irony in the fact that where Lévesque had been, way back then, Bourassa is now: sovereignty association for all!

Back then, in the sixties, Parizeau remembers people thinking, "'Oh my God, if we become a sovereign country and Canada applied to us the Canadian tariffs, while the U.S. tariffs are still very high, where are we?' In that sense, sovereignty association — the word 'association' was a point of departure — it was a way to prevent Canada from raising its tariffs against us. Originally, we were talking about how we'd avoid getting caught between two sets of variables — the U.S. and Canada. Twenty-five years later, the context is very different. A — There's a free-trade agreement in North America. And B — In any case, tariffs are so low that all kinds of things are possible with the result that now it's sovereignty and what we call a common-sense association which is important for both parties to maintain. And, shall we say, the answer can be yes or can be no, but either way nothing will be very traumatic."

In any case, this should tax the conscience of the Business Council on National Issues, those faceless free-traders, and enrich the nightmares of the conspiratorial school of historians. Could it be that the leap of faith was a plunge into an abyss? But it does explain the disproportionate enthusiasm of Quebeckers for Mulroney's Tories, as well as Bourassa's cold-shouldering his federal Liberal bedfellows, not to mention the sly endorsement of the deal by Parizeau, speaking from under the shadow of his economist's hat. This is the sort of business, in the celebrated Canadian indulgence for postmortems, to stir the furies and inspire the zealots: imagine the feast of remorse a severed country would enjoy!

I ask Parizeau, would the circumstances now be different if, for example, the country had elected Stanfield in 1972, instead of Trudeau? It is impossible "to remake history," he replies. He goes on to speak of John Robarts, who had been premier of Ontario through the 1960s: "I knew the man very well. Robarts's illness probably changed the course of history in Canada. He was the first one among all the Canadian politicians I've known — and I've known many of them — who really understood the position of Quebeckers. A remarkable man, the premier of Ontario.... The history of Canada might have been very different. And then, as you say, the fact is that with just a few more seats, Mr. Stanfield would have been in power."

The last sentence may have been spoken out of some deference to present company. But yes, comes the thought, there were similarities between Robarts and Parizeau. Both of them were implacably civil, moved with the same feline grace, an air of languid detachment about them, but in each deep reserves of strength and staying power. Only a fool would mistake the easy conviviality for pliability; Robarts could be tough when crowded and ruthless if crossed. Parizeau seems a man cast from the same mould.

One of Parizeau's first assignments as a government adviser was to slim down a provincial public service overburdened with functionaries of dubious value to a new government bent on rebuilding all in its purview. He came to Kierans with his organizational flow charts for each of the various departments, showing the lines of authority leading to boxes of responsibility, many of them circled in red ink, indicating those designated for redundancy.

Kierans, his heart forever on his sleeve, could not conceal a twinge of compassion: "My God," he said, "all those red circles are people."

"I know," Parizeau answered.

Lévesque, for whom economics was a dark mystery, struggled to suppress his visceral longings for an independent Quebec. His inner struggle was not shared by Parizeau who, when the subject arose, would reply by saying Quebec would first have to decide to provide its own currency. Lévesque appealed to Kierans, another economist, and was told that Parizeau was right. The question remains today, although Parizeau has since changed his mind, something he claims to have done "around 1980."

For a man of nearly perfect certitude, the economic theorist and the politician fused in a common enterprise, the monetary question — which troubled Lévesque — has not been entirely resolved. Could Quebec become independent while its monetary policy was made in Ottawa, its currency in Winnipeg? Ventilating the question, possibly the most vexing of all for Parizeau, takes one into the higher altitudes of banking and commerce, into thinner air. Could a ground-level observer, looking up, see wisps of doubt?

"Technically speaking," Parizeau says, "it's not all that difficult to answer the question. However, every time you mention — in any society — money, all kinds of emotions flow in all directions. I've never been particularly emotional about these things. It doesn't prevent me from speaking; it never did. There's no doubt, as far as Quebec is concerned, a distinct currency has been in the past — less today, much less today — considered something extremely dangerous, something that would move all kinds of people to make emotional statements: 'We'll go down the drain.'"

Since then, he continued, these emotions have been tempered by experience. The monetary policy conducted by the Bank of Canada in 1981, and the policy conducted by the Bank last year, had been — "and I'm not the only one to say so" — contrary to the interests of the Canadian and the Quebec economies.

"That should never happen. And therefore, I'm faced here in Quebec by two groups of people — no, by two reactions — and from week to week they're never quite the same. Those who say it would be more comforting if we had the same Canadian currency, but does that mean we'll have the same monetary policy? And I say, well, you can't have it both ways. If it's the same currency, it's the same monetary policy; it's how our system works. Our banking system and our financial system are so structured that you can't have one monetary policy on one side of the country and another monetary policy on the other."

But regardless of monetary policy, you can have more than one fiscal policy?

"Oh yes," Parizeau says, enjoying the opening. "Canada is proof of that." For example, when the Bank of Canada tightened the monetary screws, largely because of inflationary pressures in southern Ontario, the fiscal policy of the Ontario government headed in the opposite direction — fiscal restraint be damned for a policy.

Then, returning to the monetary question, "Of course, a lot of people in Quebec are ambivalent about this; but they are much less afraid than they were ten years ago." There are now spokesmen for Quebec's business community who are saying, "If we need to have a Quebec currency, we'll have it."

"Ten years ago, the issue was never discussed in these terms. In English Canada these days, I hear all kinds of reactions about this question: 'Who are these guys in Quebec who think we're going to have the same currency? That's pie in the sky. We'll never accept that.'"

Indeed, we are all hearing these things. Canada's currency has become our karma, a comfort to our own ambivalence. And to the karmic force of the money supply, add some good, old-fashioned Anglo-Saxon common sense, which yields our strategy: since Canadians would refuse to share their currency with an independent Quebec, what would it do for money?

"The problem with that, you know, is that eventually one has to go back to techniques. Even if or when there is a Quebec currency, Quebeckers remain the proud owners of a quarter of the [Canadian] money supply. There is no way, in our financial system, where the Bank of Canada could reduce the money supply in one area. If they wanted to reduce the money supply, they have to do it throughout the country. And Canadians would find themselves with a floating debt — thank God for each and every dollar — a floating debt of $100-billion in Quebec. And when you start looking at simply the technicalities of this, well, you do just about what I do these days: I say we'll have to look at a common currency.

"Everyone is very sentimental and emotional about these things. Let us pray after a few months it will pass; eventually the technicians will have to handle the issue. I just leave you — I always repeat the same thing — with one thought. When Ireland left the United Kingdom in 1921 — in a very difficult atmosphere — the pound sterling remained the common currency for twenty years. Money talks. Actually, I would think everyone will realize that technically speaking, it is much better to have a common currency."

Was it too craven of me, at that moment, to agree? I imagined myself driving from New Brunswick through Quebec to — perish the thought — Ottawa. Should I stay overnight in Quebec, would not the common currency be a convenience? A convenience to anyone doing business in Quebec?

"What you raise here is something different," Parizeau says, to my surprise, since it had not been my intention to change the subject. For the first time in the conversation, it was possible to detect a shift in tone, signalling something more serious about to be said.

"A lot of people in English Canada, at the present time, are saying about economic association: 'No way, no way. They won't have their cake and eat it too.' A lot of what they're talking about, in terms of economic association, isn't really connected to having your cake and eating it too. Transportation, for instance — water, the St Lawrence Seaway, railways, roads. There are all sorts of arguments with respect to transportation. If Canada came to be divided in two parts, do we keep the present arrangements or do we change them? The first country that would raise these questions would not be Quebec. It would be Canada. In a number of such areas, the idea is not Quebec asking for something, hoping to get it, and Canada saying, 'Well, let me think about it.' It isn't that way at all."

But if one wants a second opinion on economics, one need only ask a second economist. Kierans doubts economic theorists live in the real world. "You know, we used to say: 'With an "if" here and an "if" there, you can put Paris in a bottle.'"

And I used to say politics, like recessions, were cyclical. How else to explain the ebb and flow of nationalism in Quebec? Is Parizeau now so anxious for an early referendum, and Bourassa so reluctant — and the rest of Canada so silent — because the separatist tides are high?

The nub of the question is to learn from Parizeau how come the unprecedented popularity of his cause. A week after the death of Lévesque, forty-four percent of Quebeckers polled favored sovereignty, more than at any time Parizeau could remember. Today, the numbers in favor are closing on seventy percent. For over fourteen months, separation has enjoyed a bull market.

"I think the story starts in the first months of 1989, when several business people came forward in Quebec and said, 'Well, maybe sovereignty for Quebec is not such a bad idea. Maybe we could manage; maybe we'd be better off, just maybe.' But the impact here was extraordinary. Remember, the main objèction to sovereignty has always been economic, and that argument was all the more impressive for people who didn't know anything about business. But when they heard business people saying, 'You know, it might work,' the impact was very strong.... Then, just about the same time, there was — all those stupid things."

Do we need to ask? Like Brockville? Yes, Brockville, and the resolutions against bilingualism that became the fashion among Ontario municipal councils, and Meech. That too.

"You know, there was pretty abusive, very abusive treatment. When rational people in business say 'Maybe we should attempt [independence]' and very strong emotional images are coming from English Canada and hit the same people at the same time — even before Meech was definitely a failure, support for sovereignty was already close to sixty percent; from forty to sixty percent in less than a year. What the failure of Meech seemed to have done was to consolidate us.

"So you ask me, is it cyclical? Can it change? Well, it could be reduced, sure. On the other hand, few people see signs of this. As a matter of fact, the most impressive thing we've seen over the past four months is the inroad of the idea of sovereignty among traditional Liberals."

Soon after, Parizeau returns with an afterthought: "You saw the Gallup Poll — what was it — a month ago? Seventy-five percent of English Canadians say no additional powers for Quebec." He smiles; we light fresh cigarettes.

My clear memory of this moment in time was of feeling a need to say something cheery and conciliatory: people are wild about putting their kids in French immersion in Alberta; I have a friend in Brockville who is not a bigot; no-one in (the rest of) Canada takes municipal councillors seriously; you know what Yogi Berra said? It's never over till.... Instead, I recalled the policy conference at Montmorency, in 1966, when Tories fell upon one another — indeed, nearly came to blows — in a heated debate over the issue of *deux nations*. The media seized upon the debate as the issue of "two nations"; it became an excuse for Diefenbaker to run again for the party's leadership; it drove the leadership convention to passing a resolution of self-rebuke; candidates took oaths, swearing they never had, never would, believe in two nations; Trudeau milked Montmorency for all it was worth (in English Canada). We have made some progress, have we not? You could hardly start an argument on *deux nations* today, even in the Tory party.

This proves inspirational to Parizeau; we depart the economics seminar and join one in politics: "During the Meech Lake debate, it came as a surprise to me that Trudeau had been very successful in transforming a legal document, the Charter of Rights, into a true symbol of Canada for Canadians. That was particularly noticeable in the West, and it was particularly noticeable among immigrant and multicultural communities. A symbol that seems to have such power now that a lot of people will say, 'Well, anyone who does not want to be a Canadian like the others is not a Canadian. The Charter should apply to everybody; all Canadians, whether they speak English or French, whatever their origins, should be subject to the same Charter of Rights.' In fact, the Meech debate was on that, you see."

I interrupt to mention Quebec's Bill 178 on signage, a question already in Parizeau's mind.

"If all citizens are equal, then their political expressions of polity should be equal too. There is a remarkable historical logic in this. Canada, in a sense, is probably coming to maturity in its insistence on equal rights and its political expression of these rights. It's one hell of a change from the situation that existed twenty-five or thirty years ago; it becomes a very different kettle of fish. But this takes place at a time where, in Quebec, it is now accepted as common sense here that we feel we need a Charter of Rights — and we have one — but we take it as obvious that the Charter of Rights in Quebec would be different from that of the rest of Canada. This we don't plead. It is obvious."

This argument goes to the heart of the matter of Quebec's collectivity, its "specificity," which is in the matrix of its being. In another context, Lévesque said the same, while saying it differently: "I pity those who, in the name of an artificial and misguided concern for the individual and for human values (which they feel [Quebec] would be unable to respect, unless properly hemmed in), superciliously isolate themselves from the errors as well as the collective achievements of French Canada. This kind of attitude ... is what withers men most. It is a caricature of individualism."

Parizeau seems always prepared to reason his case; Lévesque was always ready to pour scorn on the argument against it. In Parizeau, one sees less of the politician and more of the bureaucrat and theorist whose function has always been to know what is best but not to insist upon it. The politician in the man is as elusive as his answers are direct. There is about him a matter-of-fact, take-it-or-

leave-it, like-it-or-not ultimacy which one would expect from a fiercely dog-
matic mind — certainly one already made up — or one serenely confident there
is nothing any longer left to doubt. After all, I suppose the inevitable least needs
either politics or politicians.

Long ago, in a conversation with Lévesque, when I had asked him what an
independent Quebec would do for a military force, he launched into a lengthy
and discursive reply, searching for an answer he did not have. Asked the same
question, Parizeau replied, with a slight smile, that Quebec would obviously
need some sort of force for the purpose of maintaining the public peace, "and in
order to keep our bridges open."

What does it mean, I ask Parizeau, when people say that Quebeckers want
what you want, which is sovereignty, but they want Bourassa to make the
arrangements? I suspect this choice between the professor of applied economics
and the chartered accountant, between the bureaucrat and the technocrat, suggests a preference for a blurred distinction between independence and a form of
sovereignty association not yet defined.

Parizeau shrugs off the personal comparison to say Bourassa himself cannot
define the meaning of sovereignty association — "and he never will."

But if there were a referendum on independence, and the vote was in favor,
Bourassa would still be in power, and then who would need the Parti Québécois?

Parizeau, animated, leans forward in his chair. "We would then all be as one,"
he says. "We would all be united as Quebeckers."

We had talked enough, smoked enough — God knows — the coffee had run
out, and darkness pressed against the windows. Standing now, bracing for the
cold walk back to the hotel, I told Parizeau that having spent a life in Canadian
politics trying always to be responsive to Quebec, trying to understand what is
now called its "specificity," and remaining sensitive to its concerns, I and many
Canadians like me are now fearful, should things turn out badly for us — and
well for him — that all of us, including Quebec, might lose in the end.

"Lévesque used to worry about that," he said, turning away to his desk. (The
response sounds brusque; it wasn't.)

But Lévesque again, with his federalist heart on his separatist sleeve. The
viability of an independent Quebec worried him: "Our greatest weakness," he
once said, "is economic." It was always "the number one problem." No longer.

The differences between Lévesque and Parizeau are a measure of the differences between the Quebec of the Quiet Revolution, when both professed to be federalists, and Quebec today, where the word federalist is passing from the language. It has been difficult to redefine a federalism drained of meaning by so much desperate innovation and well-meaning improvisation. It is hard to tell, rereading the collected speeches and papers of the innovators and improvisers, whether any of them knew what they were doing. For the record, one of the few who did was Parizeau, the true opportunist in that milieu of driven over-achievers. Had he lived, Lévesque would have been comforted to know that Ottawa's "great weakness" was also economic.

Certainly, for Canadian onlookers, the differences between the two principals in Quebec — Bourassa and Parizeau — do not involve economics but nuance. Quebeckers will be left to choose between the chartered accountant and the economist; the rest of Canada may choose neither. The renewed federation that survives these choices will be beyond the comprehension, or worst fears, of a Diefenbaker or a Pearson. For all anyone knows, the result may even be an improvement. This tentative conclusion kept me warm against the winter chill as I made my way back to the Château Frontenac.

The next day, to join Peter Gzowski, Kierans, and Stephen Lewis on "Morningside," I drove a long way out Laurier Boulevard to find the CBC radio building. On arriving, I told one of the studio technicians, "This is the first time I've ever been here."

"It could be the last," he said.

7
Denise Chong
THE CONCUBINE'S CHILDREN

MY UNCLE Yuen was born with his feet turned backwards at the ankles, and in traditional China no-one had the means to fix them. Following him up a set of stairs wasn't easy; we had the sensation he was going down instead of up. At the top, he led Mother and me behind the screens of a storeroom in the house their father, my grandfather, had built fifty years ago in Chang Gar Bin, a village in Guangdong province in the south of China. The wood of the screens was decaying, though the marks where carved panels had been lifted out were still faintly evident. Yuen rummaged around, looking for whatever it was Ping, Mother's sister, had said she wanted to return to her. What could Ping have to give back? As a child growing up in Canada, my mother had sent only letters, copied at the insistence of Grandfather as an exercise in Chinese brush-writing, to her elder sisters, Ping and Nan, and her younger half-brother, Yuen, in China.

Ping beckoned us out to the balcony, where the light was better, to look at the faded brown bundle Yuen handed to Mother. Shaken out, it fell into the shape of a child's coat. In halting yet sure motion, Mother went straight for its collar, searched for and found its velvet trim. She threaded her arms through the sleeves, tugged the coat over her shoulders, leaving knees and wrists exposed that betrayed when it had last fitted her. When she pulled the sides of the collar together to wrap velvet around her neck and chin, it was as if the coat itself reunited her two families, one in Canada, one in China.

Mother had last worn the coat when she was thirteen. She had paraded the sidewalks of Vancouver in it, arm in arm with her girlfriends. Never had she guessed it had lived out its life in China, that Grandfather had sent the coat in one of his regular care packages to his other family there. Ping herself had sashayed along the village paths in it, enjoying the taunts of the other children: "Foreign lady, foreign lady." The coat had then passed to Nan, the sister who died in her youth, and later to Yuen. He kept it in safekeeping for almost forty years, away from looting Japanese soldiers and Communist vigilantes — stored along with Ping's and his hopes that Mother, their sister, was still alive in Canada.

I had known all my life there might be relatives in China. As a child, I was curious about the black-and-white photograph of two children in the bottom drawer of the cedar chest upstairs in our home in Prince George, British Columbia. If I stared long enough, the two girls blinked. They had to: how could they not, waiting so long for Mother, the sister they would never meet? They even looked ready to be presented, as if they had run in from school, hurriedly rolled their socks to the ankles and smoothed their dresses. I didn't have to use my imagination so much on the other family photographs in the drawer. I had known Grandfather and his concubine, my grandmother, in real life. In fact, I preferred Grandmother's silent beauty in the photographs; in real life, she had scared me. The one portrait of Grandfather showed him with his jaw set, hinting at the temperament that supposedly made Grandmother leave him. Nowhere in the drawer was there a photograph of them together.

Years later, I noticed that Grandfather's portrait had disappeared. I saw that ones of the two sisters and of Grandmother had found their way into an album, each image scissored from its background and pasted down. But it was passing faces in crowds in China that would finally reawaken my childhood curiosity about these relatives. In 1987 I was near the end of a two-year stint working in Beijing, and I wrote to the Chinese authorities asking for help tracing Mother's ancestry. Mother, now a widow, had accepted my urgings to visit and, for my sake, brave her complicated feelings about China. I thought chances were remote that we would find any immediate relatives alive. China's political turmoil would surely have claimed them, lost them among her billion people. I thought the purpose of taking Mother to Grandfather's birthplace would be to fill in some blanks on the family tree, take some snapshots for the Canadian family album.

But the reverberations from the collision of the two worlds shook dust from mirrors. Before this visit, Mother had felt only the shame of her deprived childhood in Canada, the errant ways of her mother, the fact that both of her parents had gone to their graves unloved by her. From Ping and Yuen, she was to find out that Grandmother's money and Grandfather's love had actually been siphoned away from her to the family in China. But the discovery didn't make her bitter; instead, it lifted the burden of her shame. Over the years — through war and revolution in China, and the growing acceptance in Canada that Orientals could be Canadians too — events had evened the score between Grandfather's two families. Mother's parents, whose ways she had for years tried to forgive, had endowed her with the gift of a life in Canada. That realization finally turned Mother's shame to gratitude and made her own life at last all of one piece.

My Grandfather, leaving his family behind in rural China, set forth in 1922 to find work in North America. Chinese men before him had gone to the land they called the Gold Mountain, seeking their fortunes in the 1848 Sacramento gold rush; later, they'd been lured to work on the great transcontinental railways. But in Grandfather's time it was not money so much that drove men abroad as it was the constant turmoil and instability that paralysed the economy in his southern province of Guangdong. Canton, not far from Grandfather's village, was the stronghold of Sun Yat-sen, the founding father of modern China. Sun was arming his Kuomintang nationalists and fomenting revolution among rival warlords. Men like Grandfather didn't have the means to buy off warlords and keep roving bandits away. In his early thirties, he had to support one nearly grown daughter from his first wife (who had died), and a second wife — now titled Wife Number One — who had yet to produce children. His one hope of prosperity lay in going abroad.

After an eighteen-day ocean voyage, Grandfather stepped onto the pier in Vancouver, Canada, a fedora gracing his head, his gaunt, nearly six-foot frame attired in a three-piece gray suit. Never was he to be seen in any less casual dress. With his black hair combed to expose a high forehead, and his large, melancholic eyes staring from wire-framed glasses, he didn't look at all like the shifty-eyed, pigtailed Chinamen in the Fu Manchu movies of the day. Grandfather made it on one of the last boatloads of working-class Chinese allowed into the country before Ottawa passed the Chinese Immigration Act of 1923, also known as the "exclusion act." From then until the act was repealed in 1947, Chinese were barred from entering Canada unless they were students or merchants, or had proof of Canadian citizenship.

Chinese fathers who left their families to work in Canada lived in lonely exile. They weren't allowed to bring their families over, yet the white community condemned them as morally depraved, dirty, and disease-ridden, believing them to be undesirable citizens who worked only to remit money to China. Grandfather himself took a room in Vancouver's Chinatown and found work running a few tables of mahjong in a gambling parlor, but he resisted the bachelor's condition.

In 1924, a friend of a friend arranged for him to buy, sight unseen, Leong May-ying, a girl from another village in China. She was my grandmother, then seventeen years old. When her aunt, to whom she was probably a child-servant, told her she had been sold as a concubine to a Chinese man in Canada, she kicked and screamed in protest: "I might just as well be a concubine in China!" In her own country, Grandmother, with her penetrating, radiant, ebony eyes and delicate features set in pale skin, could probably have escaped becoming a beast of burden — the usual fate of Chinese women. In wealthy households, concubines led a pampered life. But in China girls did as they were told; it was that or suicide. So Grandmother readied herself to leave, even cutting and curling her hair to look older to conform to the illegally purchased birth certificate Grandfather had sent her. To Canadian immigration officials, she passed as twenty-four-year-old Chung Gim-ching, born in Ladner, British Columbia.

Work was almost all that Grandfather had in mind for her. At first he seemed kindly enough, taking her directly from the boat to have dim-sum at the Peking Restaurant on Pender Street. But then the owner joined them, and Grandfather introduced him as her new boss. It took Grandmother two years to work off the $500 Grandfather had borrowed from the restaurant owner to pay her passage. Lest she dream of running away, Grandfather kept a hunting knife under his side of the mattress. Out of threats, two daughters, Ping and Nan, were born.

If Grandfather was a hateful husband, he was a dutiful father. In 1929, he made plans to take his family to China. As was the custom among Chinese sojourning abroad, he wanted to give his children, then five and two, a Chinese education. For two years in China, havoc reigned as Grandfather tried to keep his two wives under one roof. As a concubine, Grandmother was supposed to be the subservient one, but she took advantage of Wife Number One's gentleness to argue with her, push her around, and humiliate her, often reducing her to tears. The one dignity on which Wife Number One stood was that she slept in the privacy of the back room of the two-room house and, usually, in the company of Grandfather. Grandmother was assigned the front room, with the children.

But of the two wives, Grandmother became pregnant first. In her eighth month, she consulted a blind soothsayer — considered closer to the truth than a sighted one — who predicted that she was carrying a son. Grandmother wanted him born in Canada where she thought he would have a better chance in life. Grandfather agreed. Ping and Nan were left behind to continue their educations in the care of Wife Number One. In the spring of 1930, fully expecting to return for their two daughters, Grandmother and Grandfather left for Canada. Three days after the boat docked in Vancouver, Grandmother gave birth to my mother in a room above 79 Market Alley in Chinatown.

Grandmother immediately tried to run away to Vancouver Island, to Nanaimo, then a bustling coal town where there were teahouses that always needed waitresses. Grandfather bundled up the baby and followed. He needed Grandmother: only she could put rice on the table for his families in Canada and in China. He couldn't get work with the Depression on and the trade unions agitating against Chinese men taking jobs from whites. But Grandmother was much sought after as a waitress. Restaurant owners knew that male patrons found seductive the way she wired curls and chignons to her hair, stained her lips red, and pinned silk flowers at her neck.

When Mother was five, Grandfather again began to make plans to return to China for the sake of a daughter's schooling. But he also wanted to build a house in Chang Gar Bin, as home villagers expected of an overseas Chinese. Grandmother at last saw her chance to get him out of her hair. She offered the money for him to go, but only if she and Mother remained in Canada. To pay for his passage, for the construction of the new house and furnishings, and for the extravagant gifts he must take, Grandmother borrowed heavily. Going empty-handed would be to lose face, or so Grandfather argued. One day in 1935, he set sail for China on an American freighter, *The Presidential.*

"One day of happiness in China is better than a hundred days of happiness in Canada," was the saying Grandfather invoked when he saw Wife Number One again. She was certainly happy not to have the concubine underfoot and was unaware that Grandfather's apparent wealth was not of his own making. Now there was just herself, Ping, and Nan — as was her duty, she loved them as her own — to enjoy Grandfather's affection and indulgences: the crates of grapes, salted crackers, and condensed and evaporated milk he brought from abroad. Within months, Wife Number One became pregnant.

Compared to when Grandfather had first left China in 1922, the country was less chaotic. Chiang Kai-shek, who became leader of the Kuomintang upon Sun's death in 1925, ruled a somewhat more unified country. What was left of the Red Army, led by Mao Tse-tung, was in retreat, on the Long March to Yenan, thousands of kilometres to the northwest. In the south, feudal landlords and rich peasants still held sway. Upon his return, Grandfather used some of Grandmother's money to purchase twenty-eight mu (five acres) of land on the edge of the village; he marked off a courtyard and hired workmen to lay the foundations of Chang Gar Bin's first-ever two-storey house. In the countryside of Guangdong, such houses — balustrades and balconies hinting at Western architecture — identified like pins on a map the families whose fathers had gone abroad.

But the cache of Grandmother's money that Grandfather had taken to China was gone before all his fanciful plans for his new house could be fulfilled. Letters were sent to Canada for only one purpose: to ask for more money to complete the house. And Grandmother was willing to work, borrow, do anything, to pay the price of keeping Grandfather in China. Then long before the house was finished, Wife Number One bore Grandfather his first son. The baby, Yuen, was born with crippled feet, but that didn't dent Grandfather's paternal pride. He put on a thirty-table banquet that spilled into his new courtyard.

From their perch on the wrought-iron gate opening into the courtyard, Ping and Nan watched as workmen affixed porcelain tiles to the rooftop. Oversize double portals swung open to reveal the house's expansive reception room, with its fourteen-foot-high ceilings. The balcony that swept around the upper floor's five rooms commanded a view of the entire village and the fields beyond. The overseas furniture crated in the courtyard was at last carried in. Craftsmen began carving wooden panels and inlaying stained glass in screens. Artists were hired to paint landscape scenes on porcelain and portraits of Grandfather and Wife Number One.

But hardly had Grandfather enjoyed the villagers' admiration of his accomplishment than he was booking a return passage to Canada. His son was another mouth to feed. He may also have feared that staying away too long would jeopardize his re-entry; who was to know how the unwavering anti-Oriental mood in North America might harm him?

He issued last-minute instructions to his daughters. Keep clean, he said. Keep your clothes folded away. Study hard: "If you don't, you will be nothing but peasants chasing bugs in the field." Two years later, in those fields, Ping, clutching Nan by the wrist and with Yuen strapped to her back, would be fleeing from Japanese bombs. But for now the fields were for frolicking. After school, the girls in their overseas dresses would offer rides to their playmates in their overseas pram.

During the two years Grandfather was away, Grandmother had taken to dressing their third daughter like the son she had been deprived of. At six, Mother, in short pants, a shirt, and suspenders, was still going to the barber in Nanaimo. When it came time to go to school, she enrolled herself. When the teacher wouldn't accept her as "Hing" — it wasn't an English name — she, and her best friend, Elsie, came up with the name "Winnie."

When Grandfather returned from China, he decided that his youngest daughter must learn to read and write Chinese if only to correspond with the family in China. But his teaching and Mother's letter-writing lasted only a year. Grandmother and Grandfather argued constantly — about nothing and everything from Grandfather's putting jam and ketchup on his rice to his buying bonds to help Chiang Kai-shek. Grandmother finally refused to live with him. After he moved out, Grandfather came around only if there was a letter from China that he wanted them to see — and the reality of Ping and Nan soon began to fade.

Grandmother mentioned her older children only in gambling-table chatter — when she won big, she boasted, she would bring them to Canada. Grandfather himself soon became little more than a cardboard figure to Mother. He could find work only out of town, usually bundling shingles. Months, eventually years, passed without contact. Once Mother caught sight of him buying groceries on the other side of the street. Grandmother forced her to turn her head: "Don't address him; he's not your father."

Grandmother, on her own with a young daughter, led a transient life, packing their one metal trunk to follow jobs to Nanaimo, Victoria, or Vancouver. The two of them saw little of each other; by the time Mother had come home from public school and then the Chinese school after that, Grandmother had already gone to work at the restaurant or the gambling parlor. When she had no homework, Mother went off to catch the seven o'clock performance of Chinese opera at the local theatre. Well past midnight, she would wander over to the gambling parlor, where she would sit silently by Grandmother's side watching her play fan-tan or mahjong. At about two in the morning, the two of them headed back to the rooming house for a late meal. Never did Grandmother cook anything ordinary: sometimes it was lady-slipper-bulb soup; sometimes a quick slaughter of a pigeon or chicken.

For Mother, Grandmother was at times an embarrassment, at times a burden, but always a stigma that had to be lived down. But in the playground Mother was the challenger to beat at marbles, jacks, and double-Dutch. In the classroom, the first desk, the one reserved for the top student, was usually hers. If she had to study for English and Chinese tests in one night, she would sometimes tie the end of a string to her hair and the other end to a light fixture overhead. If she nodded in sleep the string was just long enough to give her a sharp tug. Mother didn't like wasting time. As she watched repeat performances of Chinese opera, she knitted in the dark of the theatre. One year she turned out 112 cotton-knit washcloths, winning the public-school competition for the most washcloths knitted for Canadian soldiers fighting the Second World War.

Grandmother knew nothing of Mother's achievements; she cared less. All she wanted from Mother was obedience, and obedience she got, enforced daily, whether necessary or not, by a stick of discipline on her daughter's legs. The bruises were nothing compared to the shame Mother felt on the day she and her fourth-grade classmates were walking home and noticed a raid in progress at the gambling parlor. "Isn't that Hing's mother being put in the paddy wagon?" the children asked. "That's not her," said Mother.

More and more often, Mother was sent to buy herbs to make the teas Grandmother used to soothe away the effects of too much drink. Then there were trips to B.C. Collateral, the pawnbrokers on Hastings Street. Mother dreaded having to translate as Grandmother bargained a price for her jade and gold jewellery.

In 1940, Grandmother tried to claim back the rites of love and courtship denied her by Grandfather. She gambled her love on Chow Guen, a loud, shrewd gambling-parlor banker twenty years her senior. She met him when she was working at the B.C. Royal Café; he came in every day for a fresh butter-horn. While Guen cared for Grandmother less than she cared for him, he did have the money to help her get what she had always wanted: a son. It was Guen's $300 that Grandmother paid to Granny Yip, a Caucasian midwife who knew expectant Chinese mothers in dire straits. Granny Yip procured a newborn baby and registered Grandmother and Grandfather as its parents. Grandmother named him Gok-leng, but Mother called him Leonard.

Neither Grandmother's husband nor her lover appear in the family portraits she then commissioned — only mother, son, and daughter. But Grandmother soon began to board her children out as she chased after Guen in an on-again, off-again relationship that lasted fifteen years. Until Leonard was four, he lived mostly with the mid-wife, Granny Yip. Mother, like checked baggage, waited for Grandmother to claim her in rooms shared with elderly couples or Grandmother's women friends.

When Mother was twelve, Grandfather made one of his infrequent visits in order to tell Grandmother that their second-born daughter, Nan, had fallen ill and died. Mother's sharpest memory of the news was that Grandmother didn't shed a tear.

Mother's last foster home was back on Market Alley in Chinatown, steps from where she had been born. Her last guardian, the rather thick-headed Mrs. Low, worried more about juggling her boyfriends than about her teenaged daughter or Mother. Like their other friends, the two girls whiled away hours at cafés looking for the initials of future loves at the bottom of their tea cups. Mother found what was written at the bottom of the menu — "White Help Only" — ultimately more upsetting. At seventeen, and in the tenth grade, she began to worry about her own and Leonard's financial security; Grandmother's drinking bouts were worsening. Mother quit school and with the help of a recommendation from her former principal, Mr. Webster, became one of the first Chinese students to enter a three-year nursing program at Essondale Psychiatric Hospital near Vancouver (now Riverview Hospital).

It was 1948, and a good time for Mother finally to get away from Chinatown. Talk in every restaurant booth in the place was of the Communist advance in China. Many of the old-timers were Guangdong compatriots who had helped raise money for the Kuomintang; they were filled with fear for their wives and children back home. Few of them had the money or the connections to get their families out, even though the Canadian government had finally lifted the ban on Chinese immigrants. Grandfather certainly didn't.

After 1949, many old-timers feared the new Communist regime was intercepting their remittances. Grandfather himself feared he was a victim of extortion; recent letters from Yuen and Ping bore little news and asked only for more money. One from Ping said that unless $700 was sent, she would have a nervous breakdown. Mother agreed with Grandfather that recent letters written on Ping's behalf — she wasn't schooled enough to write herself — were unmistakably in a different hand from earlier ones. Grandfather agonized over it, but kept writing and sending money.

The ripcord that would help set Mother free from such obligations was John Chong, a man of quiet resoluteness, who won her heart. She met him when she was eighteen. He was handsome, athletic, and from a family of eleven children. After two years of driving up to Essondale on the chance that Mother could avoid curfew by sneaking out a lower-floor window of her dormitory, he gave her an ultimatum — nursing or marriage. Grandmother objected to Mother's choice of husband: a laundry-truck driver, she said, was a nobody. Mother went to Grandfather. Six months short of graduation, she walked down the aisle on the arm of her father.

In keeping with tradition, the new bride moved into her mother-in-law's house. There were three living in the attic once my parents had their first child, a girl. With six other adults and a baby living downstairs, there was rarely enough water pressure to the attic to wash rice, never mind diapers. When Mother became pregnant again, she and Father found a two-bedroom apartment near Chinatown. But they couldn't afford the $40-a-month rent on their own, so Mother invited Grandfather to share the space and the rent. This was home when Mother had me, her second-born, in 1953.

A few months later Grandfather decided that Mother should move again; that she should own a house in Canada; and that he should install her in one. He insisted on giving my parents $900 towards a down payment. Mother wondered how he had come into the money; it turned out that she had been his unwitting accomplice. Months before, she had gone with him to the immigration office on the Vancouver dock to swear that she had a sister in China named Ping. Later, a "Ping" did arrive in Canada, but it wasn't Mother's sister. It was Grandmother who eventually found out that Grandfather had sold Ping's Canadian birth certificate for $3,000, just as he had made money years earlier selling Nan's. She demanded a share of the money, but Grandfather wouldn't give her a penny, reminding her that Guen had never paid *him* for taking his wife.

In return for Grandfather's $900, he moved into the second bedroom of the modest house my parents bought on Gladstone Street, off Kingsway's commercial strip. A letter from Ping arrived at this address, in handwriting again arousing suspicions, telling Grandfather that if more money wasn't sent, his family would have to sell the glass in the windows. Grandfather asked Mother to help out. Father put his foot down: "Let them take the glass out; it will let fresh air in."

Grandfather stayed a little more than a year with us. Though he liked the idea of living in a house, Chinatown was a half-hour away by bus. For company during the day there was only old Mr. Penny tending his flowerbed on one side, or the reclusive Mr. and Mrs. Stewart on the other side, and none of them spoke Chinese. Grandfather went back to living in Chinatown.

At the time, Grandmother and Guen were running the Nanking Restaurant in London, Ontario. But Guen was getting exasperated with Grandmother; the more she drank, the more monosodium glutamate she put in her cooking. He ran out on her, and the bank moved in — foreclosing on the place. Leonard, too, had run away because of her drinking, and was placed in a foster home by the Children's Aid Society. Grandmother left him behind and came back to Vancouver to move into the bedroom Grandfather had vacated. Soon it was our garbage bins that were being filled with her empty bottles. After a year of this, Father asked Grandmother to leave. He ended up almost carrying her out of the house, depositing her at Grandfather's door in a hotel above Chinatown's Ho Ho Restaurant.

Two days later, in a rare united act, Grandfather and Grandmother showed up at our door. They served Mother with a lawyer's letter announcing their intention to sue for Grandfather's $900. Mother countersued, demanding back rent. Both suits were dropped.

Home and family in Chinese are represented by one and the same character — a pig under a roof, a symbol of contentment. Never was there domestic harmony in the Canadian family; rarely had all members lived under the same roof. But in China, Grandfather's family and home were one and the same, though the house, built on his instructions, and Grandmother's money, was almost the ruin of them.

War between China and Japan broke out in 1937, and by 1938 Japanese bombs were falling on Guangdong province. When Chang Gar Bin village became a battleground, Japanese soldiers chased Wife Number One and her three charges, Ping, Nan, and Yuen, from the house. "Don't be afraid, don't be afraid," Wife Number One chanted, as she and the children stepped on dead bodies and shrank from anti-aircraft fire. When they came back to their village, the bombs had stopped falling but the Japanese occupiers had turned their house into local headquarters: they could keep watch from the second-floor balcony. When the soldiers moved on, they ransacked the house, taking any valuables they could carry.

But Grandfather's Chinese family believed that his lot in Canada was worse. Wife Number One read in Grandfather's letters that the concubine drank and gambled her time away; about how they had separated because he couldn't stand her quarrelling any longer. The fact was he had no trouble being fatherly from afar. He regularly sent care packages. He wrote, encouraging his crippled son to find a way to ride a bicycle. At his insistence, young Yuen learned to write Chinese so he could take over from the schoolmaster the task of writing letters for Wife Number One. On birthdays, Grandfather sent an American coin or two, sometimes even a dollar bill. His children treasured most the gift of three Big Ben alarm clocks, the kind with a loud tick-tock, large faces, and two-legged stands, made in Peterborough, Ontario. His remittances, in a foreign currency, bought the family stability, especially during the rampant inflation of the war years.

Still, the family couldn't live on his affection or his money alone. Like all unmarried daughters, Ping and Nan went to work in the fields. One day in the fall of 1942, the fourteen-year-old Nan headed out as usual. Ping and Yuen remember the commotion as she was carried home, haemorrhaging. "Someone scared her in the field," was all Wife Number One would say. After a month in bed, Nan died. That same year Ping was married off. Grandfather wrote wondering if she, at eighteen, wasn't too young, but he said he would approve if Ping was a willing bride. He granted her in-laws three mu of land from his holdings; and for the wedding feast he arranged from afar for one whole roasted pig.

That was to be the last banquet for more than three decades. The first of several serious famines hit Guangdong in 1944. In 1946, the country was plunged into civil war between the Kuomintang and the Communists. By 1948, nothing could stop the Communist advance, neither Chiang Kai-shek's disorganized troops, nor American aid, much of which found its way into the personal coffers of Kuomintang leaders. In October, 1949, Mao proclaimed the People's Republic of China. Chiang's last southern stronghold fell, and he and his troops fled to Taiwan.

Grandfather's house again brought the family trouble. Communist leaders labelled Grandfather's family as "black elements" and set about redistributing his wealth. Grandfather's land was organized into a village cooperative. The "unsightly" opulence of his house was remedied. The wrought-iron gate, the dressers, the wool blankets from Canada, the carved panels in the wooden screens, the stained glass, the tiles on the roof: all were removed or destroyed. The huge portrait of Grandfather that watched over the reception area was cut down, and his house was divided, making apartments for two more families. Villagers were called on to "speak bitterness" against Wife Number One, Yuen, and Ping, who were forced to stand for hours on one spot, hands tied, heads bowed in penance for the shame of Grandfather's wealth.

Yuen wrote to Grandfather to tell him it wouldn't be possible for him to return: "You would be too heartsick to see what has happened to what you worked hard for, with your sweat and your ten fingers." Letters arrived from

Canada only sporadically, remittances even more so. The last letter came in 1957. In it was a Vancouver Chinatown newspaper notice announcing Grand-father's death at seventy. A note was attached, with Grandmother's name at the bottom, extending condolences to Wife Number One.

Though I was only four years old when Grandfather died, I have vivid recollec-tions of him. I can still see him coming through the back door of our house on Gladstone Street, his arms laden with groceries, him setting the bags down and scooping me up. The first present I remember receiving from anyone was the red and white tricycle he showed up with one day. I remember, too, sitting with my sister in pails of water in the back yard, cooling off on warm summer days, while Grandfather, dressed in a suit, worked nearby in the garden. To Moth-er's consternation, he would run hot water over the garden tools to clean them off.

I can also remember standing by his graveside, and that there was no weep-ing. Grandmother wasn't there: she was in hospital with tuberculosis, which she suspected she caught from coughs filtering over the half-partitions in her rooming house. But the first chance she had, six months later, she went through the rituals of worshipping the dead. I remember she prepared several steaming dishes and there was wine and tea in thermoses. I was astounded when she left it all in the shadow of Grandfather's tombstone.

My earliest memory of Grandmother is that she intimidated me into silence. At two, I held out my palm to her, burned on the wood stove, as she applied a stinging salve of fermented oranges. At five, I tilted my head back as she plucked my eyebrows, and then forward as she plaited my hair, always too tight. I couldn't cry out. Grandmother was herself fearless and wouldn't stand for it.

The year after Grandfather's death, Mother decided she wanted to make a final break with Vancouver. Even if Father had changed his mind about it, Mother didn't want Grandmother to live with us again because of the risk of exposing her by now four young children to tuberculosis. The federal govern-ment was advertising for radio operators; Father applied and got a job at the Prince George airport. On Christmas Eve in 1958, Mother bundled us into our 1949 Meteor for the 800-kilometre drive north along an icy highway to this northern logging town. We pulled into the driveway of a substandard surplus wartime house on the airport grounds — our home until another house became available — to find frozen water pipes by night and, by morning, neighbors frowning at the prospect of Orientals on the block.

The airport community of twenty-one families, with its own clubhouse and one-room school, was a crucible of assimilation. Mother's advice to us was to feign hard-of-hearing to the taunts of "Chinky, Chinky, Chinaman"; she soon made it clear to other mothers that she wasn't going to put up with their kids throwing stone-embedded snowballs or waiting in ambush to knock us off our bikes. She was determined that we should be as robust as our playmates: the milk in our glasses was enriched with extra cream. She worried about Leonard too; once he was old enough to be released by the Children's Aid, he came to live with us for a year. At Mother's suggestion, he applied to Essondale Psychiatric Hospital, was accepted, and graduated as a psychiatric nurse.

Grandmother, now in her mid-fifties, would visit us in the summers. From what I remember of her lightning-quick quips and laughter, she was happy to stay with us, especially since, of five of us children by now, three were grandsons. Visiting her in Vancouver was a different story. The Chinatown of my early childhood — a sensuous place of steamy smells, squawking chickens, and the clacking murmur of mahjong tiles — was already gone. In the early 1960s, cut off from new blood and commerce and sanitized by local bylaws designed to clean up the "squalor," the Chinatowns of Canada, like the old-timers who lived in them, were dying.

Father would stop in front of whichever rooming house Grandmother was living in and Mother would wait in the car as he and one of us children would climb up the stairs. He would knock on the door and then we would wait in the hallway to see if it would open to us. If it didn't, we knew, but didn't say, that Grandmother would have to dry out first. Her main pastime was still mahjong. But now, when she wanted to gamble, she had to get a ride across town to the suburbs out of the sight of the city police. Grandmother didn't much like riding in cars, trusting only Father and a mahjong buddy, Mr. Pang, to drive her. Just after midnight one night, the elderly Mr. Pang was driving Grandmother home to the Garden Hotel in Chinatown. Two blocks from the hotel, the car was hit broadside by a pick-up truck driven by a teenager, out for a spin with his pals.

The story on page fifteen of *The Vancouver Sun* said that a traffic accident had caused the city's third fatality of 1967, killing a sixty-four-year-old woman named Chung Gim-ching. Crushed between two people in Mr. Pang's back seat, Grandmother died of a punctured lung: discounting the false birth certificate, she was only fifty-eight. Mother made one last trip to B.C. Collateral to claim Grandmother's jewellery. Among the pieces, she found a diamond ring that had come from Grandmother's lover. The sale of that ring paid for the funeral.

At the inquest, the coroner found that no-one had been at fault. Of more importance to Mother, the pathologist had found no trace of alcohol in Grandmother's blood. When the coffin was lowered into the ground, Mother thought her own past had been laid to rest.

Twenty years later, in her own mind at least, Mother had turned that past to dust and ashes. If she felt anything about Grandmother, it was a slight remorse that no-one had left food on her grave — but then, Mother had never worshipped at Grandfather's grave either. Since his death, there had been no word of any relatives in China, nor did Mother know if anyone there knew that she still existed. For a time, all overseas Chinese lost contact with their families in China, because of the xenophobia that reached its height during Mao's Cultural Revolution. When Mao died in 1976, The Gang of Four was officially blamed for the persecution, torture, and execution of China's intellectuals and for the wanton destruction of cultural property. Only then was the stage set for leader Deng Xiaoping to usher in the era of an "open door" to the West.

Mother finally walked through that door in the spring of 1987, at my insistence. Still, if she hadn't already been in Hong Kong when she got word that other siblings were still alive, she might have called the whole trip off. The news alone sent her on a roller coaster from shock to jubilation to disbelief and fear.

The Chinese government's instructions were terse: "Go to the Chinese side of the frontier at Macao in two days. Officials will meet you, with your two sisters and brother. Look for a white van." Two sisters? Mother was no longer certain that Nan had died. Could Grandfather have fabricated the story to justify having sold her birth certificate? Perhaps the family had sold Nan? What if, worse, the Chinese authorities had dragged up fictitious relatives? Was the woman using Ping's name in Canada really the fraud? Who was to know who was authentic?

We decided to go no farther than the border, but the decision was in vain: the officials in the white van were an hour late and had no-one in tow. After a three-hour ride into China, the van dropped us in the compound of the overseas Chinese office in Chang Gar Bin village. We waited while news of our arrival was sent. Then a thin man, with wavy hair and a face with Grandfather's quiet strength and squareness, shuffled into the room. His feet made a sweeping sound, one at a time, as he limped towards us, like a broken doll whose limbs had been twisted and stuck — Yuen, Mother's half-brother. I had deliberately withheld from officials our knowledge of his deformity; how could this be contrived? Mother embraced him, feeling the sorrow of his crippled feet but also the joy that they swept away worries that he was not of the same blood. He answered the question of Nan. Yes, she had died, many years before; the officials had just got it wrong.

We went into the courtyard, and there Mother hugged her sister Ping for the first time. The proud fine lines of Ping's face were like Grandmother's. The quickness of her movements and her girlish laugh were Grandmother reincarnated. Both sisters fumbled for the photographs each had brought for this moment. Mother showed the one photograph she had of her two sisters as children and one of Grandmother posing with her and Leonard. Ping unwrapped the cellophane protecting a photograph of a beautiful young Oriental woman, cradling a baby — Grandmother and Ping. She turned the photograph over. It was imprinted as a postcard, and in the lower left corner was "Vancouver, Canada."

The two sisters walked like schoolgirls, arm in arm, through the village, their younger brother riding his bicycle ahead. They wove their way among black pigs that scavenged for food in the market, past the stalls where one of Ping's sons sold pork and where Yuen's sons sold fresh fish from baskets. They passed the hardware store when Yuen kept the books. Ping stopped often, hailing villagers, to show off "Younger Sister," and some of them remembered a last sight of Grandmother, leaving pregnant for the boat in 1930.

At the other end of the village, through a gate, was an imposing chalk-blue house. We entered its main room through a small swinging door hinged into massive sienna-painted twin portals. Here, Yuen lived with his wife and three children. This was the house that Grandfather — and Grandmother's money — built.

"Heaven and earth have eyes," said Yuen, as he and his two sisters finally sat in Grandfather's front room, laughing and crying at the triumph of being reunited. For the three days of our visit, Ping poured out the lost stories of family life in China, illustrated by Yuen pointing to the back room where he was born and Nan died, to the places where once stood overseas dressers, where once hung decorative mirrors. To the field beyond where Japanese bombs fell and where now stood a cluster of modern flat-roofed two-storey houses, television aerials on their rooftops. The Communists were allowing limited home ownership again. If Yuen could raise the money to build new houses for the two other families living in Grandfather's house, he could have it to himself. "I am scrimping and saving for the pride of my father," he said.

In the face of Ping and Yuen's devotion to the memory of Grandfather, Mother held back many of her stories — and that she believed he had exploited Grandmother and sacrificed the family in Canada for the sake of the family in China. Let them hold dear their idea of him as a model father. Let them believe the concubine brought him only unhappiness and that Wife Number One, the woman who raised them, was the superior wife.

Ping wanted one memento of her past: she asked Mother to find proof that she had been born as the postcard photo said, in Vancouver, Canada. When times were bad, she had had to endure the villagers' taunts that she had been left behind in China because she "must deserve to suffer." Time and again, she had thought her plight was unfair: "I don't deserve this; I was not born here." Mother didn't have the heart to tell her than another Ping had lived all through those trying years, safe in Canada.

Grandfather had come to Canada to throw off the cloak of poverty, though he and Grandmother never managed it in their lifetimes. The family in China, who had harvested some of the spoils of the Gold Mountain, now had only a few relics of the goods Grandfather had sent from Canada: a metal crib, badly rusted; an RCA Victor phonograph that once played 78rpm records; Yuen's Big Ben alarm clock; and a $10 American bill. The truth was that Grandfather's penchant for showiness had brought his family in Chang Gar Bin persecution. For Mother, who lived her childhood in the shadow of sacrifices made for the family back home, her parents' act of immigration had been a liberation.

When our Chinese relatives saw us off at the bus station in their village, the weeping was as much for the parting of flesh and blood as it was for the realization that Mother had ended up the luckier of the children. Mother, having left behind her long ago the rooming houses of Market Alley, would return home to Prince George and a life of her own choosing. Ping and Yuen could expect to die in Chang Gar Bin, the birth and burial place of several generations of the family, the village to which the Communist government had assigned them. Ping could nurture only faint hopes that Yuen's or her own children's children — the youngest of which she strapped to her back every day while its mother went to work — would not be peasants. That they might get off the land. Mother's children were college-educated and living their own lives.

The phrases of gratitude that Mother would now express to her parents, if they could be heard in the grave, might be borrowed from a letter Yuen pressed into her hand just before she left. It asked for help in getting one of his children into Canada: "I hope my children can take root in Canada. Then the roots of the tree will grow downward. We will be fortunate; the children will be fortunate; our children's children will be fortunate. The family will be glorious and future generations will have a good foundation."

Mother left the brown coat with the velvet collar behind in Chang Gar Bin. It seemed it still belonged in China, where the threads of Grandfather's hopes were still woven in his children's dreams.

8
Ann Diamond
ZEN IN AMERICA

IN JANUARY of 1986 I decided to
move to a Zen Center, a sprawling complex of buildings located in a crime-rid-
den neighborhood near downtown Los Angeles. I had met the teacher, Kaesaku
Roshi, in 1983 and had studied with him quite intensively over a period of three
years, during which I participated in more than a dozen week-long retreats in
California, New Mexico, and New York.

At seventy-nine, Kaesaku Roshi was famous in Buddhist circles for his rig-
orous adherence to traditional Rinzai Zen, a militaristic form too severe ever to
be popular with Americans. Kaesaku's seven-day retreats were marathons of
physical and mental endurance, designed to force students into "awakening" to a
Self beyond that of the conceptual mind. Once I'd learned to cope with the pain
and exhaustion of sitting in lotus position for eighteen hours a day, I found
Roshi's teaching absolutely compelling. I even wrote to friends, suggesting they
come down and share this incredible experience. Luckily, no one accepted the
invitation. The fact that I thought they'd "enjoy" a Zen retreat shows that I did
indeed transcend my ordinary mind for a while there.

The winter of 1986 was a low point for spiritual communities in America.
The Rajneesh scandal had erupted the year before in Oregon; some prominent
American Zen Masters in New York and California had recently been implicat-
ed in scandals over alcohol and/or sex. Not only was Zen no longer drawing
floods of students, but disillusioned ex-devotees were deserting the practice in
droves, hoping to salvage a future for themselves in mainstream America. Communities that had thrived in the sixties and seventies were left half-empty, while

the few members who elected to stay were racked by doubts about their spiritual vocation.

Kaesaku Roshi's organization seemed in some ways immune to these disasters, having precociously hit bottom during the late seventies when other Zen groups were still flourishing. The severity of Kaesaku's teaching had frightened away all but the most loyal, or desperate, practitioners. The skeleton crew running his organization was a strange assortment of men and women who shared two characteristics: devotion to Kaesaku and his terrible but potent practice, and a self-effacing cynicism which I considered healthy and very un-cult-like. Roshi had once called his Bodhidharma Center "the dirtiest Zen Center in America." Various people held differing interpretations on what exactly he'd meant by that, but everyone repeated the remark with a certain pride.

As an additional reason for my decision to live at the Center was an interest in a monk from South Africa whom I'd met the year before. He was tall, blond, blue-eyed. I entertained fantasies of marrying, and either adopting the Zen life or eventually luring him back to the outside world.

My duplicity on this point had immediate negative consequences. From the moment of my arrival, a strange symbolism seemed to operate, as if some force had decided to sabotage my attempts to make the Zen world my new home. The Challenger Shuttle crashed a few days later after I landed in L.A., and triggered national grieving and much speculation about the death of the Space Program. As America mourned its dead astronauts, the monk with whom I had shared passionate moments was suddenly promoted to Abbot, the highest position in Roshi's organization. This unexpected career move rendered him terribly overburdened with administrative responsibilities. From then on he became immersed in complex political struggles which sapped his energy and put many strains on our time together.

I thought of bowing out gracefully, but Roshi himself got on the case, and encouraged me to stay. Most of the monks were celibate, but Roshi was no Puritan.

"Sex okay!" he said encouragingly, in one of my sanzen interviews. "You stay, have sex with Abbot!"

I liked this idea. Besides, it was minus 30° back in Montreal, and Mexico was still recovering from its recent earthquake. I decided to stay at Bodhidharma, see my sweetie when it was possible, and work on writing. I had a Canada Council grant for four months to write a book exploring "primitive" rhythms in poetry. Before leaving Montreal, I was invited to give a reading in a loft along with a group of African drummers, one of whom was actually Haitian and had talked to me about Voodoo. He'd described it as a life-affirming religion very unlike Christianity.

Bodhidharma Zen Center proved to be a less than life-affirming place. When I sat down to write, I found myself totally paralysed. Outside the walls of our all-white community, crack-pedlars and professional burglars shared the streets with schoolchildren from middle-class black families. Few days passed without the sound of gunfire somewhere in our vicinity. The police helicopter circled our block an average of three times a day for ten minutes at a stretch. This tended to create the impression that we were living in an occupied country.

Visitors never parked in the street outside the Zen Center: instead people drove their cars into the courtyard, which was surrounded by a ten-foot cement wall. Many people in this neighborhood augmented their high fences with razor wire or barbed wire, but the Zen Center had proved fairly immune to break-ins. The local criminals seemed to know we had nothing worth stealing, although in 1979 someone had entered the unlocked zendo and run off with some imported metal gongs and wooden drums, as well as a priceless statue of the Kannon Boddhisattva of Compassion (known to the Chinese as Kuan Yin).

However, on our daily excursions to buy tofu and vegetables, it was not unusual to see cops, with high-powered rifles and sunglasses, arresting the dealers who used our tall white walls as a landmark and partial screen for their activities. Day and night they parked in cars or met on foot under the eucalyptus and olive trees, where they exchanged their little parcels. While being arrested and frisked, they would stand with their up-raised hands pressed against our walls, while the police held rifles to their heads.

Our days began at 4:45 a.m. with sutra-chanting in the zendo, then ninety minutes of meditation followed (around sunrise) by a twenty-minute work period. I was sometimes given the job of sweeping up the plastic Ziplock bags and junk-food containers left outside our gates by dealers and their customers the night before. In the soft light of early morning I might also come across a spent bullet, a stolen credit card, an empty wallet, or the contents of someone's glove compartment. Now and then there would be the bare skeleton of a car from which all the parts had been stripped before it was abandoned.

I had stayed at the Center before, for several weeks at a stretch, and had found the place restful and friendly. But on this visit either the neighborhood had deteriorated, or some filtering mechanism in my mind had dropped away (from too much Zazen), causing me to experience American life as a gigantic carnival of violence. On previous visits I'd always been impressed by the calibre of people who practiced Zen. They'd struck me as balanced, intelligent types with a refreshing sense of humor.

I had never fully entered into the disciplined breath-and-posture fetishism preached by some of Roshi's monks, who distrusted mental activity ("thinking mind") and spent their days totally absorbed in the Zen of plumbing and carpentry, when they weren't "working on their breath."

Unless Europeans or Canadians were present, conversation was limited to the exchange of information on important topics. Americans, it seemed, did not converse in an open-ended way. They traded points of view; they argued; or they fought for control.

Everyone had his own personal method of stress-reduction. One visiting resident had an electronic device that, if strapped to your leg, would induce a state similar to that of deep meditation without all the needless effort of sitting zazen. She would fasten it to her ankle and drive to work with the dial set at "Alpha." She had recently run away from a group of witches in Phoenix, Arizona. She told me that she often saw ghosts occupying the empty cushions in the zendo, and that our Zen Center was an extremely negative place. I couldn't have agreed more — but a drive down any street or a visit to the local shopping center was likely to be equally negative. Grocery stores had armed guards protecting the check-out counters. It was unsafe to cross the street to mail a letter after dark.

Looking back, I see this was a low point in Bodhidharma's history. The young wife of the head monk liked to tell us about the time she was taken prisoner by ex-Nazis in Paraguay, tortured and beaten senseless, and then miraculously rescued by Marines in an American airlift. At first I thought her yarns might be partly true. Her life seemed crammed with scenes of fantastic violence and many hairbreadth escapes — she had a penchant for car accidents which were fatal for others but never for her. She claimed to hold a Ph.D. in Artificial Intelligence, and constantly complained because the Zens believed in the value of human labor and ignored opportunities for computerization.

Sometimes at the dinner table she would assail us on topics that interested her: Aviation Fuels at one meal; Chemical Warfare at the next. She openly hated Zen but entertained fantasies of starting a Zen Center on their organic dream-farm, which was to be in Arizona, or "anywhere the aquifers aren't poisoned yet." She pretended to have ideas for improving the Center. She proposed a scheme whereby the next time our plumbing backed up during a rainstorm we would let the ground floor flood and then sue the City of Los Angeles for an astronomical sum, thus ensuring our survival as a spiritual community. She had friends who did this sort of thing — successful people with brains, unlike us. Apparently her friends were all "scientists and intellectuals."

Another, older student spent her days stalking rats in the kitchen. She would watch them at close range through binoculars as they nibbled the poisoned chocolate she put down for them. She was also the bookkeeper for the Center. Once she offered some of this "chocolate" to a student who was behind in his rent, without telling him it was for the rats.

There were endless arguments and battles for control over the daily operation of the center. Lengthy debates would erupt over minor details and result in major deadlocks which never seemed to get resolved. People appeared uninterested in any activity that could not be polarized into bitter, open conflict. Cooperation was impossible, since everyone held fixed positions on every conceivable issue.

In the written Record of Rinzai, various monks approach the master to have their realization confirmed. Some are highly trained and intellectually brilliant. Rinzai hits them all with a stick and sends them away.

Our Roshi's dictum was: No one forces you to stay here. If you don't like this Zen Center or this Roshi, go find another practice. Democracy is time-consuming and concerned with the pragmatic. Before Americans can give themselves to Zen irrationality, they have to be shocked out of their habits. Forcing them to live like Japanese monks in the middle of Los Angeles is a way of inducing culture shock. In a state of simulated exile, normal thought patterns dissolve, and unusual things may begin to happen.

Roshi continued to encourage my secret hopes and desires. "Twice a week not enough. Should have sex more often!"

But despite hours in the zendo, things were growing tense between my love and me. Now that he was Abbot, he was much sought-after, an object of resentment and envy, as well as fawning attention. Where I had been "that nice Canadian girl," I was suddenly seen as an opportunist, an interloper, one of those marauding women who, under the pretext of studying Zen, would cynically seduce some unsuspecting, sex-starved monk, and cart him off to live with her in the Real World forever. This had happened before, to a talented student who according to local legend had been a shoo-in for dharma succession. Thereafter, people were on the lookout for repetitions. Power and position were known to magnetize a monk, and make him a target for female attacks. I was warned that a girlfriend could shipwreck a man's spiritual career...

During mountain-top retreats, Roshi was always saying, "After you realize mountain, go back to the world. Don't stay here too long." I took this to mean that being a monk is not enough. To understand Zen, one has to embrace ordinary life, human relationships.

It's said that Shakyamuni Buddha had the ability to speak to crowds in such a way that each listener thought he was being addressed personally. In some of Roshi's talks, I heard little hints that seemed to urge me to run off with the new Abbot. But some of the monks seemed to hear something different.

One day my love and I went to Little Tokyo in search of ginseng for Roshi. On the sidewalk outside a row of stores all specializing in herbal remedies, we encountered a walking apparition. It was a man, or the wreckage of one, wrapped in a blanket, barefoot, his head shaved, with something dripping from the end of his nose. A strange parody of a Zen mendicant, he drifted by without seeming to be there, like vacancy-in-motion. A strange, palpable chill surrounded this human ghost.

My sweetheart, the Abbot, was appalled: "Maybe he got bad teaching. Or maybe that's me in five years."

No, my love, no, no ...

We drove back to Bodhidharma, where a new practitioner awaited us in the tea-room, a black woman called Carol.

I was having a nap in my room at 9 a.m. one morning, having dozed off while waiting to use the shower. In my dream, some people were chanting the Dharani of Removing Disaster, a text Zens recite every morning, three times. It starts out slowly and gains speed and volume on each repetition, as if its purpose were to drive away demons. *Na mu sa man da. Mo to nan no. Ha ra chi ko. Ha ra chi ko. To sha so no nan to ji to en gya gya gya.* I woke up with a feeling that something terrible was going on.

I heard a woman talking on the pay phone downstairs: "Hello? Is that the newsroom? This is very urgent. I am a black person who has been staying at the Bodhidharma Zen Center. I am being harassed by racist white people and I think you should do a story on this situation. They are threatening me with the police. I can hear the helicopter circling the block. Yes, would you send a reporter over here right away? Hello? Hello?"

The police helicopter roared by overhead. From downstairs there was the sound of frantic dialling. "Hello? NAACP? I am a black person ..."

The head monk burst in on me while I was having my shower. He urged me to get dressed and leave the building immediately. He said Carol had reacted badly to her eviction notice. She had never really taken to the rigors of Zen life. She would get up around 8:30, fix herself breakfast in the kitchen, and sit around all day, in a sort of trance. So the head monk and his wife had asked her to leave.

The police arrived while I was still hearing the details. Apparently in her rage she'd called everybody a white devil, and laid hexes on the head monk, his horrible wife, and the whole Zen Center. But she'd reserved her most virulent curses for the Buddha statue. He showed me the broken incense sticks scattered around the zendo, the ashes that still lay on the bald head of Shakyamuni.

While we were talking she must have fled on foot: she had vanished from her room without a trace, except for a trail of crossed incense sticks that began outside her door and continued all the way up the carpeted stairs to the door of my bedroom, where it ended with a little spray of broken red geraniums.

I felt a pang of guilt. I'd been too caught up in my disintegrating romance to pay much attention to Carol during the three days she'd been with us. I bent to pick up the flowers, conscious that I had been singled out for special treatment. In some way I knew I deserved it. The broken flowers seemed symbolic of something. They seemed to testify, not so much against me as against my so-called "love affair," which I had begun to sense was doomed. With one hand I held the geraniums, and unlocked the door to my room. I don't know what I expected, but everything was just as before. The couch where I took my naps. The open window with the missing screen, through which now came the voice of a man in the yard below.

"Hey, Whitey! Come on down here and get what's coming to you!"

I froze in terror. Was I hallucinating? This never happened. We were on good terms with the neighborhood...

"What's the matter? You scared of something, White Man?"

It was approaching noon. I was alone in this building. I couldn't remember if I had locked the back door behind me when I came in. The only phone was in the hall downstairs. I might be able to get to it, but it was a pay phone and I was out of dimes.

I had an impulse to run in every direction at once. I was alone on the second floor and there was a man down in the yard who seemed to want to kill me, for some reason.

This was the worst coincidence of my life. Wait a minute — this was no coincidence! This was a Curse. I had brought it to life by the simple gesture of my hand touching those geraniums.

I dropped the geraniums and focused my mind. What would the Zens say? It is important to extend the out-breath fully ...

O Sariputra, form is here emptiness, emptiness is form.

I'd heard of cases of Voodoo where the victims died of fright. The whole secret, of course, was not to panic. I could talk my way out of this. I would lean out the window, and make things perfectly clear. "I'm an innocent Canadian! I'm not a white man, I am a white woman!"

I imagined myself dead already: Zen practice was supposed to prepare you for that.

I waited for the sound of the back door opening, of heavy footsteps on the stairs, but the shouting had stopped. I looked down from my window: there was no one in the yard. After a minute I found a quarter in the pocket of my other pair of jeans. I tiptoed down to phone for help.

This time the police just sat in their patrol car and asked questions. The white cop was driving; the black cop had the clipboard.

"I heard a voice in the back yard. He was threatening to come up and kill me."

"What did he look like?"

"I didn't see him."

"What do you think his motive was?"

"Well, there was this lady staying here; she thinks we're racists. Maybe she called up one of her friends."

"Why does she think you're racists?" The black cop looked interested.

"Uh, I don't know." I tried to smile. "Maybe because ... because we are?"

Later, when I was dramatizing the story for the other residents, I went to my room to get the geraniums. I wanted to display the Voodoo objects. I could have sworn I'd dropped them on the carpet in my panic, but now where were they? I searched the cupboards, the waste basket, even the bathroom down the hall. But I never found the geraniums.

Near the end of my stay, the Chicano man who drove the neighborhood ice-cream wagon was murdered. I had always enjoyed the tinkling music of his little truck as it passed in the street, and often I'd thought of running out to buy an Eskimo pie or some little treat to break the monotony of living in a combat zone, but something always prevented me — perhaps I was already developing Zen intuition? Later the story came out: he had been dealing more than space bars and popsicles out of his freezer.

The ice-cream man's violent end seemed symbolic of many things. Reagan had just dropped bombs on civilians in Libya. I sat in a bar in a little town in the San Gabriel mountains one evening, and watched the news on TV. Around me people celebrated the great national victory. One man I spoke to was particularly jubilant that America had finally recovered her "pride." I asked him what there was to be proud of in killing women and children. I learned that he and his drinking companions thought Libya was a country in Central America, poised to invade the United States via Mexico.

I said, "You mean Nicaragua?"

On the TV over the bar, the 24-hour-a-day Horror and Fantasy network flooded the room with images of spacemen or evil female vampires. There seemed to be a huge explosion approximately every minute on that channel.

I was looking forward to my flight, still some days away. Even bumper stickers looked threatening: "You toucha my car, I breaka you neck." Traits and attitudes that would have been considered psychopathic or at least extremely anti-social back in Montreal were seen as normal, even admirable, down here. I imagined America on the brink of some paroxysm — a race war? A second Viet Nam?

I remembered the words of Carol, the Voodoo Lady, who said that the fate of the space program was tied to the treatment of blacks in America. When we shopped in the black shopping malls, I began to feel like the black people. There was a great depression, an enormous weight of pain concentrated in their bodies. But if you were white, you were programmed not to feel it.

Under the circumstances, there was little to do but record the little things people said. About walking to the store in broad daylight: "Nine times out of ten, nothing will happen to you...."

Or about the daily shooting around the neighborhood: "Most of the gunfire you hear is just people firing in the air."

When a parole officer was shot in the alley behind the Zen Center, I was alone in one of the houses. I phoned across the street for advice on what to do. "I think someone's just been killed in the back yard."

"Turn off the lights and stay away from the windows."

A monk from another Zen organization visited Bodhidharma a few days before I left. His teacher led a "rival" center located a couple of kilometres from Bodhidharma, in a safer, largely Korean, neighborhood. It was a dynamic community with a strong organization and a high profile in spiritual circles.

Laurence, now thirty, was growing his hair back and applying to law schools. The reason: a sex scandal involving his Roshi. The large and thriving community in which he had lived and worked for twelve years was falling apart over disclosures of the Roshi's drinking problem and involvement with female students. An attempt at Zen *glasnost* had shattered everyone's faith. Apparently the students had grown to depend on certain seductive illusions, Number One being that of membership in a group of superior, "spiritual" people. When the place was exposed as just another hive of passion and intrigue, the spell was broken, and an exodus began.

We had tea in the courtyard, near the oleander bush. Traditionally, a Zen garden should contain no poisonous plants, but this was Bodhidharma, the dirtiest Zen Center in America. No one came or went during our conversation; there was a general deadness which was very characteristic of the center. The phone rang once or twice but as a visiting student I was forbidden to answer it. Laurence tried to convince me I was making a big mistake by coming to a place like this. His center might be going down the tubes, but Bodhidharma had always been something of a sewer.

I suggested it was partly a difference of style. His center practiced Soto Zen, a softer school. Soto, according to our Abbot, was "slow and beautiful." At Bodhidharma we followed the Rinzai school — "fast and messy" Samurai Zen. Sudden enlightenment as opposed to gradual.

But if our brand of enlightenment was so sudden, why did certain people hang around the place for years? Laurence was sceptical about everything. "There was always something sleazy about Bodhidharma. I mean, look at the kind of student you have coming here."

I gazed around at our tranquil garden, devoid of any human presences. I looked across the alley at the razor wire that crowned the fence of the kindergarten next door. A group of black children, led by their teacher, were holding hands in a circle and slowly singing:

A tisket, a tasket
A green and yellow/basket
I wrote a letter to my love
But on the way I dropped it

I dropped it, I dropped it
But on the way I dropped it
A little girlie picked it up
And put it in her pocket.

It struck me that this was the only song I had ever heard them sing, that maybe it represented their entire repertoire. It struck me that maybe I hadn't paid enough attention to the background during my stay here. In place of meditative silence, I might have investigated some of the spoken/chanted/sung texts, audible and half-audible, which were woven into the fabric of life in America.

The singing of those kindergarten children. The innocent off-key chimes of the ice-cream wagon. The drum-accompanied Sino-Japanese chanting of the incomprehensible Heart Sutra, which translates, in part:

O Sariputra, form is here emptiness, emptiness is form.... all things here are characterized with emptiness: they are not born, they are not annihilated; they are not tainted, they are not immaculate; ... there is no suffering, no accumulation, no annihilation, no path; there is no knowledge, no attainment, [and] no realization...

The roar and swoop of the police helicopter. The curses and predictions of the Voodoo Lady. "You are all white devils, and the whiter you are, the deeper in Hell you will burn."

The African drums and rap music blasting out of some dealer's slow-moving vehicle, making its daily rounds outside the walls. I imagined a half-dismantled, multi-colored van, spray-painted with names and initials. This too was a kind of text, very difficult to decipher.

And then there was the text of a letter I was writing to my love, who had escaped South Africa to become a Zen monk in America.

I wrote a letter to my Love, but on the Way I dropped it. Or the Voodoo Lady took it with her when she fled.

9
Moira Farr

WOMEN AND WANDERLUST

Someday there'll have to be a new world. A new kind of woman. Or a new world for women... In that future time a woman will be a strong warrior: free, strong, proud, able to control her own destiny... Meanwhile things stink."

Kathy Acker, *Kathy Goes To Haiti*

I WAS SEVENTEEN, working weekends as a waitress at what was locally known as "the Bypass Texaco" restaurant, on Highway 7 just outside Peterborough, Ontario. It was a viciously cold afternoon, mean pellets of snow falling out of a slate-gray sky. The lunchtime panic was over, but a few customers lingered — elderly farmers passing the time, truckers drinking coffee and eating slices of the restaurant's renowned coconut cream pie.

From behind the counter, I could see beyond the gas pumps and out on to the highway. As I watched, a car pulled on to the shoulder, and a woman got out on the passenger's side. The car drove off and she bolted across the road, into the Texaco parking lot. She was wiry, with short-cropped gray hair, a taut face, wary eyes. She wore a thin navy-blue ski jacket, pants that flapped above her ankles, a battered pair of crepe-soled shoes. She pulled open the door, walked inside and plunked herself down on the stool in front of me. "I have no money," she said in a clear, loud accented voice. "But I am hungry, and I vill vash dishes, or do any other vork."

I guess I gaped, like everyone else in the place. There was embarrassed silence, a bit of coughing, eye-rolling. Frank Kulas, the restaurant's owner, stood with his big fists on the counter, looking slightly amused. He went back to the kitchen, slapped together a hamburger and french fries, shoved it through the hatchway, and barked at me to give her a drink. She asked for coffee, and proceeded to eat hungrily, but with dignity. When she'd finished, she said: "Now I do dishes." Frank waved his hands. "No, no work, just go now." She eyed him suspiciously for a moment, then simply nodded and said "Thank you." She left the restaurant with the same determined gait that had brought her in, sprinted across the road and stuck out her thumb. I turned away to serve some customers and when I looked up again, she was gone.

I remember wondering how on earth a woman who looked to be my mother's age could end up alone on a highway in the dead of winter, hitching rides and cadging food. (Now it isn't so inexplicable to me.) I'll never know whether that particular woman chose to do what she did for reasons other than dire distress, but I thought then and think now that she was remarkably courageous. It was the mid-seventies, a time when hitchhiking was on the wane, even among the adventurous young. Fewer people were inclined to pick you up, and those who did, more likely to do you harm. I'd hitchhiked occasionally with friends in my early teens. But then the mother of a friend was found dead in a ditch along a lonely back road — she'd been murdered, the police said, by someone who'd picked her up when she was hitchhiking. I couldn't bring myself to get into a stranger's car again.

Fuelled by songs like Connie Kaldor's "Wanderlust," and Bonnie Raitt's gutsy "The Road Is My Middle Name," I've been thinking about what possibilities have ever really existed for women who feel the desire to head out. Questing is an ancient urge not bound by gender, but historically more men than women have acted on the impulse. Paeans to the romance of the road have come primarily from the male imagination, articulating masculine notions of personal freedom.

That's why a book like Jack Kerouac's *On the Road* is difficult reading for a woman. I gave it a go five years ago, while living with a man who said it had changed his life when he'd devoured it years earlier. You might say that as a teenager in the late fifties, my friend had been part of the book's target audience; you might say that as a woman in her mid-twenties in the mid-eighties, I was not. Kerouac's Beat argot was, it's true, a bracing antidote to talk of bull markets and *Bright Lights, Big City* — and when he confessed that he "shambled after as I've been doing all my life after people who interest me, because the only people for me are the mad ones, the ones who are mad to live, mad to talk, mad to be saved, desirous of everything at the same time, the ones who never yawn or say a commonplace thing, but burn, burn, burn like fabulous yellow roman candles" — well, my heart warmed.

But when Kerouac used the word "people," he really meant men. I may have been seduced by his lyrical recklessness, but I had to be magnanimous to finish the book, to swallow the sexism in the boys-club bonhomie. From Dean Moriarty's "beautiful little sharp chick," Mary Lou, to the whores of Mexico, there isn't a woman who exists to do anything but cook, clean, look cute, and copulate. Early in his journey, Kerouac tries to hustle a "little blonde" in Montana, but finds her morose and unyielding. She tells him she wants to get out of the backwater and head for New York. "Ain't nothin in New York," he tells her dismissively. "Hell there ain't," she replies. Jack doesn't get laid, and the blonde with her yearning to break away is left behind in the dust.

Nothing I've read since about the Beats has altered the feeling of sadness and exclusion I had reading *On The Road*. (*Minor Characters*, by Joyce Johnson, who consorted with Kerouac for a couple of years in her youth, poignantly reveals the fates of the women of her generation who tagged along with their men for the adventure. At the time, even tagging along was iconoclastic. But most of them abandoned or deferred their own artistic ambitions; and many died untimely deaths by suicide, drug addiction, and murder.) I began to wonder whether any woman could journey through the world — through life — experiencing it and writing about it with the celebratory expansiveness that Kerouac at his most lucid achieves.

Could there ever have been a female Kerouac? Are there role models for women who want to travel alone and write about the experience today? I went looking, and found spunky adventurers, earnest anthropologists, lovelorn desperadoes, atrociously bad writers, and one inspiring radical hobo named Boxcar Bertha, whose story is told by a man.

Yes, women have travelled alone in the past, under a wide array of circumstances, and more are doing it all the time. But how and why they do it, the risks they take and dangers they face when they do it (not to mention the emotional baggage they unpack when they write about it) still differ greatly from men. Bookstore travel sections swell with annual additions to the genre by male authors, but those by women are still scarce. For men the burden of a crowded market means that gimmicks abound and at this very moment someone is no doubt windsurfing down the Amazon or pogo-sticking across the Outer Hebrides.

Women's voices can be found, it's true, and more are being retrieved from obscurity by feminist scholars, collected in anthologies such as *The Blessings Of A Good Thick Skirt* and *Girdle Round The Earth*. From Mary Kingsley, who forged her way through West Africa in the late nineteenth century, to Dervla Murphy, who rode a bicycle from Dunkirk to Delhi in 1963 (and has been gone on quirky expeditions to exotic locales ever since), they are plucky, indomitable women, whose travelogues are often witty and astute. But en masse, the "what a gal I am!" tone of their memoirs gets tiresome. Their own inner terrain remains largely unexplored, and if they had any sexual encounters along the way (I mean pleasurable ones, of their own choosing), they certainly don't write about them. Mercy, no. For that, move to the opposite extreme, and find the tortured Maryse Holder, brought to harrowing life by actress Jackie Burroughs in the recent film, *Winter Tan.*

Holder, a New York feminist academic, boozed and screwed her way across Mexico in the seventies, on a journey she described as a "vacation from feminism." The vacation came to an end when she was beaten to death and left by the side of a road near Mexico City. Her posthumous account, based on her letters home to friends, is called *Give Sorrow Words*. Holder's book did indeed give me sorrow. Her searing intelligence and wicked wit are shot through with a bitterness and pessimism that is painful to regard. She drinks to ever-increasing excess, she dances in discos, she glories in a cavalcade of cocks, on an apparent mission to prove that "the feminista is really a whore."

Holder didn't live to overcome her profound self-loathing, which was, it is so painfully clear, only a despairing inversion of legitimate anger — anger that desire in a woman diminishes her in the eyes of a male-dominated world to the level of a pathetic, expendable slut. "How men hate the sexual in women," she rages. "How incredibly oppressed women are, for surely they all want exactly what I want, and men want, and they are crucified for it."

The crucifixion continues. Despite a powerful political introduction by Kate Millett in the Avon paperback edition of the book there is something offensive about the breathless jacket blurb: "A SISTER, AN ADVENTURESS, A MADWOMAN ... Maryse Holder went to Mexico to live, to write and to learn how to love. But as she moved from one man to another ... she ignored her own sense of impending doom — and too late, discovered that in some places a woman can't live by her own rules." It's just a fancy way of saying the little hussy asked for it.

Though she expressed suicidal thoughts in her last, booze-addled letters, and even though her closest friend concludes in the epilogue that Holder engineered her own death, I don't buy it. Maryse Holder, like everyone, wanted love and affirmation, and when she couldn't give it to herself or find it in the world, she grieved. Several times she talks excitedly of one day writing a series of travel guides for women, which would draw on her own experiences and those of the tough and resourceful women she met on her travels. These are the thoughts of someone who envisions surviving, not someone asking to have her head smashed in.

I eagerly anticipated reading Mary Morris's recently published story of her solitary journey through Mexico and Central America in *Nothing to Declare: Memoirs of a Woman Travelling Alone*. A slim volume with a pretty pink cover and quote from a rave review in *Cosmopolitan* should have set off warning bells. Comparing Holder and Morris is a bit like comparing Virginia Woolf and Jackie Collins.

There's grace in Holder's vicious candor; Morris's prose galumphs from one banal observation to the next. When she arrives in San Miguel, she notices that the name of the townhouse complex she's moving into is the Departamentos Toros. "I am a Taurus and as I stood beneath the sign with the name of the apartment, I thought this must be a good omen," she proclaims.

In presenting herself as a courageous lone wayfarer, Morris is a bit of a poseur. In fact, she is rarely alone. She is drawn into San Miguel's little community of tedious expatriates, and travels with a Seattle art therapist named Catherine. On one jaunt, when Mary doesn't get a seat on a hot and crowded train, she starts to cry. Indeed, she spends a lot of time weeping, particulary over the (to her) insurmountable cultural differences between Alejandro, her Mexican lover and herself. When not commenting on the tackiness of the furniture in Alejandro's apartment, or rhapsodizing about his profile, Morris strays into stale New Age musings about ancient Aztec and Mayan mysteries.

A friend suggested I look at Kathy Acker's contribution to the genre, *Kathy Goes To Haiti*. My friend had read it when it was first published in 1978 by Rumour Press, a small now defunct Toronto publishing house. "I seem to remember a lot of descriptions of her cunt." I must admit, this wasn't exactly the inner terrain I had in mind when I contemplated the ideal female travelogue, and I gloomily anticipated a pain-fest in the Holder tradition.

Like Holder, Acker's persona is that of the alienated New York intellectual, pissed off at men, confused about her longings, desperate for some kind of reconciliation between lust and love. As she steps off the plane in Port au Prince, she presents herself as a fallen innocent, wide-eyed nonetheless.

It isn't long before the entire male population of the town gets wind of this strange creature in their midst, an attractive young white woman who says she likes being alone. Men follow her everywhere, explaining that it simply is not possible for a woman in Haiti to be without a "boyfriend." Soon, poor Kathy feels she is running around like "a cunt without a head." The situation improves when she meets Roger, a playboy son of a wealthy plantation owner. Kathy and Roger have some blissful times together (the Rumour Press edition comes complete with charmingly explicit wood-cut illustrations that have captions such as "Oh oh oh"), and Acker's descriptions of sex are about as honest and unembarrassed as any you're going to find.

But there's a disturbing subtext to it all, one that Acker herself queasily acknowledges. Despite her best liberated intentions, Kathy, lost in a sex fog, falls in love with Roger, even as he is revealed to be a slimeball of huge proportions. The longer she stays in Haiti, connected to the unsavory Roger, the more dangerous life becomes. What's a girl to do? This being Haiti, Kathy goes to a voodoo doctor. Here, the requisite strange rituals are enacted, and cryptic advice dispensed. But Kathy doesn't feel enlightened. As the book ends, "Kathy turns around and walks outside into the sun. She's more dazed than before." Well, better dazed than dead. Kathy did at least survive her trip. Moreover, she continues to write, and recently was paired on a joint book tour with William S. Burroughs.

My favorite tale of a female sojourner is *Boxcar Bertha: Sister of the Road.* Originally published in 1942, and recently re-released in paperback, it is the moving story of Bertha Thompson, who hoboed across the United States during the twenties and thirties, documenting her experiences as she went. The book stands as a sweet revelation that Kerouac and his cool cronies didn't invent the twentieth-century road-trip to self-awareness.

Bertha Thompson came by her hobo leanings honestly. Her parents were "free-thinkers," stalwarts of the communal anarchist colonies and hobo camps of early twentieth-century North America. Near the beginning of the book, Bertha recalls her first encounter with a female hobo. "I saw one in dusty black sweater and striped overalls flip a freight that had stopped at our switch to take on an empty ... the look on her face as she talked about going on west, and the sureness with which she swung under the freight car, set my childish mind in a fever. The world was easy, like that. Even to women. It had never occurred to me before."

Bertha set out on her first hobo excursion from San Francisco when she was seventeen. "I was wildly happy with life," she says, in a passage redolent with the headiness of the youthful Kerouac, who would write as he hitched one of his first rides, "I ran for it with my soul whoopeeing."

Bertha's story, if not as lyrical in the telling, is equally packed with adventures and misadventures, strangers met and conquered, mistakes made and lessons learned. What's different, though, is that the members of the opposite sex she encounters don't come across as stereotypes or ciphers; even those who reject her (all of them, basically) are accorded compassion and humanity.

More interesting still is her clear-eyed social commentary. In the original edition, Bertha's narrative is followed by an appendix entitled "What Makes Sisters Of The Road?" which catalogues the ways and means of hobo women of the era. It's one of the most poignant things I've ever read. Under "Factors As To Why Women Wander," she lists: "To escape from reality, to get away from poverty, misery and unpleasant surroundings; to run away from husbands, lovers and admirers; inability to find expression at home; freedom and adventure; romance — to find lovers and a husband; some drive compelling them to go away, some call beckoning and seducing them."

Bertha was certainly a romantic, but she didn't gloss over the horrors of a woman hobo's life — stories of violence and exploitation dot her account. She wanted to remedy that, make the road a little more civilized, and so she championed the idea of hostels for roving women that would provide a temporary safe haven — complete with poetry rooms! (Try getting that one by today's urban housing officials.)

The book ends on a brave note. At the age of thirty, after more than a decade of rambling, Bertha decides she's had enough. She settles down to care for her eight-year-old daughter whom she had entrusted until then to anarchist-camp friends. "I had achieved my purpose. I had wanted to know how it felt to be a hobo, a radical, a prostitute, a thief, a reformer, a social worker and a revolutionist. Now I knew.... It was all worthwhile to me. There were no tragedies in my life."

Wonderful as the book is, there are, I learned, some doubts about its veracity; it's billed as "an autobiography, as told to Dr. Ben L. Reitman." He was a flamboyant anarchist of the time who penned a number of what he called "outcast narratives," detailing the lives of hoboes he'd met on his own down-and-out travels. *Boxcar Bertha* is his *pièce de résistance*.

Still curious about *Boxcar Bertha*, I wrote to the publisher to ask if anyone knew what became of her. I thought it odd that neither the introduction (by none other than our girl in Haiti, Kathy Acker), nor the afterward by Reitman's biographer, Roger Bruns, made any mention of Bertha's subsequent life. She was thirty in 1942, so it seemed to me there was a good chance that she might still be alive. I confess to having some fuzzy fantasies of tracking down the grand old lady, to find her still feisty and full of great stories.

Well, it's nice to dream. Don Kennison of Amok Press wrote back to say that the Bertha of Reitman's chronicle was probably an invention, a composition of several women hoboes Reitman encountered in his travels. All the same, I was informed a 'hobo king' by the name of Steam Train Maury Graham maintains he heard of Boxcar Bertha, though he never met her. He is convinced she did exist and lived a full life after her written story ends.

The fact that there is such mystery surrounding Bertha Thompson (which no one seems to have been bothered to solve) has, in my view, a lot to do with sexism. As with travel writing in general, books by and about male hoboes are legion. But finding anything by and about women is difficult. A book published in 1934 called *Canada's Untouchables*, by one Reverend Andrew Rodden, concerns itself with the thousands of male transients making their way across the nation, but makes only a passing tut-tut reference to the fact that even some women were resorting to this too. All the minister's solutions and compassion are aimed at the men. Another account of the time, written by a psychologist, puts the phenomenon of women on the road down to "heterosexual maladjustment." I wish Maryse Holder were alive to cackle at that one.

I also wish Holder had lived to write her travel guides for women. What rankles most when surveying the literature that does exist, when considering the whole exercise of travel writing from a female point of view, is how central a factor violence remains. There isn't one account I've read that doesn't contain at least one incident of assault, and there isn't one author who doesn't at some point ruminate seriously on her own fear. "To wing it feministically is not possible," Holder laments. "Like fighting the ocean ... one finally wants to escape eyes. It's so potentially dangerous here."

Making the world a safer place for women is surely one of feminism's most ravaged dreams — we're not safe from harassment and assault on the streets where we live, so we certainly can't expect to be when we set out alone to far-flung destinations. Unfortunately, all the Wendo in the world won't lower the weirdo count, or shield us from the random harassment that isn't life-threatening but just a goddamn nuisance. A woman embarking on a lone journey still has to arm herself — psychologically and physically — take more real risks and be braver than a man doing the same thing. And until there's a new world for women, I have to agree with Kathy Acker, it stinks.

10
Don Gillmor

CLUES

I HAD two best friends when I was eleven, as others did, grouped in secret-keeping, punching trios on the way home from school. One member of every trio was bound to learn about sex first, by rumor, education, or reckless imagination, and then become the authority for the other two. Denny Marks was the first in our trio; Brian Fortner and I came to rely on him for the big news. Kneeling on the asphalt outside Oakenwald school, Denny drew a line with two dots on it with a piece of chalk, offering us our first glimpse of the female reproductive system. "One is for sex," Denny said, pointing to the top dot. "The other is for having babies. If you pick the wrong one, you'll kill her instantly."

Like most fabrications of childhood, Denny's plan had the quality of fable and the possibility of truth. It illustrated the gory themes from "Mutual of Omaha's Wild Kingdom," where death was a routine part of every animal's day. There was a risk to consider every time out, every hour, if Denny's statistics could be relied on. I stared at the woman behind the Tom Boy Drugstore counter with new respect as she handed over my Fat Emma bar. To have lived to such an age, to have gambled — on bad men, myopic men, parked cars, marriage — and won.

There was a section of woods on the way home from school, not a park, simply an undeveloped block of residential property with a path running through it. It was called the Witchy Path and it was full of legends and quirks: once, walking home through its overgrown channels, I found Brent Kiesman tied to a sapling with his own belt. He could have freed himself easily but had been instructed to wait for fifteen minutes by Dean Hemp or Dean would be forced to drown Brent in the flooded golf course. I chatted with Brent for a few minutes and went home to Campbell's chicken noodle soup and liverwurst sandwiches.

Another day in the Witchy Path, in late autumn when the foliage had thinned, I saw a classmate standing stupidly by a tree, smiling.

"Want to see something?" he asked.

"What?"

"Just do you want to see it. Yes or no."

I was wary. This could so easily be something odd, but finally worthless: a dead squirrel, my classmate's dwarfish dink.

"How do I know if I want to see it if I don't know what it is."

He walked over and showed me two color photographs from a magazine, the color spotted by white where the pages had faded from being hidden outside. There was a woman sitting naked on an exercise bicycle, her breasts pointed outwards like setters sighting a bird. I was tickled and my breathing became giddy. The schematic Denny had diagrammed was nowhere in evidence, the whole business made more dangerous by disguise. I looked at the woman for quite a while, fixing her in my memory.

"I can get more. Any time I want."

"Can I keep these then?" I asked thickly.

"No way." He grabbed them back and folded them along the worn creases.

The Red River undulates through Winnipeg, forming switchbacks as the banks are imperceptibly gouged each year. My neighborhood lay in the lee of one of these, protected and finite, the river a source of daily warnings. It moved past with an opaque heaviness, a thick brown color rather than the advertised red. Occasionally we saw a rat dart along the slick banks. Crayfish were sometimes retrieved, gray and blind, from the water. There was a stand of trees lining the river bank; beyond it was open short-grass prairie before the dyke road and then houses. A nine-hole golf course lay adjacent to our homes, a private course that flooded in the spring if we were lucky. We all lived in the park, our source of information limited by geography.

Brian's family had taken in a boarder, a twenty-one-year old man with a job and a Ford Fairlane. He told us that no engine, foreign or domestic, could pull the kind of duty the slant six could. Never was one, never would be. He told us that his pubic hair grew so quickly he had to trim it with a pair of barber's scissors every month. Sometimes he got his girlfriend to do it, he said with a wink. We never saw his girlfriend.

On a Saturday, Denny and Brian and I walked along the river path, wearing the same brand of checked shirt in different colors. We climbed the curving trunk of a river-bank tree, cleaned the mud from our desert boots with sticks, and each took a cigarette from the package of Alpines Denny had brought. He took out a Zippo lighter and opened it by flicking it against his thigh; with a backwards stroke he brought it back up and lit it against his jeans. It was a trick Brian's boarder had taught us in the garage, but Denny was the only one who could do it with aplomb, and the only one with a Zippo. We dragged on the Alpines wilfully and discussed teachers and women. Below us, in a small clearing, Brian spotted the anthropological remains of a riverside meeting. We climbed down to investigate, the cigarettes clenched tightly in our teeth.

There were several stubbed cigarettes, an empty package of du Mauriers, and a used condom. Denny picked up the condom with the end of a stick and bounced it lightly as we squatted in a circle around it. This was proof of some kind, someone had done it. Dean Hemp was a candidate; in the wake of the Beatles' success on "The Ed Sullivan Show," he had kept a black pompadour. We discussed possible partners, naming girls at random, some from our school, some of them movie actresses. Denny flicked the condom with a sneaky wrist movement and it landed, briefly, on Brian's face, before it was brushed away hysterically with flailing hands. Denny screamed "Coodies!" and we broke through the brush blindly, running as fast as we could. Sixty yards onto the prairie scrub we stopped, exhausted, bent over and panting. Brian punched Denny on the shoulder twice, the second time hard, and we sat down and lit three more Alpines.

When we were twelve, Denny's sister, Alva, who was sixteen, told us dirty jokes. We laughed at every joke and she would say, "You don't get it, do you?" Quite often we didn't get it, some of the jokes may even have been traps, ungettable, but we always said we did. Alva asked us to explain the joke — *why* it was funny.

"If you don't know, we're not going to tell you," Denny said.

"You don't get it because you're too immature," Alva said. "You wouldn't know what to do if you were in bed with a woman."

"Would so," Denny said at the same time as I said "Doubters."

"What would you do?"

It hadn't been completely articulated in my imagination, the mechanics were still in soft focus, slightly mystical. I waited for Denny to answer with something devastating, like "Wouldn't you like to know?" Our hesitant silence condemned us in Alva's eyes.

"See, I told you." Alva walked up to me in an exaggerated Marilyn Monroe walk. "You're going to go to bed with me right now," she said.

It was hard to grasp why this wasn't good news, but I was nervous and stood mute. I was rescued by Denny, who issued an Ozarkian summons. "*I'll* go to bed with you," he said, grabbing her breasts. "*Denny!*" she screamed, "God, you ..." They were off, Denny rocketing down the stairs and out the door and into the broad safety of the yard. Alva followed as far as the door in her socks and yelled threats. I squeezed by her sheepishly and stood to the side, enjoying their escalating taunts.

Denny said he had naked photographs of her which he was going to sell to the *Winnipeg Free Press*. Alva said she would pound Denny. "I used your brassiere for a school project," he yelled.

When Alva left the house, Denny and I went into the basement, staked out positions behind furniture, and shot our BB guns at each other. We occasionally hit one another but the guns weren't very powerful and the BBs didn't hurt much. Denny became disappointed with the lack of injury; he took his gun, pressed it to his thigh, and pulled the trigger.

"*Jesus Christ!*" he yelled, hopping and limping in a small circle. Tears were beginning to form. He took down his pants and examined the welt with pride. The BB hadn't broken the skin, a letdown, but it looked like there would be a bruise.

In one of those spontaneous bursts of adolescent bad judgment, each party abdicating responsibility to the event itself, we experimentally chucked one of Alva's Dave Clark Five records the length of the room. It sailed forcefully and erratically and smashed into the far wall, leaving a pie-shaped gap. With the impulse of creation, we took up our previous positions, this time armed with a stack of forty-fives. We had destroyed most of Herman's Hermits' oeuvre when we noticed Alva suddenly at the bottom of the stairs.

She went for Denny, and I inched towards the stairs. She got in some good shots before Denny squirmed by and we hightailed it down the lane, checking over our shoulders regularly. Denny couldn't go home, that much was clear. I felt it was unlikely that Alva would repeat her offer of sex. It was time to do our paper route anyway.

Our paper route was a mutual burden, more than a hundred houses. Once, when we were collecting in the summer, Mrs. Kimpton in H Section answered the door after a lengthy delay wearing a robe, which she clasped together with one hand. When she turned sideways to yell behind her, "It's the *Free Press*, collecting," one breast was exposed in profile, the nipple barely obscured and vividly imagined. When she turned back to face me, I stared downwards at the kitty-litter box on the landing and said I could come back later. Perhaps that would be best, she said. I noticed small beads of perspiration on her upper lip when I looked up to say goodbye.

Our route included some of the magisterial river-front homes, most with long driveways and several cars. One of them was owned by the Luptons, whose daughter Gloria sunned herself in a pink bikini. Denny and I split the route but we both delivered to the Luptons, resting the paper on the doorstep and looking into the bay windows. When we delivered the paper that day, the door opened and Mrs. Lupton and Gloria were standing there, wearing summery two-piece outfits. They were tanned; not a garish, oily brown but the soft, faded, buttery hue of a September tan. Their blonde hair was sprayed into short, sweeping helmets. Gloria was wearing gold sandals; a skein of fine blonde hairs trailed downwards from her navel into her short skirt. The air inside the house was cool and rich. Mrs. Lupton told us that they were moving and we could stop delivery the following Thursday. Gloria smiled politely and Mrs. Lupton closed the door.

"She wanted it," Denny said.

"What?"

"Couldn't you tell? She was dying for it."

Gloria Lupton was out of our lives, another missed opportunity. Denny and I split up on South Drive, headed for our respective houses with our slack canvas *Free Press* bags. In recent months Denny had quietly abandoned the fatal-choice theory of human sexuality. We had moved towards more plausible accounts, informed by our ontogenic hormones, by some atavistic impulse coursing towards our brains. When we shouted obscene suggestions to girls from the safety of packs, they were uninterested. Their silhouettes moved closer and they whispered smugly, their school books clasped to their breasts. They seemed to lack our worldliness.

I turned to walk through the park, past oak trees, dogwood, and the fading lines of newly mown lawns. A young wife was bent over at her garden, wiping the perspiration from her forehead with her wrist, her madras shorts stretched to the shape of a pear. Past the houses, the open interior spaces of the park sat wild and secret, the echoing shouts of children carried occasionally on the wind.

11
Hugh Graham

LIFE AND DEATH IN ONTARIO COUNTY

I WAS seven in the winter of 1959 when my parents and I went to look at a farm house near Greenbank, about twenty-five miles north of Whitby, Ontario. It was occupied by a ferretish old man with faded blue eyes, and his wife, and their sixty-year-old son. They lived in one large room and my mother discovered that they slept under coats upstairs. Everything they had was old and worn out. The ceiling was low and buckled, the blistered wall-paper was from the twenties, and the air thick and dry with stove heat. Puzzles of Scottish castles had been framed and hung on the wall. Everything that could be saved was stacked in another room behind a door closed and stuffed with rags.

We returned several times that winter, sometimes after dark, and entering that house was to cross into a warm and dim place that was otherworldly and unsettling. The son, a lumbering giant of a man, shaved in front of us beside the stove in his undervest and suspenders using a cracked mirror, a straight razor, and a basin with steaming water from a blackened kettle. The old man sat idly in a rocking chair among other chairs around the stove with flattened torn cushions. The old woman was the only one who was moving, large and bird-like, giving me and my friends candy and pictures. Out in the back, on the unfinished planks of the woodshed wall there was a tattered collage of pasted-up magazine illustrations that included a painted thirties advertisement of an old countryman in a suit playing the violin. The evening light in the picture seemed to be like the light in their house, the night sky was the color of his suit, and for a long time I was certain that the fictional fiddler was the old man. Beyond the woodshed a track through the snow led to a hand pump. In the depths of that hard winter when they were snow-bound, food had to be brought them from the village. I had never seen such people. My mother explained to me that it was poverty. They maintained the land for a beef farmer, their name was Beedon, and I later realized they were the forgotten; tenants of a type commonly associated with the American south.

When we took possession and began work on the farm house, they had moved down two concession lines to a solid ancient field stone house on high and bald melancholy farm land. The old man, John Beedon, and his son Alf put in our garden, built livestock fencing, and taught us how to manage our woodlot and sixty acres of pasture. And now we seemed to be visiting in the new place, where they had brought the same heavy smell of mildew and stove heat, just as we had visited the old. Mrs. Beedon still had a miniature museum she had created in an aquarium that displayed a growing and changing collection of postcards, dolls, doll furniture, miniature flags, and buttons, which she called her "funny box."

I had been afraid of them at first. They were crude, spoke with "don't" and "ain't." Beedon was slight, bantam-like, testy, and irascible, and the son, haunted and moronic, towered over his parents. The three looked alike, with sharp eyes and big noses and thin flat mouths and the two men had abscess scars in the right cheek, which gave them a look of wild inhaling. One winter Mrs. Beedon was talking to my mother, when, in a moment of womanly confidence, steadying her thick glasses, she pulled down a black stocking and then pulled up a leg of long underwear and showed a faint blue mark where the old man had given her a kick.

The son, Alf, as Beedon told us outright, was dim, subnormal, while Alf himself, with his monumental craggy face and deepset gray eyes seemed to agree with equanimity. All his life he had held menial jobs and worked with his father in laboring or picking up highway tree-trimmings in a horse and wagon for Ontario Hydro. Alf spoke with a solemn nodding expertise about cutting post tops to a slant to keep out rot and expounded with an air of grave foreboding on the common details of maintaining the property. He had a high hearse-like black '48 Dodge and at every opportunity he opened the hood to display the engine with my father listening and nodding politely while trying to get on with things.

But when his father was discussing the plans for the day with mine, and Alf attempted to add a detail, the old man snapped, "There, we heard enough from you," with a swift short kick in the shin.

On weekends Alf drove home from a cleaning job in Milton and spent the time with a case of twenty-four in front of the television mildly sloshed; the program, which he highly recommended, was *Popeye.* "I've courted every girl in Reach Township," he told us, with the implication he'd turned them all down, but it was when my mother hired him to drive her into Port Perry to do shopping that he talked. My mother, who was easily bored, was impressed with his skill as a raconteur as he told his stories with reverence and amazement, saying he'd been overseas during the war and that an English girl had slapped him for proposing they go to Petticoat Lane. His father told us flatly that Alf had never been out of the country and had been turned down for the service "because of bad nerves." My mother later gathered that Alf had taken stories he'd heard from braggarts, farmers, and servicemen, and honed them into his own imaginary past.

In the summers when I got to know the old man, he was eighty and cycling six miles a day to our place over hilly gravel concession roads. I recall him always in indigo twill trousers with suspenders, a light-colored fedora he never took off, hawk-like without teeth and with alert pale eyes that never seemed to change; an expression of amused, open-mouthed, almost delectable outrage, as if he had caught you doing something he had predicted you would do. In those summers I was a city kid with no friends in the country and I spent my days with the old man. He taught me how to build livestock fencing, to use an axe and a scythe, to cut and trim timber and till a garden. He worked slowly and with certainty and economy. He used an axe gently and perfectly, everything he had was immaculate and shop-worn, his tools white with wear, fastidiously sharp and clean. He had nothing new, but rather items that seemed to be part of the derelict inside of our barn: rags, pegs, bottles, wire, and a jealously guarded enamel drinking ladle. For stretches of summers running, my only life was his, as we replaced rods of fencing in hot dry pasture ringing with crickets. He stretched fence wire by hand, strand by strand with a crowbar, set posts in straight, dug-out stones four feet in the ground, planted solid anchor posts, and cut exact and tightly notching brace poles. With a pale wild eye he could line up posts so that lengthwise they appeared as one from here to the horizon. I stayed with him while he ate his gum-soft lunch out of the same old Wonderbread bag and drank Pepsi (Coca-Cola was "poison") in the noon shade of the driving shed.

He and his family had lived dirt poor with no plumbing in the same kinds of houses for close to sixty years. He had visited no city since he'd been to Toronto in 1908. He had gone to see the Exhibition, then a celebrated agricultural fair, disliked the city, condemned the fair, which was nowhere near as good as the one in Lindsay, and went home quickly never to return. His time was that of teams and traces; he operated no machinery, would not even touch a tractor. He had no use for television, found football ridiculous, could just read headlines and sign his name, and kept their money in cash at the post office. But all his life seemed to have been lived in a struggle to prove he was, or had been, right. He argued tooth and nail with my mother about putting in the garden and was always vindicated; when my father's car arrived on weekends, Beedon looked up with a smile, ready to show him his errors. The old man's tales were of cleverness and cheating, triumphant accounts of meanness and dishonesty and in these he seemed to stand alone in a world of rural propriety. Where the conversation of the farm wives and close-mouthed farmers that we knew was filled with righteous anodynes, tact, and caution, Beedon's eyes lit up at recollections of incompetence and shabbiness. Perhaps he had nothing to lose by such stories; he seemed to have fought with every employer he had ever had; he walked out on fence-building jobs because the farmer insisted on hanging the wire upside down. His suspicions of malice were often senseless and extravagant, for example, that a shovel of ours found in the pond had been thrown there by a man we hardly knew, for spite.

We on the other hand were city middle-class, devoid of the natural suspicion of farmers, and since we had the money to pay him what he wanted without welshing, he seemed, for that practical reason, to respect us — even if he always told us we were wrong, or was amused by our ignorance and capriciousness. After my father hung a stark contemporary conceptual piece over the mantel, the old man smiled toothlessly and said, "What you doing with a picture of a shovel?" His affections were indeed practical and determined his loyalty, and yet when local painters accidentally set our house on fire, he ran in alone through dense smoke and tried to drag out the furniture before he was pulled out by firemen.

He had lived and worked longer in the county than almost anyone and yet for all his stories almost no one seemed to know him. In turn, the world he described seemed to have passed, a spectral place devoid of witnesses where he fought two men to court a woman, where he had been able single-handedly to lift a full-grown heifer into the back of a wagon. When he'd dart in laughing and jab at the tail of my pony just to make him kick, he seemed very much of another age. Likewise, his entertainment was in talking: in denials, claims, and tales; the brush with death riding the famous long slope at Sandy Hook after his bicycle chain broke; a renowned giant elm near Goodwood, which he said had yielded seventy-odd cords of wood in its death, and then regretted, "I never did get down to see that tree."

The stories he told were redolent of the abandoned farm houses that were scattered around Greenbank, of suicide, fraud, and arson, of vandalized, trashed, melancholy places where frozen overalls still hung by the door over boots ghosted with dust and among the mites and mildew of a medicine cabinet where you could find a dusky tin of brilliantine, still viscous and marked by the scoop of fingers; where the son of a man whose farm had a broken dam decorated with a cow skull had died drinking strychnine. Those very places that smelled of mildew and damp plaster but hadn't fallen to dereliction were the places lived in by Beedon and his family. In a house rented in Uxbridge the attic had been closed and several nights running he heard a heavy chain dragged the length of the house across the floor above. In the daytime he investigated and found nothing; it was bare and completely sealed, but a few days later he learned that two years before the butcher who lived there had hanged himself. There was a story of the thirties that began with a column of smoke he had seen over near Uxbridge and ended with the owner of a blazing house tearing out of the front door with a baby carriage draped for protection with heavy blankets. And what made Beedon look at you as if he dared you to believe anyone could be courageous or honest, was the fact that the carriage had concealed no baby but four expensive folded suits. The implication, of course, was insurance fraud.

After five years I could scarcely remember the time when I had been afraid of him and now he was the first person the prospect of whose death made me sad. By then I knew he didn't mind me, and his gone world, which seemed to live on in the stillness before thunderstorms and the dry decay of barns, had become mine as well, a ghost world of Reach Township which followed me back to the city and to school. He had become a major figure in my life and in my imagination.

When my father hired an old farm couple from Quebec to live and run a mechanized operation on our place, it now seems we were pushing Beedon on as the world was pushing him. While he was still working for us, I remember the two old men talking in lawn chairs and my mother's remark that they were rivals and fundamentally disliked each other. Indeed, he moved on but even the riot of the sixties and what appeared to be relentless and ineluctable change were well on their way before I saw the last of him, and one spring when he didn't come round to the farm, it seemed only inevitable. We visited him and I saw him pale as parchment, small and hatless in his rocker. Then they were gone from that house too; the world seemed determined to move them on.

About eighty-five years ago, John Beedon, the eleventh or twelfth son of a Wiltshire game warden, came to Canada as a Barnardo Boy: one of the thousands of orphans sponsored by the Barnardo homes in England to populate the Empire from a pool of unskilled labor that Great Britain couldn't feed. This was how he had made his way to his first job turning over vegetable gardens with a horse and plough in Uxbridge, Ontario, in 1906. He also did the ornamental flowerbed that spelled CNR at the Uxbridge railway station. But it was in the network of walking and wagon-hopping itinerant farm labor that he met and courted and married a hawk-faced woman, his female doppelganger, a farmer's daughter from a remote hamlet at the end of the Marsh Hill road. Even when Beedon was old, you could see from his arms and hands, elongated and burly for his small frame, that his life had been the eternity of ploughing, pitching hay, managing horses and cattle, and all the other endless and thankless work of a time now unknown to us.

Two daughters who had disappeared seemed to us long gone and mythical. "Oh, she was wayward," they had spoken in gruff euphemism of one who had run off with a variety of men, perhaps in the twenties or thirties, and whom they had never seen since. Cannier, perhaps more worldly than the first, the other had married a lawyer in Whitby and, apart from meager financial help, refused to acknowledge her parents, having risen into a middle-class town world where such people as her parents supposedly didn't exist. So the Beedons and their son lived on in a world without clan or extension, where the old woman noted, remembered, and honored every birthday in every neighborhood they moved to. With the mechanization of farms and the reduction of country labor after the war, the old man took to his bicycle and travelled the same circuits tending gardens, and in that quiet time when we first went to Port Perry, many of the handsome gardens around the commodious Victorian villas would have been his work.

In the summer of 1970 I was nineteen, they were long gone, and with education and travel, childhood had become remote, when I heard somewhere that they were still alive and living on in another old house, inevitably in Ontario County — this time in the village of Kinsale. It would be their last. I went down with a couple of friends and we found a listing frame peaked Victorian farm house covered in insulbrick and we knocked. The old woman, vague and almost blind now, told us to come in and again there was the hot odor of old plaster and stove heat I had smelled twelve years before. She had no idea who any of us were and told us to sit down and began without comment to give us tea. I asked her where Beedon was, and she waved a massive work-hardened hand dismissively in front of her face and croaked, "They killed him. He's gone. They took him away two months ago." She couldn't explain more than that. She couldn't remember either of the farms where we had known them, and apologized and directly began to recall her youth in Marsh Hill at the turn of the century. We spoke to a neighbor who confirmed that Beedon had died in hospital two years before, and not two months, and if we wanted to know more we should wait till Alf came home.

Alf came by and Mrs. Beedon offered us dinner with her son. Close to seventy, he was just as massive, still a bachelor but had whitened and was a different man. He jobbed at country fairs and came home irregularly with money for his mother. He ate a corn cob with giant forearms on the oil-cloth and spoke with a sober hardness as if finally wakened by the death of his father. "We always lived in the houses like this, old houses, every damn one built the same way, four-square, mortise and tenon joints, the same roof joists." But he remembered me and even my best friend who was with me: "the little yellow-haired fella." Our place, which had remained in my mind their original place, he remembered tersely as "the place with the pond" — turning out to be but one of myriad tenancies. I asked him about his father and he said, "They said he died, but they took him in the hospital and cut off his leg, they killed him." As we left, I saw him watching us leave, shadowed and headless behind a drawn blind.

In a year I came back to that house in the winter, the insulbrick had been half stripped off and the door was answered by downtrodden people I had never seen. A young and toothless woman told me the old woman and her son were gone. Mrs. Beedon had died, and he had been committed to a mental hospital, but they believed the gravestone of Beedon and his wife had been erected in the cemetery at the next concession road. In blowing snow that formed wells around the monuments I found no stone, not even an unmarked plot.

When they disappeared, the Beedons had lived in twenty-two houses in a single county since he had arrived in 1906. Unmarked in death, John Beedon, his wife, and son left almost no impression either among those who knew them or had hired the old man; few could recall them well, fewer could really distinguish him in their memories of the gone world into which he had dissolved like a footprint in pasture.

12
Ernest Hillen
BACK ON JAVA

I SAT near the edge of the pond and
watched for fish jumping; I never saw any, only the widening rings they left
behind. The ample pond was stocked with carp and gourami. Monsoon rains
had raised the brown water almost level with the lush lawn and shrubs. My
wrought-iron chair stood beside the front door of a two-room guesthouse overgrown by an orange bougainvillea. It was light but the sun didn't yet show;
ordinary birds had taken over from the noisy creatures of the night. This was the
best time. Once the sun appeared the heat would soon follow — heat that you
breathed and tasted and could see dancing in the hazy air.

There was time; by now a routine had evolved. Renni wouldn't come over
from the main house with the tray of tea and sliced papaya for another half hour.
I had been awake for hours already: tropical nightlife was still disconcerting. In
the dark, inside my little house and around it, there was much rustling, whirring,
and the odd squeal, and around 4:30 the muezzins' voices calling the faithful to
prayer would swell to a great wail.

During most of a short stay in Indonesia last winter, I moved along in a kind
of dream state — every sight and sound and smell set off waves of memories.
Back in Canada I had made no specific plans. I wasn't a tourist. This morning I
would be leaving the city of Bogor on a small journey that would take me about
100 kilometres south into the mountains in search of a tea plantation, difficult of
access. My father, a Dutchman, had been one of the administrators there before
the Second World War. I had lived on the island of Java from three to the age of
fourteen. For me, remembered consciousness began there. In a sense I was
going home.

Somewhere back in the garden a woman began to sing tonelessly, on and on. I watched big red ants marching along a branch of the bougainvillea up to the roof, one behind the other. It would be good to get away from Bogor's closeness. To escape the swampy coastal heat you have to travel at least twenty kilometres farther south. Yet Bogor is cooler than Jakarta, the capital, sixty kilometres to the north. Jakarta, with a population of around 11 million, is just bearable at night; to survive during the day takes immense stamina and patience.

A week earlier I'd landed there, as most visitors to the country do. The city is a magnet for Indonesians, the nerve center of their remarkable — and little-known — country. Indonesia comprises 13,677 islands, which, when imposed on a map of the United States, stretch from Oregon to Bermuda. Its 180-million citizens from 300 ethnic groups speak 250 languages and form the world's fifth most populous country. One hundred and ten million Indonesians live on the island of Java, which is only as big as England — and every year uncounted thousands of them drift into Jakarta. The city boasts luxury hotels, handsome boulevards, fine museums, a number of office towers, twelve daily newspapers, and Southeast Asia's largest mosque. About eighty percent of foreign investment stops in Jakarta first; the deals are made there and the rake-offs dispensed. But what the newcomers are more likely to encounter are endless expanses of slums — easily the equal of those of Calcutta or Dhaka or Lagos — garbage-choked waterways, snarled traffic, thousands of starving, diseased, and crazed individuals roaming the streets, and a sewage and drainage system so outdated that when the rains come two-thirds of Jakarta is flooded. And there's the heat.

We had lived in Jakarta for a few years after the war, my parents, my brother, Jerry, and I. There was much unrest in the streets: fighting had started almost immediately after the Japanese occupational forces capitulated to the Allies in 1945. The Indonesians wanted independence, but the Dutch, who had dominated the islands for 350 years, said no. "Police actions" and "pacification exercises" were launched and bloodily pursued until the Indonesians, cheered on by world opinion, finally managed to toss the Dutch out in 1949.

Our family had already returned to Holland by then: my brother and I needed proper schooling. The war years had been spent in Japanese prison camps and before that on the isolated plantation. In Jakarta, between shoot-outs and rabies scares, school closed almost every other day. By leaving in 1948, we missed the independence celebrations put on by the new republic's flamboyant President Sukarno, with the crowds screaming *Merdeka!* (Freedom!) in the heart of his capital, a one-square-kilometre neglected park — right across the street from our house.

A sleek high-rise had replaced our home, and government buildings, banks, and hotels now crowded the square. In the middle of it rose the 130-metre National Monument, a marble obelisk with thirty-five kilos of pure gold gilding its crowning flame, built to commemorate the struggle for freedom. I remembered the empty field where goats had grazed. Once it had held mystery for me. Where the obelisk now stood there had been a dry and rusted fountain. By day I had dared approach it with a friend. By night yells and wild laughter could be heard, but I never got close enough even to distinguish men from women in the light of their little fires. On our day excursions we saw only women, as many as twenty, their faces white with make-up powder, young, middle-aged, some nursing babies, cooking, washing, picking at each other's heads, sleeping in the shade of lean-tos made of trash. They wore their blouses unbuttoned, or no blouses, and their long oily hair hung loose. Their arms and shoulders were burned nearly black, like those of beggars. They would screech and flap their small hands for us to come closer and take teasing little runs at us; they moved so it looked at first as if they were gently dancing. Cackling, they would make gestures with those small hands that we understood at once. We laughed with them and then turned and trotted home, feeling older.

On the way out of Jakarta's furore, I had asked the English-speaking driver, Rusli Sunanjaya, if we could find out whether anything was left of the last prison camp I'd been in at age ten. Located outside Jakarta, on a small road to Bogor, Kampung Makasar, one of many on Java, had held about 3,500 mostly Dutch women and children. Rusli and I discovered that the village of the same name that had been near the camp had grown into an entire city district. Clerks at the municipal offices had never heard of a camp, but then none of them looked over forty. They wanted to help, though, and were able to guide us to the house of Hajji Mohamad Nur, a retired fruit farmer, who had been a village official in the 1940s.

Tall, straight, seventy-five years old, and a chain smoker of Indonesia's clove-spiced cigarettes, Nur waved his big hands around and was inclined to shout though he wasn't deaf. It was a pleasure, he said, to have us in his house, though unexpected. He was called Hajji, I should understand, because he had made the pilgrimage to Mecca. The camp, he said, had been a "bad and secret" place — bamboo barracks surrounded by a high fence in the middle of vegetable gardens. White women and children worked there. Nur thought his wife, his blind, ninety-year-old mother-in-law, and he himself were probably the only ones left who remembered. About three-quarters of the people in the area had died in those years, first when the enemy army took away the food the farmers grew and afterwards during the revolution. He pointed at my driver, at me, and then at himself, clapped his hands, and laughed loudly: "We have all survived!"

I didn't know what to say.

And neither did he then, I think, so he showed us around his small stone house. Oil-lamp smoke had blackened the ceiling of the front room. In a second, even dimmer room hung an oil portrait of Nur in the 1940s, as tall and straight as now.

I asked if anyone had ever felt *kasihan* for those whites? The exact word for pity had leapt to mind.

"Of course!" he said. Young men from the village would make their way to the camp after midnight with fruit or other food, to exchange for clothes or jewellery. But sometimes they'd feel such *kasihan* they'd just throw the food over the fence and run home. He shrugged.

After the women and children had been evacuated from Makasar, the Allies filled the filthy barracks with Japanese prisoners. Today it is an army garrison built of stone, but there's still, as then, a lot of barbed wire about. We drove by later, en route to Bogor. The road is wider and busier, but the main gate, through which as a child I'd peered at freedom, is just where it used to be. According to Nur, neighborhood people are superstitious about it: since 1945, accidents in which someone is always killed have been happening in front of the gate. "Many people died inside that place," Nur explained, "and their spirits are still there!"

Once in Bogor, whether by luck or by the connivance of the ever-present "silent forces" — it's easy to accept the mysteries of the spirit world there — my lack of planning began to prove providential. An acquaintance in Canada had asked me to drop off a couple of paperbacks at the home of a zoologist friend, Kathy MacKinnon. She promptly used her credentials to arrange a room in the boarding house for scientists visiting the world-famous Bogor Botanical Gardens. It was late when we drove into the deserted grounds of Kebon Raya, the 87-hectare park and research center. Stopping by a tall house looming in the dark, she directed me to walk ahead to a small light aswarm with insects. The motor's sound faded quickly in the high-pitched thrumming from the trees and bushes beyond the road. The air was hot and moist and overhead things whooshed by, receding fast, coming back. In addition to the flora, the gardens were host to a colony of bats with huge wingspans and bodies the size of rats. Don't run, I thought.

Out of the blackness at that moment came a thin bent old man, wrapped in a sarong, barefoot, smiling, folded hands out in greeting: I was safe. On the plantation there had been men like that staying up all night, cigarettes gleaming in the dark, guarding us whites, our homes, our trucks, the tea factory. Old men usually, but they kept away the evils of the night. When it stormed and the souls of children wept in the trees, it was good to know they were out there, smoking, watching.

The next morning, when I delivered another package from the same Canadian acquaintance, I met Renni Samsoedin. Renni has degrees in botany and chemistry and works in research in a building ten minutes' walk from Kebon Raya's main gate. The gardens are in the middle of Bogor; the city has grown up around them. An attractive, immensely cheerful woman in her early thirties, Renni spoke fluent English and asked why I was in Indonesia. I told my story of wanting to see the place where I'd lived as a boy. She nodded and smiled and nodded. When you talk to Indonesians, it seems sometimes that part of their consciousness is elsewhere, as if they are dreaming and yet awake.

"Ah well," Renni said suddenly, "we must make a plan. You must come and stay where I live — there's lots of room. Of course, you will want to meet my father. He will help with the plan."

Renni was intrigued by the idea of someone returning to where he'd been small — and in *her* Indonesia. It would not do to muddle on alone, though. Just rent a car and go? It wasn't that simple. Or maybe it was, but it was no fun. Or at least it was more fun if Indonesians came along to explain things. Her whole family would help make a plan. There were three girls and seven boys, all adults; Cucu, the youngest, was twenty-two. What's more, her father had been Kebon Raya's chief administrator until he retired in 1978, and their house had been right on the grounds. That her family and I should now meet was, well, "magical."

Would I return to her office at the end of the day when Cucu picked her up in the Land Rover — and would I like *saté ayam* (chicken roasted on bamboo skewers in spicy peanut sauce) with *nasi goreng* (fried rice) for supper?

Much of that day I roamed through Kebon Raya, with its rolling lawns, holy banyan trees, cactus gardens, lily ponds, and forest groves. Opened in 1817 by the Dutch, the park contains 15,000 species of tropical plants and trees (including 400 types of palms) and the nurseries house more than 4,500 orchid varieties. It was green and still. Upside down from the branches of a dead-looking tree hung the bats from the night before. Now and then one would wake up with a cry of grief, spread its cloaklike wings, float to another branch, and fold up again. The massive, many-trunked holy trees possessed immense self-assurance: roots grew down from their branches into the earth, enlarging and renewing them forever. It was safe in their shadow.

Beyond the gardens' main gate the street was noisy, busy, the air gray with exhaust fumes. Returning to Renni's office, I followed the narrow, crowded sidewalk that hugged Kebon Raya's fence of iron bars. I spotted the figure from thirty metres away. She squatted motionless with her back to the traffic, her head tucked face-down between her knees, her arms around her shins nearly touching the fence. She was a small, not old woman, stark naked, pressed together as once in the womb, her skin streaked with dirt, crusts of it in her hair. She was in no-one's way and no-one paid attention. Her turned-away body begged to die. Despair speaks out everywhere, but sometimes there's a long echo.

Later at Renni's house the rest of the family wasn't home yet. She first showed me, spread out on the floor, polished and ready, enough flutes, bamboo xylophones, gongs, and other percussion instruments for an entire *gamelan* ensemble. On Sundays the Samsoedins get together and perform Indonesia's rhythmically complex, liquid, thousand-year-old music for hours on end; but I missed that. Renni walked me around the family's terraced fairy-tale garden, full of still places, to the little guesthouse by the fish pond where I would sleep.

Most of the family came around that evening. Word got out about Renni's foreigner, though none of them has a phone. All knew some English. Pak Samsoedin, the father, also remembered a few words of Dutch. Soft-spoken and much less direct than his daughter, he did eventually ask why I was in Indonesia. Halfway through my reply his attention shifted in that curious Indonesian way.

"So," he said abruptly in English-Dutch, dropping in a word of French as well, "you are going on a journey of *nostalgie*?" He stared ahead. The room was quiet. "I too would like to go on a journey of *nostalgie*. And in the same area. It is beautiful. High in the mountains with the tea.... I was stationed there, you know — in 1947, with the army."

That would have been the revolutionary army fighting the Dutch.

"I remember we were put up in a nice house," he went on. "In the morning I would go out and do my exercises on the big flat lawn...."

He paused, remembering.

I thought I felt some neck hairs rise. I reached for my camera bag and felt inside for a half dozen tiny black-and-white pictures taken before the war.

"And then I would walk to the edge of the lawn," he resumed, "and look down at my friends playing soccer on the field below...."

I held out a photo.

"This house?"

He looked.

"That house, yes."

It was a picture of *our* first house on the plantation. We'd been trucked away in 1942. The population of Java is *110-million* ... and *forty-seven* years later ...! The family was amused but not awe-struck: these things happen. Renni laughed and said, "Magic!" Her father took it entirely in stride and continued to reminisce about his army days. But yes, the journey of *nostalgie*....

Cucu should drive me. Cucu was on a break from law school and had time. In a corner on the floor with his seven-year-old niece Dini in his lap, Cucu nodded sleepily. Short and slight, he rarely spoke and always looked sleepy — but he handled the powerful Land Rover as if it were a toy. Pak Samsoedin thought his son would probably want along as navigator his best friend, Yadi, also a student of law, and free. Cucu nodded. Renni said that if I could wait a couple of days, she'd take time off and come as interpreter. Absolutely. Other Samsoedins suggested they'd like to go. By all means. The map was spread out on the floor, the jug of chilled coconut juice did the rounds, a route was plotted. The "silent forces" were at it all right. There was a great honking of frogs in the fish pond.

The road started to ascend on leaving Bogor and the air grew drier and cooler. Every day since I'd arrived in Indonesia there had been the season's sudden rain squalls, but today it stayed dry and mostly sunny, allowing the views along the twisting, climbing roads to come spectacularly into their own. Early on, patches of mist had raced over the valleys, over the tender green, terraced rice fields. Where the hillsides carried cuts or stood too steep there was unruly jungle growth from which poked the familiar heads of coconut trees. Later, high up where the tea plantings began, the terrain acquired the long sweep of mid-ocean waves: the flat-topped black-green bushes fell and rose in patterned clusters against the red earth from the shadows of one mountain into those of the next. Renni (only she, Cucu, and Yadi had finally been able to come along) called the weather "magic," as she labelled almost everything slightly fortuitous. But she was right. At a certain point the narrow asphalt roads turned into roads of rock and earth — we'd gone wrong. Had it rained, even the Land Rover might have bogged down.

We were quite alone by then, except for the occasional clutch of women tea pickers in their conical hats, chest-deep among the bushes, hands quick as sparrows pinching off the pale green youngest leaves. The car jolted along in first gear for what seemed hours, but the windows were open and the sun was gentle. A stop for pictures let the uplands' immense stillness settle for a moment.

We were getting closer to Pasirnanka, the plantation, and my mind was moving awfully fast. We turned a corner and were suddenly amidst houses and people — some of them in dark-blue uniforms, gesticulating at us with night sticks! Security guards yelling, What were we doing here? Who were we? They were clearly astonished to see us: we had come in the back way. How had we known the bridge on the main road collapsed yesterday? Renni murmured, "Magic" — and cheerfully set about explaining. Cucu, unperturbed, passed around cigarettes.

Was this Pasirnanka? Yes, it was. Nothing looked familiar, not a house, not the shape of a hill. I wandered away from the car. My mind was slowing down again. By the guardhouse a road turned left and down towards a large gray metal shed. I could hear a humming that grew louder as I came closer ... the factory! If that was the factory, then up that hill had to be the swimming pool. And to the right, beyond those new houses, the home of Mr. Plomp. A tall blond man, he had walked around a whole day with his face as red as a beet because of a telegram from Holland saying his father had died. And from way up his hill, Plomp had looked down — on us!

I started to run, and the group by the car followed. A few steps and there was the Plomp house, a dilapidated bungalow on a little rise, not a hill. And there — our house ... the garden still the same. On those fieldstone steps my father made Jerry and me promise to look after our mother; the last time we came down them, my mother, Jerry, and I were loaded into the back of a truck with the other white children and mothers. But such a little house! The shape unchanged but walls cut into picture windows, the guesthouse and the servants' quarters gone.

The others had caught up. The guards were laughing and calling to someone inside the house. A woman in a pink dress came out; a little boy and a girl followed and clung to her legs. The woman looked a bit apprehensive and didn't speak. One of the guards urged her to invite me in, which she did with her hand. But I said thank you, no — because I knew right then that I had no need to enter, and no curiosity. I took a few pictures, thanked her, and started down the steps, the group following. There were many new homes, but those the whites had lived in were still in use too. The biggest had been Mr. Witte's, the chief administrator's, my father's boss; his house was in even worse shape than the Plomp place.

Every morning, before lunch, all the white families had walked up to the swimming pool. It was the choice spot in the plantation compound: from it you could see all our houses, the soccer field, the factory, the main road. On weekends we brought picnic baskets and spent almost entire days there. My brother and I had few toys, but every day held the certainty of play in the pool. It was never denied. On birthdays we were allowed to jump in with our clothes on. If it rained, my mother said that was all the more reason to go. In bed I planned amazing jumps and tricks for the next day.

Friends and guards in tow, I now marched towards the pool on the hill. At the bottom of the slope there was a tall vine-covered wire fence, broken and flattened in places, the gate hanging open. I knew for certain that there had been no fence there in our time. Inside, high wild grass ran up the hill. I reached the edge of the pool. One rusted handrail still stood upright by the steps leading down; weeds sprouted from the cracked concrete. I wasn't five yet when I dog-paddled its length, eyes wide open beneath the sunlit surface. The guards looked around with interest. The hill top was quiet, shadowy, neglected — where once it had resounded with life. It was like an old cemetery.

A half hour out of Pasirnanka, on the way back, Cucu drove off the narrow road to let a small packed bus pass us. He cut the motor and lit a cigarette. He had hardly spoken at all on the whole trip. As always, he listened to what others said and responded with his eyes or his smile. But then he turned to me sitting next to him and unexpectedly asked:

"Are you happy now?"

I thought of the place we had just left and that I'd travelled such a way to visit, and I said: "I am, yes" — and realized I was already seeing it again, in my mind's eye, as I'd always seen it, and probably always would.

13
Michael Ignatieff

AUGUST IN MY FATHER'S HOUSE

IT IS after midnight. They are all in bed except me. I have been waiting for the rain to come. A shutter bangs against the kitchen wall and a rivulet of sand trickles from the adobe wall in the long room where I sit. The lamp above my head twirls in the draught. Through the poplars, the forks of light plunge into the flanks of the mountains and for an instant the ribbed gullies stand out like skeletons under a sheet.

Upstairs I can hear my mother and father turn heavily in their sleep. Downstairs our baby calls out from the bottom of a dream. What can his dreams be about? I smooth his blanket. His lips pucker, his eyes quiver beneath their lashes.

I have been married seven years. She is asleep next door, the little roof of a book perched on her chest. The light by the bed is still on. Her shoulders against the sheet are dark apricot. She does not stir as I pass.

At the window, the air is charged and liquid. The giant poplars creak and moan in the darkness. It is the mid-August storm, the one which contains the first intimation of autumn, the one whose promise of deliverance from the heat is almost always withheld. The roof tiles are splashed for an instant, and there is a patter among the trumpet vines. I wait, but it passes. The storm disappears up the valley and the first night sounds return, the cicadas, the owl in the poplars, the rustle of the mulberry leaves, the scrabble of mice in the eaves. I lean back against the wall. The old house holds the heat of the day in its stones like perfume in a discarded shawl. I have come here most summers since I was fifteen.

When I was fifteen, I wanted to be a man of few words, to be small and muscular with fine bones, to play slide guitar like Elmore James. I wanted to be fearless. I am thirty-seven. The page is white and cool to the touch. My hands smell of lemons. I still cling to impossible wishes. There is still time.

The house was once a village wash-house. At one end of the pillared gallery, there is a stone pool — now drained — where women used to wash clothes in the winter. At the bottom of the garden under the lyre-shaped cherry tree, there is the summer pool where the sheets were drubbed and slopped between their knuckles and the slanted stones. That was when the village raised silk worms for the Lyons trade a hundred years ago. When that trade died, the village died and the washing pool was covered over with brambles.

The house became a shepherd's shelter. He was a retarded boy, crazed by his father's beatings, by the miserable winter pastures, by the cracked opacity of his world. One night in the smoke-blackened kitchen, he and his father were silently drinking. When the father got up to lock away the animals, the son rose behind him and smashed his skull into the door-jamb. After they took the boy away and buried the father, the house fell into ruin, marked in village memory by the stain of parricide.

When we came to look at the place that evening twenty-two years ago, my father sent me up the back wall to check the state of the roof tiles. The grass and brambles were waist-high in the doorway. A tractor was rusting in the gallery and a dusty rabbit skin hung from a roof beam. One push, we thought, and the old adobe walls would collapse into dust. But the beam took my weight and there were only a few places where the moonlight was slicing through to the dirt floor below. The tiles were covered with lichen and I could feel their warmth through the soles of my feet. When I jumped down, I could see they had both made up their mind to buy it.

It is my mother's favorite hour. Dinner has been cleared away from the table under the mulberry tree, and she is sitting at the table with a wine glass in her hand watching the light dwindling away behind the purple leaves of the Japanese maple. I sit down beside her. She is easy to be with, less easy to talk to. The light is falling quickly, the heat it bears is ebbing away. After a time she says, "I never expected anything like this ... the stone wall that Roger built for us, the lavender hedges, the bees, the house. It's all turned out so well."

Her voice is mournful, far away.

A Toronto schoolmaster's daughter, squint-eyed and agile, next-to-youngest of four, she rode her bicycle up and down the front steps of her father's school, the tomboy in a family of intellectuals. I have a photograph of her at the age of ten, in boy's skates with her stick planted on the ice of the rink at her father's school. She is staring fiercely into the camera in the manner of the hockey idols of the twenties, men with slick side-partings and names like Butch Bouchard.

It is nearly dark and the lights have come on across the valley. She twirls her wine glass between her fingers and I sit beside her to keep her company, to help the next words come. Then she says, out of nowhere, "When I was seven, my father said 'Who remembers the opening of the Aeneid?' as he stood at the end of the table carving the Sunday joint. 'Anyone?' They were all better scholars than me, but I *knew*. 'Arma virumque cano ....' Everyone cheered — Leo, the cook, Margaret, Charity, George, even Mother. My father slowly put down the knife and fork and just stared at me. I wasn't supposed to be the clever one."

There is some hurt this story is trying to name, a tomboy's grief at never being taken seriously, never being listened to, which has lasted to this moment next to me in the darkness. But her emotions are a secret river. She has her pride, her gaiety and her elusiveness. She will not put a name to the grievance, and silence falls between us. It is dark and we both feel the chill of evening. She gets up, drains her glass and then says, "Mother always said, 'Never make a fuss.' That was the family rule. Goodnight." I brush her cheek with a kiss. We will not make a fuss.

She was a painter once, and her paintings have become my memory for many of the scenes of my childhood: playing with a crab in a bucket on a rock in Antigonish, Nova Scotia, and watching her painting at the easel a few paces away, her back, her knees and her upraised arm making a triangle of concentration, her brush poised, still and expectant before the canvas, her face rapt with the pleasure of the next stroke.

When I was six she painted my portrait. It was an embarrassment at the time: my friends came to point and laugh because I looked so solemn. But I see now the gift she was handing me across the gulf which divides us from the vision of others: a glimpse of the child I was in my mother's eye, the child I have kept within me. She doesn't paint anymore. For a time, marriage and children allowed her a room of her own. But then it was swallowed up or renounced, I don't know which. She says only, "Either I do it well, or I do not do it at all."

She whispers, "Have you seen my glasses?"

"Your glasses don't matter. You can do the shopping without them."

"I know they don't matter. But if he finds out ...."

"Tell him to ...." But now I'm the one who is whispering.

When I find her glasses by the night-table where she put them down before going to sleep, the lenses are fogged and smudged with fingerprints. A schoolgirl's glasses.

She says, "I know. I know. It runs in the family."

"What? Forgetting?"

"No." She gives me a hard stare. "Dirty glasses. My father's pupils used to say that he washed his in mashed potatoes."

She owns only one pair. She could hide a second pair in a jar by the stove so she wouldn't be caught out. But she won't defend herself.

I take her into town and buy her a chain so that she can wear them around her neck and not lose them. She submits gaily but in the car on the way back home, she shakes her fist at the windscreen: "I swore I'd never wear one of these goddamned things."

When we lived in the suburbs of Ottawa in the fifties, she used to come out and play baseball with the kids in the street on summer evenings. She could hit. In my mind's eye, I see the other boys' mouths opening wide as they follow the flight of the ball from her bat and I see them returning to her face and to her wincing with pleasure as the ball pounds onto the aluminum roof of the Admiral's garage. She puts the bat down with a smile and returns to make supper, leaving us playing in the street under her amused gaze from the kitchen window.

When the Yankees played the Dodgers in the World Series, she wrote the teacher to say I was sick and the two of us sat on her bed and watched Don Larsen pitch his perfect game and Yogi Berra race to the mound throwing his mask and mitt into the air. We saw Sandy Amaros racing across center field chasing a high fly ball which he took with a leap at the warning track. In life, the ball hits the turf. In memory, its arc returns unendingly to the perfection of the glove.

The *notaire* arrives as dusk falls. We sit down for business under the mulberry tree. When my mother and father bought the house and fields twenty-two years ago, the *notaire* was a rotund Balzacian figure who observed with amused contempt while the peasants from whom we were purchasing the property passed a single pair of wire-rim glasses round the table so that each in turn could pore over the documents of sale. The new *notaire* is a sparrow of a woman, my age, a widow with two young sons and a motorcycle helmet on the back seat of her car.

We pore over deeds of sale and cadastral surveys of the fields: one planted in clover once and now overgrown with mint and high grass. The goat is staked there under the walnut tree and eats a perfect circle for his breakfast. Framed between the poplars in front of the house is the lavender field. Once a year in the first week of August, the farmer comes with a machine which straddles the purple rows and advances with a scrabbling grinding sound, tossing aside bound and fragrant bunches. We watch from the terrace as the field is stripped of its purple and is left a bare spiky green. The butterflies and bees retreat ahead of the mechanical jaws and at the end of the day are found in a desperate, glittering swarm on the last uncut row, fighting for the sweetness of the last plants like refugees crowded into an encircled city.

Then there is the orchard behind the house. It was once full of plums, but the trees were old and wormy and one by one they were dropping their branches, tired old men letting go of their burdens. Father called in the bulldozer, but when it came, we all went indoors and clapped our hands over our ears so that we wouldn't have to listen to the grinding of steel on the bark and the snapping of the tap roots. In a quarter of an hour, the planting of generations had been laid waste. But it had to be done. The field is bare now, but olive saplings are beginning to rise among the weeds.

The deeds of sale are all in order. My mother runs a finger over the old papers and stops at her name — *"née à Buckleberry Bradford, Angleterre, le 2 février 1916, épouse sans profession"* — and at his — *"né à Saint Petersbourg, Russie, le 16 décembre, 1913, profession diplomate."*

"'Épouse sans profession' sounds sad, doesn't it?" she says.

They are transferring the title of the property to me and my brother. "Just once more," she asks, "tell me why we have to."

"Because," I reply, "it is cheaper than doing it afterwards."

Sometimes on airless August nights, I lie in bed and imagine what it would be like to sell the house, turn it over to strangers and never come back. I find myself thinking of hotel rooms somewhere else: the echo of the empty *armoire*, the neon blinking through the shutters, the crisp anonymity of the towels and sheets. I remember the Hotel Alesia in Paris, eating brie and cherries together on a hot June afternoon; the Hotel San Cassiano in Venice and its vast *letto matrimoniale*. I remember the next morning lying in bed watching her comb her hair at the dressing-table by the open window. A curl of smoke is rising from the ashtray and the swoop of her brush flickers in the facets of the mirrors. Through the window comes the sound of lapping water and the chug of a barge. We have the whole day ahead of us. I think of all the writing I might do in hotel rooms. Words come easily in hotels: the coils spring free from the weight of home.

In my father's house every object is a hook which catches my thoughts as they pass: the barometers which he taps daily and which only he seems to understand; the dark *armoire* they bought from the crooked *antiquaire* in Île sur Sorgue; the Iroquois mask made of straw; the Russian bear on a string; the thermometer marked *gel de raisin, Moscou 1812* at the cold end and *Senegal* at the hot end. My thoughts, cornered by these objects, circle at bay and spiral backwards to the moods of adolescence.

"Old age is not for cowards." My father looks at me angrily, as if I cannot possibly understand. "I have no illusions. It is not going to get any better. I know what she goes through. Don't think I don't. You wake up some mornings and you don't know where the hell you are. Just like a child. Everything is in the fog. Some days it lifts. Some days it doesn't."

He paces slowly at the other end of the long room, at the distance where truth is possible between us. It is late. Everyone else has gone to bed. We are drinking *tisane*, a nightly ritual usually passed in silence.

There are thirty-four years between us: two wars and a revolution. There is also his success: what he gave me makes it difficult for us to understand each other. He gave me safety. My earliest memory is rain pounding on the roof of the Buick on the New Jersey Turnpike. I am three, sitting between them on the front seat, with the chrome dashboard in front of me at eye level and the black knobs of the radio winking at me. The wipers above my head are scraping across the bubbling sheet of water pouring down the windscreen. We are all together side by side, sharing the pleasure of being trapped by the storm, forced to pull off the road. I am quite safe. They made the world safe for me from the beginning.

He was never safe. His memory begins at a window in Saint Petersburg on a February morning in 1917. A sea of flags, ragged uniforms and hats surges below him, bayonets glinting like slivers of glass in the early morning sunlight. The tide is surging past their house; soon it will break through the doors, forcing them to run and hide. He remembers the flight south in the summer of 1917, corpses in a hospital train at a siding, a man's body bumping along a dusty road in Kislovodsk, tied by one leg behind a horse. I see it all as newsreel. He was there, with the large eyes of a six-year-old.

As he gets older, his memory scours the past looking for something to hold on to, for something to cling to in the slide of time. Tonight, pacing at the end of the room while I sit drinking the tea he has made for both of us, it is Manya who is in his mind, his nursemaid, the presence at the very beginning of his life, a starched white uniform, warm hands, the soft liquid syllables of a story at bedtime heard at the edge of sleep. She followed them south into exile. She was the center of his world, and one morning she was no longer there.

"I woke up and she was gone. Sent away in the night. Perhaps they couldn't afford her. Perhaps they thought we were too close. I don't know."

Across seventy years, his voice still carries the hurt of that separation, a child's helpless despair. He was her life. She was his childhood.

I try to think about him historically, to find the son within the father, the boy within the man. His moods — the dark self-absorption — have always had the legitimacy of his dispossession. Exile is a set of emotional permissions we are all bound to respect.

He is still pacing at the other end of the room. He says suddenly, "I don't expect to live long."

I say: "It's not up to you, is it?"

He stokes the prospect of his death like a fire in the grate. Ahead of me the prospect beckons and glows, sucking the oxygen from the room. He says he is not afraid of dying, and, in so far as I can, I believe him. But that is not the point. In his voice, there is a child's anger at not being understood, an old man's fear of being abandoned. He does not want a son's pity or his sorrow, yet his voice carries a plea for both. A silence falls between us. I hear myself saying that he is in good health, which is true and entirely beside the point. He says goodnight, stoops briefly as he passes through the archway, and disappears into his room.

On some beach of my early childhood — Montauk Point? Milocer? — he is walking ahead of me, in those white plastic bathing shoes of his, following the line of the water's edge, head down, bending now and again and turning to show me what he has found. We decide together which finds go into the pocket of his bathing suit. We keep a green stone with a white marble vein in it. He takes it to a jeweller to have it set as a ring for her. In some jewellery box back home, it is probably still there.

I don't believe in the natural force of blood ties. There is nothing more common, more natural than for fathers and sons to be strangers to each other. It was only on those silent beach walks together, our voices lost in the surf, our footprints erased by the tide, our treasure accumulated mile by mile, that we found an attachment which we cannot untie.

There was a period in my twenties when that attachment foundered on my embrace of victimhood. It is a natural temptation for sons of powerful fathers. I was elated with destructiveness, righteous for truth. They had sent me away to school when I was eleven, and I wanted to know why. We had ceased to be a family in the flesh, and became one by air mail and transatlantic telephone. Once a year, for a month, in this house, we tried to become a real family again. Such is the story which the victim writes. I wanted to know why. I see his hands covering his face.

Why did I cling to the grievance? The truth is I loved going away from home, sitting alone in a Super Constellation shuddering and shaking high above Greenland on the way back to school, watching the polar flames from the engines against the empty cobalt sky. I won a first-team tie in football. I listened to Foster Hewitt's play by play of Hockey Night in Canada on the radio under my mattress after lights out in the dorm. I was caned for a pillow-fight, a wild and joyful midnight explosion of feathers, the only true uprising that I have ever taken part in. After such an uprising, the punishment — twelve stripes with a bamboo cane — was an honor.

I read *King Lear* in Gallimore's English class. He frog-marched us through every scene, battering us with his nasal southern Ontario intonations: until I fell in love, for the first time, with the power of words.

I went to my first dances and breathed in that intoxicating scent of hairspray, sweat, powder and the gardenia of girls' corsages, that promise of lush revelations in the dark. I became an adult in a tiny tent on a camping ground north of Toronto. The gravel was excruciating on my knees and elbows. The girl was very determined. She guided my hands in the dark. Afterwards she slapped my face, like a caress.

I did what I wanted. Because I was at school, I didn't have to bring her home; I could keep sex a secret. But I clung to the grievance of banishment.

I clung to another grievance too, but this one as much my making as his. I said to him, You have crushed her. She used to paint. Not anymore. She has wishes for you and for me, but none for herself. Not anymore.

He never forgave me for that, for the absolution I had given myself in blaming him. I see his hands covering his face.

"Truth is good, but not all truth is good to say."

My son is sitting on his grandfather's knee, working over his grandfather's hands with his gums. I notice that his signet ring, a carving in amber of Socrates set in a gold oval — one of the survivors of exile and the pawnshop — is missing from the little finger of his left hand. In its place there is a small university ring which seems to pinch. He notices me looking at it.

"I gave it to your brother. You'll get the watch."

The tops of his hands are strong and sunburned, but the palms are gullied and clenched with arthritis. He no longer wields the axe.

He is tender and wary with his grandson, this messenger of life and his mortality. He strokes the child's chest absently, as if relearning a long-forgotten gesture. My son turns in his lap, and with infantile deliberation removes his grandfather's spectacles. They exchange a blue glance across seventy years. "In the year 2000," my father says, "he will be sixteen."

When I come through the beaded curtain with my breakfast, my mother is whirling the baby around slowly beneath the mulberry tree, cheek to cheek, holding his arm out against hers in the old style and crooning, "Come to me, my melancholy baby." My son has a wild look of pleasure on his face.

"You dance well," I say.

She whirls slowly to a stop and hands him to me: "No, I lead too much."

She whispers in the baby's ear, "Crazy old granny, crazy old granny." She is not crazy. She is afraid. Her memory is her pride, her refuge. The captions of *New Yorker* cartoons not seen for forty years; lyrics of Noel Coward and Gerty Lawrence songs from the London of the thirties; the name of the little girl with Shirley Temple curls in the desk next to hers at Bishop Strachan School for Girls; the code names of all the French agents she helped to parachute into France during the war: her memory is a crammed shoe-box full of treasures from a full life. It is what happened five minutes ago that is slipping away — the pot on the stove, the sprinkler in the garden, what she just said.

The memory which frightens her, which portends the losses still to come, is of the last time she saw her mother. They spent a week together, and as they were leaving, her mother turned to my father and said, "You're Russian, aren't you? And who is this charming girl?"

Your daughter.

When I was eight, I spent a weekend with my grandmother in the large dark house on Prince Arthur Avenue in Toronto. We ate breakfast together: tea on a silver service, Ryvita biscuits imported from England, with the London *Times* in a feathery edition two weeks late. I sat on the end of her bed and we had a conversation, tentative and serious across the gulf of time. I had never seen her hair down before, masses of it — gray, austere and luxuriant against the pillows. There is a kind of majesty in some old women, the deep red glow of a banked fire. I talked on and on, and she followed me with her eyes and a whisper of amusement on her lips.

Then there came a Sunday, not many months later, when I was ushered into the dark mahogany dining room and knew at once from the slope of her shoulders, the terrible diminution of her presence, the slowness with which she turned to meet my eye, that she had no idea who I was. She stared out through the window at the blank wall of the new hotel rising to block her view. She said nothing. Her eyes were still and gray and vacant. I was speechless through lunch with her, and, when I left, I knew I would never see her again. She died several years later in a nursing home north of the city. Her will, that last relinquishing gesture of generosity in a generous life, enabled my father and mother to buy this house.

My mother is cool and lucid about her own prospects. I do not believe these things run in the family, and I tell her so. She nods and then says, "I'm sure I would make a cheerful old nut. Don't you think so? In any case," and here she picks up her drink and walks into the kitchen to look to her cooking, "it's much worse for those you leave behind."

In the next village, a theater troupe is staging *Oedipus* on a tiny stage built into the sandstone cliffs at the foot of the village. There is a little boy in front of us in the stands, sitting between his mother and his father. He is about five. Oedipus and Jocasta circle each other slowly against the towering folds of sandstone: the eternal story unfolds in the night air. Oedipus turns his bleeding eyes upon us: "Remember me, and you will never lose your happiness."

The little boy rocks backwards and forwards on his seat. He says to himself in a small voice, "Now I understand everything."

Then he falls asleep on his mother's lap.

We stay behind afterwards while they dismantle the set. From the top row of the stands, the valley stretches out below us in the amber afterglow of nightfall. The vines and cane wind-breaks are drained of color. The first lights in the village appear. It was this landscape which made me into a European: man's hand is upon it, the millennia of labor, the patient arts of settlement. The stillness is human: the rim of light at the edge of a shutter, the snake of a headlight, the swish of the irrigation sprinklers drenching the earth in the dark. In Canada the silence among the great trees was menacing. No light for miles. The cold. I had no quarrel with the place. I just wanted to get out.

She is standing beside me looking out into the dark valley. She leans her weight against my shoulder. I met her in a street dance in London eight years ago. Within two weeks I had brought her here, knowing that this was the place which would reveal us to each other.

My favorite photograph of her was taken in the first week we spent in this country. She is on the terrace walking towards me, wearing a white dress and a red Cretan sash. Her right hand is pushing the hair back off her forehead. She is smiling, her gaze directly into mine, shy and fearless. It is the last photograph in which she is still a stranger, approaching but still out of reach, still on the other side of the divide, before we fell in love.

The valley below us is black now. A breeze lifts up from the earth and the olive groves. She points to the sparkling village perched ten miles away on a promontory of ochre: "It's like an ocean liner."

I am thinking of the *Andrea Doria*. She went down off Nantucket when I was nine. They sent divers down, and they took photographs. She was lying in shallow water, and the lights of her bridge, by some impossible chance, were still on. Like the livid eyes of some great beast staring at the hunter who has brought her down, the ship's lights streamed through the ocean darkness. As a child I used to dream about those pictures of the great ship glowing on the bottom of the sea. It seems to me now that those dreams were an image of what it would be like to die, sinking in the folds of the ocean, your own eyes blazing in the salty dark.

On the way down the hill from the village, through the vaulted tunnel of the plane trees, white and phosphorescent in the headlights, she sings to me. Verdi as always. Flat as always, her head leaning back, her eyes staring up at the trees rushing by through the sun roof.

"I am *not* flat."

I am laughing.

She ignores me and sings on in a husky voice, "*Libera me ... de morte aeterna.*"

From the village road, the house looks low and small, its back hunched against the mistral. By Christmas, when the *notaire* has filed the deed, it will belong to my brother and me. But whatever the deeds say, it will always be my father's house. I cannot sell it any more than I can disavow the man I became within its walls, any more than I can break the silences at the heart of family life.

The lights are out. My parents are both asleep, and our son is in his cot.

She says, "Let's not go in yet."

We climb up into the field behind the house where the bee-keeper has his hives, and where you can see the whole of the Luberon mountains stretched out against the night sky. The shale is cool and the dew is coming down. We watch for satellites and for the night flights to Djibouti, Casablanca and Rome. There are many bright cold stars. A dog barks. In the house, our child floats in his fathomless sleep.

"Cassiopeia, Ursus Major, Orion's Belt ... I must learn the names, I want to teach him the names."

Out of the dark, as if from far away, she says, "What do you need to name them for?"

14
Marni Jackson

GALS AND DOLLS: THE MORAL VALUE OF "BAD" TOYS

IN THE days before I actually had a child, child-rearing was a clearcut proposition: simply Raise Them Right. Minimal TV, no hooker-type dolls or plastic Uzis and a constant flow of high-fibre ideas from the morally evolved parent to the vulnerable, blank-slate child. I felt sorry for parents who didn't have the gumption to stick to this plan. Then I had a son, and the rest is — well, not so much history as culture.

Not since the days of Spock have we had so much parental advice in the air — how to raise kids, how to ruin them, how to "juggle work and family." This is why it's so refreshing to read someone like Alice Miller, the psychoanalyst-turned-writer whose books explore the childhood roots of violence and creativity. She doesn't have a theory about raising kids. In fact, she argues that *any* system of moral values imposed on children is potentially damaging, because too often the rules are there to serve the emotional needs of the parents, not the children. In the name of morality, we try to keep the unruly passions of children — not to mention memories of our own childhood — safe, tidy, and under control. Most pedagogy, good or bad, sends a hidden message to the child: "Your desires and feelings are not good enough. Feel this, think that, instead." If children require so much correction, then deep down — so they reason — they must be bad. Sooner or later the child who only hears this message learns to assemble an other-pleasing, false self around a core of inexplicable shame.

This doesn't mean that Miller thinks children ought to fingerpaint with their food and otherwise disport themselves as gods. Post-Spockian permissiveness is just another form of pedagogy, really. But the experience of her own patients convinced her that it was the ones who were raised rigidly, with an overabundance of "good values" who were most likely to grow into benumbed adults, lost to themselves and predisposed to violence. The violence erupts in response to long-stifled childhood anger, which began as a perfectly human response to a voice that said "Don't be who you are, be good." The moral here — if we dare draw one — is that excessive handwringing about the values we are giving our kids may be as much about peer vanity as anything else. Values are not external; they are intrinsic to the sort of relationship we have with our children, arising out of the ordinary, humdrum way a family works and plays. The boy or girl who receives fair treatment, as opposed to "moral" correction, quickly develops an exquisite sense of justice — one that is more likely to shame the parent, rather than the other way round. (I'm moralizing here, of course.) Even young children bring a surprising amount of savvy and shit-detection to the moral bargaining table. To assume otherwise is to inflate our roles as parents into the architects and owners of our children's souls.

Now, Miller was talking about some fairly rigid, loveless households — Hitler's and Goebbels', for instance. She wasn't necessarily addressing the problem of whether or not to buy your son a Nintendo, or to give your niece a Wet 'n' Wild Barbie. Nevertheless, I detect a lot of dubious pedagogy in our much-cogitated attitudes towards "good" and "bad" toys.

I know what happened with toy guns in our own household. I went from a serene pre-child conviction that guns would never cross our threshold to the ridiculous but amiable compromise my seven-year-old son and I have reached. Childish logic is impeccable. If you give him an innocent green water pistol for the bathtub, then why not the hideous toy M-16 in the backyard? If he can brandish a popsicle stick, why not a space laser? So he now owns a bow and arrow and a noncombat rawhide whip (history? art?), but he knows I have a "thing" about realistic guns, so he doesn't ask for them. He watches plenty of TV (all right, too much), but after flat-out indoctrination on my part — moral interference in the name of what I can or cannot stand to overhear — he now flips past the more violent kids' shows, of his own volition. Of course, our definitions of "violent" are continually being refined. But he's kind by nature, and always has been. I try not to improve on that too much.

There was a time, not so long ago, that Barbie dolls were considered the worst sort of sex-stereotype propaganda. Barbie, with her foot permanently arched in the shape of a high heel, her long, scissoring legs, her high, hard, de-nippled breasts. It's true she's unswervingly represented a career gadfly, a weak-chinned Caucasian princess and a fashion flibbertigibbet — 11½ inches of beige plastic that has been accused of encouraging eating disorders, mindless consumerism and low self-esteem in little girls. Small wonder that to the Birkenstock generation, Barbie was bad.

But little girls are not pushovers. They know what they like and they like Barbie. Now 31 years old (but ever ageless and firm of chin), Barbie has triumphed over pedagogy, to the tune of over $500-million annually. Last year was the biggest year for Barbie sales in history. Some 98 percent of Canadian girls aged four to ten have a Barbie — or four — in their bedrooms. Like Coca-Cola, she has insinuated her hourglass, bottle-shaped self into 67 countries around the world. None of this will surprise parents with daughters, but it was news to me.

I went into several department stores to get a blast of Barbie, a feel for Barbie, and there she was — row upon row of her and her almost identical pals, including li'l sister Skipper, brown-skinned Christie, freckle-faced sporty Midge, Hispanic Nia, red-haired vixen Ashley. Her countless outfits run the gamut from the tiny tubes of her pantyhose to wild salsa dresses, purses that turn into skirts and skirts that turn into hair bows. Her eminently loseable accessories include teacups, toe paint, Ferraris, guitars and running shoes.

After twenty years of feminism, you may ask, why don't little boys play with Barbies? What *is* it about girls and dolls, anyway? Boys play with He-men and Ninja turtle figures but the marriage between girls and their Barbies seems more enduring. Girls' sense of pink and blueness also seems more acute, more precocious, although I base this only on the fact that I bought my son some plain but *purplish* boots last year. They didn't bother him until he came home from school one day and announced he couldn't wear them because they were "girls' boots." Who had decreed this? "The girls in my room."

Are girls more proprietorial about identifiable girl things because they've already detected an imbalance in the adult world, between boy toys (tanks and guns) and female fun? Or is it something simpler — that at a certain age, children want some kind of sex identity. Just because adults have bequeathed them a culture that offers only testosterone-poisoned orange He-men and anorexic beige Barbies, must we insist on snuffing out any sign of gender?

An eight-year-old girl in the neighborhood lugged over her five Barbies, in two pink vehicles, for my inspection. While twirling and braiding the long blonde tresses on one of them, she explained that although she doesn't want to *be* Barbie, she really likes to play with her. "We make up stories that are like real life and then we make the Barbies act them out," she said with admirable succinctness. "Her body isn't very realistic," she admits, pointing the ballistic bosom of one towards me. "In fact, the only realistic thing about it is her ears." If she were designing them, she would go for more variation. "Like, it would be neat to have a tattooed Barbie, or one with a bigger head. Her head is too small for her body." And Ken's definitely in a rut. "I wouldn't mind a bald Ken, for example."

The sad truth is, Barbie has left the bland, rug-haired Ken behind in a spangled cloud of dust. Ken sales only amount to 35 percent of their combined total — and in fact, his shelf presence suggests more like a ratio of ten Barbies to one Ken. Ken is looking more and more like a rented gigolo, or the guy who takes Barbie's outfits to the cleaners and back. His accessories are laughable (a slice of pizza, a kite, a basketball) and his weekend outfits are a bore (blue pin-striped smock and navy pants). The only thing you can do with him, apart from suicidal dives off the couch, is change his hair color from a terrible fecal-mustard color to an obviously touched-up brown. While Barbie has a choice of five stylish wedding gowns, Ken's lone wedding tuxedo is deplorable, a nylon unitard with an ill-fitting white jacket and a shiny bow tie. His loafers are interchangeable little boats. No wonder Barbie seems to prefer the company of her on-the-go girlfriends.

When I saw Ken strapped stiffly into the passenger seat of Barbie's huge new pink RV trailer, with plates that say "Barbie," I felt a stab of compassion for him. As I was gazing at this harsh spectacle, a couple wandered down the aisle. "Oh there's Ken," said the woman. "We were always so mean to Ken with our Barbies, we used to do terrible things to him. I don't know why." Laughing, they moved down the aisle to inspect a Baby Uh-Oh. ("Give her a drink and uh-oh! ... time to change her diaper!")

However retrograde she appears to be, I sense Barbie is a survivor. Her maddeningly firm little bosom and fashion-victim personality, her fickle careers are all voodoo tricks to ward off parental approval. If we had given Barbie a social conscience and sensible shoes, she might have moldered away at the bottom of the toy bin. As it is, girls play with their uneducational Barbies as they always have, playing out the "mean babysitter" scenario, madly acting away, with no parent-pleasing values to inhibit their stories. Therapists may envy the Barbie blankness — she too can create a private, privileged space where any and every feeling is permitted. May Barbie be "bad" as long as she reigns, for it is her lack of redeeming social value that helps keep her true to the child's sense of play, instead of the parents' worst fears.

15

M.T. Kelly

THE LAND BEFORE TIME

THE grave of a child makes all ideas of oneness with the land, in fact ideas of there being any purpose at all in nature, seem absurd. This is especially true in a country that looks able to kill children so easily — east of Great Slave Lake, where the trees and the species thin out, less than fifty miles south of the Barrens. Here are the "gloomy regions of the North" as Samuel Hearne described them in the eighteenth century. They haven't changed.

Yet even in a haunted, frightening moment, as if to give hope and prove "our almost-instinct almost true; / What will survive of us is love," it becomes clear that this grave in this spot shows much evidence of thought and love. And it becomes clear that landscape, "wilderness," which appears utterly uninhabited, has been profoundly inhabited, both physically and imaginatively, for thousands of years.

To the west of the fallen, javelin-shaped log posts that mark the grave is an overturned eagle's nest. It's obvious that both the vanished birds and the vanished people were looking for the same thing: a high place overlooking water, a place of spawning fish in the spring, with two tributaries flowing into the larger river; a place where wind would keep the insects down in summer and where caribou in winter, facing north without fear, could be seen moving along the ice. There are unity and wonder here; an ancient connection.

In his book *Mounds of Sacred Earth* the late Walter Kenyon observed how the megaliths and mounds and graves of Europe are set on high ground with views over sea and fjord and inland waterways: they overlook freshwater lakes,

great rivers, and the sea; they are set on jutting headlands; they command
spreading expanses of valley; they are inland at sites to which rivers give access.
What was true for Europe was also true for the Americas. The similarity is obvious enough in the pyramids and stelae of Central America, but as Kenyon points
out "nearly every major waterway of the Midwest was bordered by clusters of
mounds." Kenyon's book is about Ontario, but the same considerations seem to
have applied at L'Anse-Amour in the Strait of Belle Isle, on the Canadian
Shield and on the plains, and even in the most inhospitable of environments,
the subarctic and arctic Barrens.

Alex Hall, who owns Canoe Arctic, has guided in the Barrens for fifteen years.
He speaks of finding graves — so many of them seem to be of children — "up,
way up, where you can see all around," or else in places "where you'd want to
camp." What was working in these choices was far more than concern about a
view for the dead, or even a sense of aesthetics. The impulse to seek out such
places seems the opposite of the word religious as it is usually understood, with
its freight of dogma and righteousness. Standing in such a spot one has a sense,
tiny, ineffable, of the human spirit searching for, and finding, comfort; comfort
in the deepest sense.
   When he speaks of his finds Alex Hall is very secretive. A tall, garrulous
man who turns his head aside as the stream of small talk pours out, he dismisses
his reticence with comments like "I don't want helicopters coming on my river."
There's far more to it, however, than an outfitter protecting his territory. Trained
as a biologist, Alex is a strange combination of fussiness and scientific certainty
as he explains his equipment and methods. His obsession with detail was perfectly understandable in light of where we were going. Samuel Hearne travelled out onto the Barrens to go to the mouth of the Coppermine in 1771, but he
and his companions hugged the edge of the woods. The portion of Hearne's
trip we intended to retrace was his route back to Prince of Wales's Fort. Next to
his "discovery" of the Coppermine, to which he was guided and accompanied
every inch of the way, Hearne's major accomplishment was the walk from
Prince of Wales's Fort, now Churchill, Manitoba, across the taiga and barren
lands to the Arctic Ocean and back. This feat is still remembered in the North.
The pilot who flew our expedition out of Fort Smith, the home base of Canoe
Arctic, said to me, tilting his head to acknowledge an achievement both extraordinary and ridiculous: "Hearne! Isn't that the guy who walked across the Barrens?"

We flew out of Fort Smith over a river system through the open taiga forest which is clearly marked on Hearne's map. Because of the archaeological remains, the graves, I won't give the exact name of the river, but we passed Hill Island Lake, or "Noo-shetht Whoie," a place that still retains its Indian name. The route Hearne took is obvious not only from his descriptions but from looking at a topographic map. The plan of our trip was simple enough. With three canoes and seven people — Alex had a twenty-foot canoe to accommodate three people, so not everyone had to be an experienced wilderness paddler — we'd drift with the current down the watershed Hearne and his guide Matonabbee had walked up. They had slogged this way over the ice in March and April, resting in protected groves, "the Indians ... employed at all convenient times in procuring birch-rind and making wood-work ready for building canoes." Our time on the river was eight days; Hearne and company stayed in one spot for ten because of the caribou, "as this was the last time the Indians expected to see such plenty until they met them again on the barren grounds." When we were there in early June the ice had only just left the river; in Hearne's time an April thaw came "so great that the bare ground began to appear in many places, and the ice in the rivers, where the water was shallow and the current rapid, began to break up." That didn't last long, however, because: "As the morning of the first of May [1772] was exceedingly fine and pleasant, with a light air from the South, and a great thaw, we walked eight or nine miles to the East by North, when a heavy fall of snow came on, which was ... accompanied by a hard gale of wind from the North West. At the time the bad weather began, we were on the top of a high barren hill, a considerable distance from any woods; judging it to be no more than a squall, we sat down, in expectation of its soon passing by. As the night, however, advanced, the gale increased to such a degree that it was impossible for a man to stand upright; so that we were obliged to lie down, without any other defence against the weather than putting our sledges and other lumber to windward of us, which in reality was of no real service, as it only harboured a great drift of snow, with which in some places we were covered to the depth of two or three feet."

After reading these relevant passages I was delighted Alex was punctilious about planning. I also realized he was deceptive. His constant conversation came from years of keeping talk going in the pressure cooker that long canoe trips can become. And in the end Alex had no objections to my reporting the location of a chipping site (for arrowheads, some thousands of years old) to the Department of New World Archaeology at the Royal Ontario Museum. He had summed up his Master's thesis with the statement: "shooting a wolf is just the same as shooting a person." His wariness *is* a desire to keep people out of his wilderness, he admits, implying that where people go interference and crowding and muddle follow. He has campaigned hard to keep the Thelon Game Sanctuary, a vast preserve in the Barrens on the Thelon River, protected in the face of new pressures. If at first Alex seems austere, a little crazy, if there is something in him of those rigid biblical mystics who fasted in the desert, it soon becomes clear that he's a mystic all right, but not one who takes his inspiration from a desolate landscape. The Barrens have been described as a "cold desert," but for Alex they are better described by the Cree word "Kistikani," the garden.

In his Fort Smith home Alex keeps books and bones, marvels of his voyages. There is a wolverine skull, and pairs of the caribou antlers that he uses for the logo of Canoe Arctic; there are teeth, pebbles, grizzly bear claws, and feathers. For years I had corresponded with him about canoeing in the Barrens and about Samuel Hearne who, Alex says, of all the writers about the North "stands alone." My own fascination with Hearne made me want to retrace some of his route. The land through which Hearne travelled has been depopulated since his day, and because of its isolation and, so far, freedom from mining, it has remained as it was when he first saw it with his brilliant, alien, eighteenth-century eye.

Hearne's book is *A Journey From Prince of Wales's Fort In Hudson's Bay To The Northern Ocean 1769-1770-1771-1772*. Along with David Thompson's *Travels in Western North America, 1784-1812*, it is one of the great, if neglected, Canadian books. Northrop Frye says that Hearne and Thompson, along with the *Jesuit Relations*, form the very beginnings of our literature. Hearne wrote in a clear style, well before the Victorian sentence made getting through historic journals and novels the literary equivalent of wading through sawdust.

There is something outlandish about Hearne as he sets out with his wig on his head and his high heels sinking into the lichen. The impression lasts all through his book as he calls medicine bundles "rubbish," symbolic paintings "hieroglyphics," shields "targets" and "lumber"; shamans are "jugglers" who "blow into the *anus*, or into the parts adjacent, till their eyes are almost starting out of their heads." He explains that the jugglers, "being naturally not very delicate," must, nevertheless, be taken seriously. "However laughable this may appear to a European, custom makes it very indecent, in their [the Indians'] opinion, to turn any thing of the kind to ridicule." Hearne respects this grudgingly, because of "both the juggler and sick person, both of whom were men I much esteemed." Although he holds his tongue because his life depends on it, in his journal Hearne remains very much a man of his time and cannot hide his contempt.

What makes Hearne's *A Journey* timeless is the depth of feeling he can display and his ability to observe — he was a naturalist of genius — and create a world that is as real today as it was when he travelled through it. Here is Hearne at the beginning of May, 1772:

> We had not been long on the East side of the river before we perceived bad weather near at hand.... We had complete sets of Summer tent-poles, and such tent-cloths as are generally used by the Northern Indians in that season; these were arranged in the best manner, and in such places as were most likely to afford us shelter from the threatening storm. The rain soon began to descend in such torrents as to make the river overflow to such a degree as soon to convert our first place of retreat into an open sea, and oblige us in the middle of the night to assemble at the top of an adjacent hill, where the violence of the wind would not permit us to pitch a tent; so that the only shelter we could obtain was to take the tent-cloth about our shoulders, and sit with our backs to the wind; and in this situation we were obliged to remain without the least refreshment, till the morning of the third of June: in the course of which time the wind shifted all round the compass, but the bad weather still continued, so that we were constantly obliged to shift our position as the wind changed.

This is not hiking. Certainly Hearne's view of the North is anything but romantic; he lets you know how tough and harsh the place can be. There are many times in the book when he finds himself "long before morning in a puddle of water, occasioned by the heat of our bodies melting the snow." Yet Hearne's creative intensity, the feeling he shows for place — much like that of his native companions, unsentimental, subconsciously pantheistic — is unlike the responses of many modern adventurers in the North. After all, Hearne took his time. The major characteristic of nearly all modern canoe trips in the North is that they take too little time.

Through nineteen years of canoeing Alex Hall has met this pattern over and over. His explanation is that "people get out of the plane, take a look around

them, and think, 'Where are we?' The conclusion they all seem to reach is —
let's get out of here or perish! Everyone travels twelve-hour days; they have
rigid schedules; they hardly get out of their canoes."

It is easy enough to understand why. The thrill of flying over Hill Island
Lake, with the oddly shaped hill in it just as Hearne recorded, was completely
offset by low sky, leaden water, the rolling, rocky land of dark evergreens and
sere color with not a hint there would ever be a spring; and here it was June.

"Pretty depressing, eh?" said one of my fellow voyagers, Kim Janda, a chiro-
practor and writer from California very much interested in native American
mysticism. Kim's specialty was the religion of the Pueblo in the warm southwest. As he looked down at the Northwest Territories I could tell he was wondering what he'd gotten himself into.

When we emerged from the plane we too looked around as if wondering
where we were. I stared out at a widening of the river, aware that falling in
meant danger from hypothermia. Because of the cold, no-one's hands seemed to
work properly as we tried to open a tin of tuna for lunch. A small group of people by this small lake, we seemed, for the moment, pathetic. I remembered how
I'd looked down at the canyon of the river as we'd flown in, searching rather
desperately what rapids I could see for "downstream V's" — the route a
canoeist must follow to navigate white water successfully. The next morning I
mentioned my search to Alex at the first rapids we came to, a roaring cataract,
utterly uncanoeable.

"People with experience get worried when novices who've had one white-
water course want to run everything. Those who know what they're doing take a
look and they're cautious. If you fall in it's not like getting pulled out of a river
on a warm July Saturday and going to the car to dry off."

My feeling of dread had grown because that morning we'd been followed by
a bear who had swum across the ice-cold lake to get to our side of the river.
We got over the first portage with no trouble from the bear — and of course the
other side of dread is elation. Once we'd finished our carrying, the sun came out
and my perspective on the danger of those rapids, and on the world in general,
changed.

"Would anyone want to run that?" I asked Alex, nodding at the surging boils
above the spot where we would put in again.

"I tried to restrain people from going down stuff like it on the Coppermine,"
Alex shook his head. "They made it, but they were foolish. I told them to
remember they had kids, what they were risking, but it didn't work. I don't

know — I guess I understand it. I was out three months once, and it was a dangerous, exploratory trip; every morning I woke up never having felt more alive. But then I look at water like this," he gestured upstream, "and I think, it's death, it's just death."

Many of those involved in sports such as white-water canoeing and mountaineering do seem to feel most alive on the edge of extinction. It is hard to imagine someone emerging from rapids, having "bagged" it — crash helmeted, Kevlar armored, Goretex clad, flotation equipped, looking like something out of NASA — thinking, "To see a World in a Grain of Sand / And a Heaven in a Wild Flower...." Adrenaline ecstasy doesn't work that way. Nor is it possible for modern sojourners in the North, no matter how delighted they feel at moments, to think like Saltatha, a Yellowknife Indian who confronted white religion in the nineteenth century by comparing the earthly barren grounds to Christian paradise: "Is it [heaven] more beautiful than the country of the muskox in summer, when sometimes the mist blows over the lakes, and sometimes the water is blue, and the loons cry very often?" One of the most canoed rivers in the Arctic, the Coppermine, is one that Hearne walked beside. The Chipewyan people Hearne travelled with used canoes to ferry themselves across rivers; they spent a lot of time with their boats on their backs, and walked immense distances with them.

This is not to say Hearne thought like a native American. He was full of attitudes and contempt. But one has only to contrast his book with that of a contemporary, *Voyages and Travels of an Indian Interpreter and Trader, 1791* by J. Long, to see Hearne's genuine empathy with the native way of seeing things, an empathy that was sometimes unconscious.

The real story of Hearne's *A Journey* lies in the love and friendship between him and Matonabbee, his guide. Guide isn't accurate; the concern Matonabbee felt for Hearne was like that of a parent for a helpless child. Hearne called Matonabbee a "famous leader." Matonabbee and his family took pity on Hearne after his first two attempts to find the Coppermine ended disastrously. They allowed him to travel with them. According to Matonabbee, all Hearne's misfortunes on his first two attempts happened because he did not have women accompanying him on the journey. "They [women] pitch our tents, make and mend our clothing, keep us warm at night; and, in fact, there is no such thing as travelling any considerable distance, or for any length of time in this country, without their assistance."

The whole issue of how the Chipewyans treated women is a controversial one. From Hearne's point of view the men were brutal: women always died first in times of starvation; they were "made for labour" and could produce as much as two men, yet according to the Indians "the very licking of their fingers in scarce times is sufficient for their subsistence." Sometimes women would kill their daughters to save them a life of cruel drudgery. Men wrestled for women; the women had no say whatever.

This was in direct contrast to other native groups, especially the "Southern Indians" or Cree who lived south of the Chipewyans. In fact most Algonquian-speaking native groups seemed to have had more humane relationships between the sexes. As early as the *Jesuit Relation* of 1634, Father Paul Le Jeune complained about the freedom Indian women enjoyed in direct contrast to their European counterparts. The independence of native women was seen as a problem by the Jesuits, who lectured the men about "allowing" their wives sexual and other freedoms. Women held "great power ... in nearly every instance ... the choice of plans, or undertakings, of journeys, of wintering."

Reading Hearne does not make it easy to understand Chipewyan views of women. Jennifer S.H. Brown of the University of Winnipeg, editor of *"The Orders of the Dreamed" : George Nelson on Cree and Northern Ojibwa Religion and Myth, 1823*, has written: "It could be ... that the wrestling over women reflected the extent to which the men really *needed* them, as Matonabbee really needed his wives. We have real problems with how one-time encounters in small groups in special circumstances, recorded by one observer with a certain amount of his own cultural and psychic baggage, become archetypal and mythic in the literature, representing 'The Chipewyan' (all of them, all the time)."

Whatever the context, it's hard to discount any of Hearne's perceptions since his observations were acute. The last chapter of *A Journey From Prince of Wales's Fort In Hudson's Bay To The Northern Ocean*, which is a report on the birds, animals, and plants in the northern part of Hudson Bay, is phenomenally accurate. Visiting the country he described I was continually pausing, amazed at what I recognized. What Hearne described remains the same.

The country is the open forest of the northern taiga. It is also called lichen woodland. Unlike much of the Canadian Shield, it is without underbrush. The lichen crumbles like dried parsley or sand under your feet. The country is so open that it invites you to walk through it, to go on and on as the trees recede, on out over the Barrens and into the sky.

This is "the land of little sticks" and the trees are scrubby, though they grow larger along the river and at rapids where shelter and moisture in the air form microclimates. Here are skinny black spruce that are very, very old, and birch. Caribou trails are everywhere, reassuring in their serpentine certainty, luring you on. These groves are where the Indians would gather to make canoes, or sledges and snowshoes. In early spring such areas, flooded with black water, stark because nothing has begun to grow, are reminiscent of wet November woods in the south. But the season still holds out its possibilities, and in spite of chill in the shadows, the bark of the birch trees, springy, resilient, invites you to make an impression in it, whether with a fingernail or a stick, just to feel its life.

Animal signs are everywhere. Signs are the polite way of saying it; there is scat or faeces galore; bear scat full of berries, wolf scat white with caribou hair and harboring a dangerous parasite, ptarmigan pellets, caribou droppings; there are mounds and tunnels of seeds from red squirrel colonies. They live underground in winter because of the severe cold.

The many sandy beaches make it easy to see animal tracks. At one ancient "chipping site" on a high sandy bluff overlooking a lake, we discovered a beautiful turquoise arrowhead and above it what seemed, at first, human prints. It was as if a young adult had been running across the sand on his toes, leaving only the impression from the front part of his foot, the toes gripping deep. The footprint was a bear's pug mark, a juvenile bear's, but because of the human associations of the place and it being a sunny day I couldn't help thinking we were in a Club Med setting. Then the sun went behind a cloud, and the sand took on the physical properties it must have had when it was frozen grit in winter.

These incredible mood swings occasioned by the weather were felt by everyone on the trip. At one minute we would be overlooking the river seeing its beauty stretch into the distance, and the next minute, as the ceiling dropped and cloud moved in, we could imagine a band of travellers from Hearne's day struggling along the ice in February. The caribou that rested out in the open to escape wolves retreated quietly. The band advanced, their dark skin and clothing looking like rags against the snow.

On the last night of the trip, after supper, I watched Alex Hall sitting with a cigar and staring out over the water. Again, the weather was changing, wind and lights sweeping across the lake. One side of the sky was totally dark, the other brilliant blue with sunset luminous on the edge of the horizon. We had talked of the arrowheads, the grave, and Hearne's journal. We would talk again, but for a moment there was silence. I walked away and looked back. Alex seemed to vibrate with excitement as he stared over the water, almost as if, though stationary, he was doing a dance. Wind blew and rain fell in one part of the world; the other was unbearably clear.

Nature may well be a "maniac," and I couldn't delude myself that this place cared for human beings. But for a moment, against all reason, as the water shivered and the light flew, I knew that this land was capable of love.

16
Myrna Kostash
PENS OF MANY COLORS

GABRIELLE Roy once wrote about Ukrainian Canadians that we possess *"une teinte indéfinissable de rudesse et d' extrème douceur, de violente gaieté et de violente protestation."* Nevertheless, she felt that we were somehow familiar to her — like the French-Canadians, she wrote, we were possessed of a "nostalgia for the past" which kept cropping up in our speech — and were relieved, therefore, of our burden as the Other, the Alien in Canadian society. Thanks to our drift away from the land and our arrival in the towns and cities where everybody else was living, we had even lost our status as a real minority group: we had, according to Roy, "completely adapted" to Canada and our "dances, picturesque costumes, and songs" had passed into the "national heritage" where they were taken up as "all of ours" by Canadians at large. And that, I suppose, is the end of the story, as Roy saw it.

I don't know when Roy wrote this essay but I would guess well before 1970, given its tone of satisfaction that the incomparably jolly and crude Ukrainians had ceased to be alien among Canadians, that our characteristics, far from marking us as strangers, reminded the writer *of her own people*, that our very ethnicity was no longer a rebuke to anglo and franco cultural habits but had somehow merged with them and brought us all closer together in a kind of reconciliation. I have no doubt that Roy approved of these processes. But almost everything she had to say about Ukrainians and otherness is now quite out of date. In the last twenty years, we have almost entirely "rethought" ourselves, as it were; and I for one no longer recognize myself in this romantic portrait of the wistful suburban settler and reconciler of paradoxes.

Or rather, to speak more honestly, I do recognize myself in that portrait but it is like an old photograph found in a shoebox: a memento of an earlier self that evokes sharp recall of what we once believed and cherished and what still resides within the more recent self, but like a kind of hard nut around which the layers of experience and reflection have formed a complex tissue.

I don't suppose there is any member of a minority or oppressed group — any woman, any person of culture, any ethnic — who has not dreamed of belonging — of escaping from the curse of the ghetto and entering the high streets of the city like an ordinary citizen. It is this dream that Roy speaks to — and also, let us never forget, to the fear held by our ruling classes of the unassimilated, hence unmanageable, stranger at their gates — and so the evocation of finality, absorption, closure (in a word, assimilation), is meant to be profoundly reassuring. We ethnics have deeply desired to be ordinary, to be "just" Canadians (as women have desired to be "just" human beings and homosexuals "just" men) and relieved of our role of the exotic, at best, sinister, at worst, newcomer whose job it is to provide object lessons to "Canadians" about their own superiority.

My parents' generation — the first one born in Canada — seems to have confronted this. By learning to speak English, by taking middle-class jobs, by raising children in the suburbs, they did more than just take on protective coloring. They served notice that they wished to be engaged in the general public debate and process of construction of Canadian society. They wanted to *be* there. As comforting and reaffirming as a ghetto is, its homeliness and solace have a price: exclusion, self-containment, set-asideness. If the ghetto is a sanctuary, it is because this is precisely the zone where the outside world, the big one, the mainstream one, cannot and does not wish to intrude.

For my generation, however, the question has been posed again, and it has been posed not as a polarized conflict between the either/or assimilation and ghettoization but as the postmodern realization that we ethnic *arrivistes* live in both conditions at once. The point, suddenly, is not Roy's dream of the reconciliation of opposites but the acceptance, even cultivation, of what Eli Mandel has called the "interface" of cultures, the "dialectic of self and other" where tension at the point of contact, ambivalence, ambiguity, porousness, is the point, not resolution — the transcendence of paradox, stasis — as had been implied in the older dream. No, this new generation does not want to *overcome* the so-called problem of ethnicity but to live with it. It doesn't want to see its "problem" as having been dealt with once and for all the moment its parents adapted to the ordinary, the unexceptional. It wants to revive the extraordinary, the dissonant, the unpresentable, and juxtapose them to the civilized center.

This is no gratuitous exercise. *This is our condition.* For as surely as the repressed material of the subconscious reasserts itself in the individual soul — as dream, obsession, metaphor — so does it come back to haunt the assimilated ethnic. To my parents' generation, it came back as nostalgia — that melancholic yearning for the unrecoverable. To an older generation of writer, as with Gabrielle Roy, it came back as a figure of speech, as though metaphor could transform the conflicted self into well-being. For my generation, though, it has reasserted itself as politics, specifically the politics of the inside agitator.

I wanted the I to be an arrow
of pure intent
instead of the flesh it tears through
I am a snake

shedding my skin
from the inside

(Joanne Thorvaldson, "Border Crossings")

Of course it is no accident that it is my generation which raises the creative possibilities of ambivalence and ambiguity: we are, thanks to our parents' efforts, at home in Canada. Our status as citizens is not in question. We can *afford* to cultivate tension. But we came to this tension through our own generational experience. I have written elsewhere about how the 1960s experience in student movements, civil rights movements, the counterculture, and the women's liberation movement have provided us the material with which to identify with the oppressed and brutalized against the violence of capitalist, post-industrial institutions and with which to identify ourselves as a group, a collective consciousness, an unalienated "we." From this experience, it was not far for the ethnic to go to embrace the "we" in ethnicity as well and, more important, to see it as a zone of resistance to the overbearing authority of the dominant culture that oppressed us as women, blacks, gays, students. For if it is true, as George Grant has said, that resistance to oppression is possible as soon as we come to know and love what is good in that which is ours, then our politics as inside agitators became a given the moment we embraced the "ethnic" in ourselves: the person with a specific history, which is to say memory, with a special sense of place — the interlocked historical narratives of Canadians *and* aliens — and with an experience of endurance and contention that did not take place only in the private fastnesses of the self but in all of us, together, relations.

To know all this, of course, is to know that one's condition as ethnic is one of flux, pluralities, tension. That one is simultaneously *of* this society but not at all times *in* it.

How this condition affects the place of the ethnic writer within Canadian writing is the obvious next question. How do we, living at the interface of culture and insisting in their contiguity, and their ultimate communicability between each other, how do we write ourselves into the dominant culture? How do we become heard within the orchestrated polyphony of CanLit? It is not an obvious question, for, even when we write in English, as most of us do, we do not stand in the same relationship to language as do the anglophones.

Under these words
Are the echoes of other words

as the Polish-English poet, Maria Jastrzeska, writes. Even when English is our first language, we have all our lives heard another one (or two or three), as though these *other* sounds — strange, fragmented utterances though they be — were natural speech, one which preceded the one we now call mother English. And so we are like the young James Joyce, Irish-born, monolingual English-speaker, in conversation with his tutor from England who suddenly realizes that though they are both speaking the same language, for one of them the language has had to be *learned* — struggled for, struggled against — across generations of Celtic-speaking peasants who were forcibly dragged into English speech by violent men from a foreign place. So, my "native tongue" is a kind of gift. It is not mine by race or ancestry, it is mine only because my parents learned it. Behind *them* stand rank upon rank of peasants who never spoke a word of it, who spoke instead a language lettered by monks of Byzantium. Perhaps it is time now to speak of sister or cousin-tongues as well as of the mother?

The second problematic concerns one's designation as a writer in Canada. I had the very odd experience of finding myself entered in the *Oxford Companion to Canadian Literature* as "Kostash, Myrna, See: Ukrainian Writing." Odd, because it seems to me that, over some twenty years of writing, I have made a contribution not just as an ethnic but as a woman/feminist, an Albertan, a Canadian, a non-fictionist, organization activist, teacher — why should the "Ukrainian" component of all this activity be the one to characterize me? Odd, too, in that I have no idea what "Ukrainian writing" is supposed to mean in my case; I write only in English and address an English-speaking audience. What on earth does it take to become a Canadian writer, a contributor to and practitioner of CanLit, if not books written in Canada by a Canadian for Canadians? Could it be that, given my origins outside the Anglo-Celtic and Franco founding nations, I shall *never* be considered to belong because I wasn't there at the beginning when the naming took place? That CanLit is a category and a practice hijacked and held captive by a very exclusive gang of men and women who all come from the right side of the tracks?

In a provocative article in *This Magazine*, Rosemary Sullivan takes up the question directly, arguing that the "national story recorded in our literature is a cumulative one and it's open-ended." I take her point: that, with each wave of immigration to Canada, the "national story" acquires new plots and characters, new sounds and images, and is never told once and for all.

Any attempt to exclude some voices to privilege others — to say that CanLit is the work mainly of male Anglo-Saxons from Ontario, say — is to do grave injury to the multicultural character of our society, of our creativity even. "What would it mean if we defined Canadian literature as the literature of a multicultural nation?" she asks, in a rhetorical invitation to consider the enriching possibilities of a literature which sees itself as multilingual and multifocal, polymorphous and resounding with a thousand different memories?

It is an exhilarating vision and yet, and yet ... I find myself sceptical and resisting. For it reminds me of that assimilated world of Gabrielle Roy with which I began, where all difference has been transubstantiated and the particular experience of ethnics at the margin of speech and audience — the experience of alienation, anger, fear, envy — is collapsed into a generic speech called CanLit. Anybody can belong. "I'm bored with 'Canadian' being a term of exclusion," writes Sullivan, with a hint of that ennui of the ladies and gentlemen of the chateau, presented ethnics for their entertainment. For those ethnics, "exclusion" is not boring. It is painful and exciting, for it is in those "interstices" of cultures that we have become writers. In other words, we may not *wish* to belong to the club. We may wish to live with tension and distress. We may wish to remind ourselves, over and over, that we live on the wrong side of the tracks, on the edge of town.

But "town" is home, is here. This is both literal and figurative. I grew up in an ethnic and immigrant working-class neighborhood east of downtown Edmonton and it has never occurred to me — not then, not now — that this neighborhood was not an organic part of the city; for all its "otherness" it was nevertheless linked by roadway and workplace and commerce to the rest of the city. Similarly, the "town" in my head is a Canadian zone: I have lived in it all my life, I understand its codes and lingo, I know how to get around, it is the place where I was given birth as a writer.

So, Sullivan makes another, more crucial error: she identifies multicultural literature with immigrant literature, as though the problems of exclusion and belonging, language and speech, were present only to the newcomer, at the point of entry, as though the Canadian-born, belonging to the generic Canadian "here," had nothing to say about the multicultural condition. But we do. We ask such questions as: What is my relationship to the English language? Do my memories of ethnic custom bear on the shape of my work? Do I, as a kind of outsider, visualize Canada differently than an insider does? How shall I balance the claims of my feminist "sisters" against those of my grandparents' ghosts? Is the Old Country recoverable?

Speaking of the theme of the torn and exiled immigrant, Sullivan asks: "When one exhausts the theme of 'there,' what does one have left?"

My God, woman. Everything!

17
David Macfarlane

LOVE AND DEATH

THE first dead body I ever saw was one I found hanging under a bridge in Paris. It was late at night. I remember being impressed with its stillness and with the calm, unprotesting way its unbound hands rested at its sides. The face, a young man's, was swollen black. When I saw it I let out a little yelp I hadn't heard come from inside me before.

Fourteen years later, I was back in Paris for a brief visit. My friend Bernard Grégoire, who is a Parisian, found occasion to remind me of the night I found the body. It was my last evening in the city, and an odd thing just had happened.

Bernard and I were playing chess at the Old Navy, an unfashionable and undistinguished café on the boulevard St-Germain. Walking past our table, slowly swaying her graceful hips, a young woman smiled. At me. And this inspired Bernard — a man who prides himself on his rakish good looks and his way with women — to remind me of the suicide.

We weren't supposed to be at the Old Navy. Bernard and I had planned to play in style at Les Deux Magots, the elegant café at the corner of the place St-Germain-des-Prés. But when we opened our chessboard there we were informed by a white-aproned waiter that playing games at the tables was not allowed. We moved down the street. The Old Navy wasn't so choosy.

Bernard, who also prides himself on his aggressive chess, was beating me badly. He lined up my defeated pieces beside his glass of Cointreau on ice. It was a lovely evening, just after the dinner hour, and the sidewalks were crowded with the sauntering passers-by who, more than any other characteristic of the city, make Paris Paris. The smell of the place — a combination of hot, ancient air from the métro and black tobacco from everywhere, exhaust fumes and flowers, stone walls and coffee, gutters and ironed linen — took me back fourteen years to when I was twenty-five and had an apartment on the rue de Saussure. The smell, and also the strange, disproportionate noise of the place — the way that the clatter of ice or the laughter of a woman can be heard across a café in spite of the loud rush of traffic only a few feet away — saddened me the way the passage of time always will, and, at the same time, delighted me with the simple fact of my being in Paris.

"You're still a terrible player," Bernard said.

I had to agree. Bernard is decisive and methodical, bent, from his first move, on destroying his opposition. My strategy amounts to little more than vaguely hoping for the best. But that night at the Old Navy, Bernard's offensive was interrupted at a crucial moment by the strolling tap of high heels on pavement. The rhythm was seductively slow. We both looked up, and we were both surprised to see a peerlessly beautiful young lady, arm in arm with a well-dressed young man, smiling warmly and directly at me.

Her brown hair was pulled back in a thick ponytail. It shone like satin in the light from the café. Her face had a fine, Pre-Raphaelite quality. Her hands were long and graceful. Her nails were red, and her eyes were wide and exotic. She was wearing an elegantly tailored silk suit, and her neck was wrapped in an ivory scarf. Her sophistication was obvious and unquestionably Parisian. She moved, swaying gracefully off the axis of her narrow toes, with a steady, measured pace.

When I realized who she was I smiled back. Only a few hours before, while waiting for Bernard, I had shared a curious moment with her. For two and a half hours I had been drinking thirty-franc Ricards at Les Deux Magots, and daydreaming happily about Paris. I was staring at a handsome young couple seated a few tables away. The light around them seemed golden in the late glow of a Paris afternoon. (Such is the effect of three Ricards.) She was beautiful. He was quiet and attentive. She was laughing and they were drinking champagne. Eventually, she sensed my steady gaze and turned towards me. Her young man was looking the other way, across St-Germain.

She didn't seem insulted by my stare. Apparently, we understood one another. She seemed to realize, or so I imagined, that I was someone who, in a guileless and slightly drunken way, was simply enjoying the pleasure she was taking in the remarkable coincidence of her being alive and happy, in love and in Paris. She leaned across the table to kiss the young man — in one of those protracted and passionate public embraces that only Parisians have the panache to pull off — and as she did she smiled at me as if we were old friends.

But when she strolled by our table at the Old Navy a few hours later and our eyes met again, I saw no reason to explain our brief and innocent past to Bernard. I preferred to leave him puzzled. "Ah Paris," I said, just cryptically and just archly enough to annoy him. "A city of coincidence."

Bernard wasn't going to be impressed. He wasn't even going to be curious. "Sometimes," he said, "I think North Americans do nothing but think of stupidities to say about Paris."

"But Bernard," I said, "it's true."

Bernard and I had met in the spring of 1976 on the train to Paris from Chartres. Then, by coincidence, we ran into one another two weeks later on the wide stone steps of the Luxembourg Gardens. In an odd, Parisian way this didn't surprise me. I had already come to realize that the city, in spite of its sprawling and exhausting size, encouraged chance encounters. The chairs of its cafés face out to the sidewalks and to the happenstance of passers-by. Its oldest streets turn back on one another in reunions of convoluted circles. And because the city's greatest pleasures are its public ones — strolls along the grand boulevards, explorations through winding streets, promenades through the parks, drinks in cafés, and walks by the Seine — it's not surprising in all of Paris to see someone you know from somewhere else, or someone you noticed that morning at a cheese stall, or perhaps just someone you remember from the line-up for taxis at the airport.

"Coincidence?" Bernard asked. He was staring glumly at me over the chessboard. "Like that time you got into trouble with *le pendu*."

"I guess."

"What was her name? That Polish girl?"

"Gabrielle."

"Now that," Bernard said, "was bizarre."

Bernard used to have a *vélo*. He has a car now. It's a green, five-year-old Peugeot that bears the battle scars of parking in Paris. During my visit we drove everywhere, and the car changed the city for me. I won't think of Paris the same way again.

When I lived in Paris, I walked. Endlessly. Gabrielle used to chide me about the time I spent in plodding, pedestrian transit. I would set out hours in advance for a film or a gallery or a quarter of Paris I had not yet seen. Even the métro was a luxury — the less money I spent, the longer I could stay, and I had no plans of leaving.

Exploring Paris on foot gave it an oddly disunified aspect — or this, at least, was the image that persisted in my memory once I left. The city seemed less a single entity than a gray solar system of destinations — the Cinémathèque, the Jeu de Paume, place des Vosges, the rue St-Denis, Sacré-Coeur, the Marché aux Puces, Père Lachaise, Le Grand Palais — orbiting at incredible distances my little apartment. I happen to read maps the way I play chess, and my most common memory of Paris is of heading in what I thought was the general direction of somewhere and finding myself, unperturbed and unhurried, back at the corner of a grand terraced boulevard and an askew little street I thought I'd left far behind.

But on this visit, I hardly walked at all. We drove, and Bernard proved to be an excellent driver — in the Parisian manner. He was fast and accurate and ruthless. "You must ignore pedestrians," he told me in the midst of his guided tour. "If you slow for them you might cause an accident."

Bernard insisted on using the car for our every outing. In fact, the only distances we ever walked were the inevitable four or five blocks from wherever we could park to wherever we were going. Once, on our way to the Musée d'Orsay to see Millet's *The Gleaners*, Manet's *Le Déjeuner sur l'herbe*, and Cézanne's *Apples and Oranges* — "You're only here for two days," Bernard said. "Three masterpieces should be enough" — we found a miraculous parking spot directly behind the museum. "For a Parisian," Bernard said, "this is better than an orgasm. I will now not need sex for a week." And my most Parisian memory of the trip — not a meal, nor a vista, nor a monument — was a glimpse of two young men on motor scooters. In front of us, they wove through traffic at breakneck speed and then, whirling around place d'Italie, shook hands without slowing down and went their separate ways.

This, I realized, was the Paris most Parisians know — the Paris of traffic jams, exhaust fumes, noise, and, in spite of all this, the civility of handshakes. I would prefer, I suppose, a Paris without cars, but Bernard scoffed at what he called touristic nostalgia for the *belle époque*. "Paris is Paris," he said. "Regrettably we are alive in the present tense." He shrugged and shifted to fourth, cutting through the place de l'Alma and heading across the river. We cut over the steel gray water of the Seine. That was when I saw the black iron bridge I had walked under one night fourteen years before.

On that evening, Gabrielle was supposed to go with me to the Cinémathèque. We'd spent the day at my apartment, but by the afternoon she'd changed her mind. Gabrielle, from the day I met her, was in the process of breaking up with her boyfriend. I'd never met him. I knew he was a student. From what Gabrielle told me I knew he was a poet and a political activist — romantic and darkly impossible. The break-up had been going on for months. When it seemed that they had finally ended things, Gabrielle spent time with me. Then, afraid because he got so upset, she'd go back to his place in the Marais. Her description of where he lived always made me think of *La Bohème*.

But the last movie at the Cinémathèque that night was *La Nuit américaine*, one of my favorite Truffauts. And that afternoon, in the little enclosure outside the apartment, Gabrielle and I had our one and only argument. We stood beside two crumbling terracotta pots of red geraniums. We both shouted our terrible French while my landlady, proper as a correctly declined noun, listened and pretended to sweep her doorstep.

I went to the movie myself. Afterwards, I had an espresso in a café behind the Palais de Chaillot. I watched the passersby at the place Wilson. An hour or so passed. It was a lovely, moonlit night. I decided to walk home partway along the cobbled banks of the Seine.

The river was black and smooth, only wrinkled here and there with the reflection of the yellow lights on the *quais*. The noise of traffic droned in the distance. My soft-soled walking shoes slopped along the bricks of the embankment. I could smell the river. Occasionally, a little wave slapped the dark stone wall below me. I approached the narrow bridge that crossed from the avenue de New York on the Right Bank to the quai Branly on the Left. I stepped out of the soft light of a full moon and, beneath the network of iron struts, walked straight into a pair of dangling feet.

Since Bernard was the only Parisian I knew during the time I lived in Paris, the night after I found the body I met him at Le Sélect and told him the story. I had imagined this would calm me down, but Bernard listened with growing consternation. He was horrified. Not horrified because I'd found a body hanging underneath a bridge; Bernard was a Parisian. Bernard was horrified because I'd called the police.

In those days Bernard smoked Gitanes *jaunes*. He lit one, and as he waved out the match he pushed his other hand through his lank brown hair. "This is very serious, man," he said. "The police here can be very weird."

I explained. I had called the police; I had waited forty-five minutes for their arrival; I had put up with two hours of their questioning while they'd taken endless photographs of the corpse — only to save someone else the trauma of finding the body. Bernard shrugged his shoulders, arched his eyebrows, and blew out a gust of smoke in the single gesture that Parisians reserve for the stupidities of anyone who, obviously not from Paris, isn't even from France. "Pffft," he said. "You should have kept walking."

Bernard was right. *Le pendu*, as the police called the body, was a young Polish student. He was in Paris studying French at the Alliance Française. By an extremely unhappy coincidence studying French at the Alliance Française was my excuse for being in Paris as well. The fact that I almost never went to classes didn't help. Neither, apparently, did he. Worse, the three hours a week that both of us spent our time avoiding were the same three hours. We were in the same class. And worse still, there were only a few Poles in the class. Gabrielle was one.

I learned this the morning after I found the body. I was taken from my apartment by two policemen for further questioning. Standing in the courtyard with her broom, my landlady acknowledged my escorted departure with the same icy formality with which she kept careful track of all my comings and goings. The police, presumably, had asked her which apartment was mine. They had, perhaps, even explained to her why they were interested. This hadn't altered her impression of me. Being a foreign student and being arrested, possibly for murder, amounted to pretty much the same thing.

"*Au revoir, monsieur,*" she said.

"*Au revoir, madame,*" I replied.

The investigating officer was a Detective Lévy. He sat behind a neatly ordered desk. The photographs the police had taken of the hanging body were in an envelope in front of him. To his left was an ancient typewriter. The walls of his office were a dirty beige, and his tall windows opened onto a courtyard. The only decorations in the room were a row of six different gauges of shotgun shells lined up across the top of a metal cabinet and a poster for a Goya exhibition at the Orangerie. The illustration was Saturn eating his children.

Detective Lévy passed me the photographs and watched me carefully as I looked at them. He told me what the police had learned. As he spoke I felt my face flush. He rested his chin thoughtfully between his thumb and forefinger. I passed the pictures back. I couldn't tell if he knew anything about Gabrielle. He asked me what I had been doing down by the river alone so late at night. He listened to my reply with the slightly pained expression that typically greeted my French in Paris. I told him I liked walking.

Detective Lévy sat back in his chair. He had a round face and gleaming, brilliantined hair. Almost certainly, he said, the case was a suicide. It was not, in a city the size of Paris, an uncommon thing. But there were, he went on, gazing up to the flaking ornamental molding in the ceiling, a few things that worried him. The first, of course, was the strange coincidence that in all of Paris it had been a classmate who'd happened upon the body.

And there was the knot. The knot would have been very difficult for someone to tie by himself. Detective Lévy swivelled in his chair and considered the height of his windows. He didn't want to bother me with technicalities, but it happened that there was something a bit odd about the position of the feet.

"*Monsieur,*" he said. "*Est-ce que vous avez touché le cadavre?*"

"*Non, monsieur.*"

Detective Lévy sighed. He held a pencil as if it were a cigarette holder and he were a movie star. He regretted the inconvenience but wondered if I could stay in Paris for the next few days. Just in case. He wanted to make further inquiries at the school. A formality, really. The family might ask about certain details.

I said that I would stay. Detective Lévy acknowledged his thanks and his regret with a slight shrug. It was, his expression managed to convey, just a question of bad luck that I was involved in this. A regrettable coincidence. I agreed and shrugged back. We both stood.

"*Vous aimez Paris?*" he asked as we shook hands.

"*Oui, monsieur. Beaucoup.*"

The next day I was on the train to London.

18
Joyce Marshall

REMEMBERING GABRIELLE ROY

I'VE been reading *Ma chère petite soeur* (*Letters to Bernadette* in Patricia Claxton's translation), Gabrielle Roy's letters to one of her sisters, called Dédette in the family, who became a nun while Gabrielle was a child. The book holds so much of the Gabrielle Roy I knew, far more than does the rather formal and studied autobiography, *Enchantment and Sorrow*, the summation of her old age, that I've found myself missing her dreadfully. The letters are so much warmer, so characteristic, and often very moving — not only the daily letters written while Dédette was dying of cancer but earlier letters too, when the beloved sister was still the unspoiled eager person of whom Gabrielle often spoke. I've always been sorry I wasn't able to get down to meet this lively and engaging woman when she came east in 1965. But I translated *Enchanted Summer* which, with its fresh, almost childlike responses to nature, its delight in all living creatures, was Gabrielle's tribute to Dédette.

We met, Gabrielle and I, in June of 1959. I've recently searched through an old journal and found these words, which I wrote after our meeting:

> She is frail but gay, simple and warm, tiny with a tortured dark face, a very deep voice and wonderful light eyes. We liked each other and I feel much happier for this liking.

I had had to go down to Quebec City and thought it would be interesting to interview Gabrielle for the CBC program "Anthology." But when I wrote proposing this, she declined very firmly: she didn't like interviews. (She'd considered suggesting, she told me later, that I "come as a friend" but was afraid this would sound silly, even arrogant.) I was very anxious to meet her — because the publication of her *Bonheur d'occasion* (*The Tin Flute*) had been such an event for me as a young writer — and luckily I had a friend in Quebec City who knew Gabrielle and was able to arrange for the three of us to have lunch together in the little restaurant on the ground floor of the apartment building on Grande Allée where Gabrielle lived with her husband, Dr. Marcel Carbotte. My friend and I were already seated when Gabrielle, looking just like her photographs, appeared in the doorway, saw us at once and came quickly towards us, her eyes — those magnificent gray-green eyes — lighting up as she came. Strange that I didn't mention this in that old journal since I remember it so clearly even now. Strange too that I neglected to say what we talked about or why I was so sure we "liked each other."

That meeting was the beginning of our friendship. (And the truest thing I can say of our long association is that I continued to "feel much happier for this liking.") We corresponded, sent one another copies of our books, talked on the phone. Twice I visited her at Petite-Rivière-St.-François, downriver from Quebec, where she spent the summer, joined on the weekends and for his own holidays by her husband. Here, I've always felt, Gabrielle was most completely herself. I can see her rocking vigorously — all her movements were rapid and somewhat nervous — in one of the antique Quebec rockers Marcel had found and finished, or outdoors squeaking back and forth on one of those two-seater wooden contraptions that are activated by pressure of the feet.

In August 1960 I stayed a week with her in that cottage high above the St. Lawrence. We walked the road and the railway tracks, observed birds, watched ships and tried to name wildflowers. And one sunless morning we saw belugas leaping against the dark of water and sky, at least a dozen of the twisting, tossing silvery hoops. On this occasion too she let me read the typescript of *La montagne secrète* (*The Hidden Mountain*) and I pointed out that Carl Sandburg, the name she'd chosen for a minor Swedish character because "it sounded so right," was in fact so "right" that it couldn't be used.

In 1967 I spent a month in a little split-log house a field away that she'd rented for me so we could do our work in private and just come together for meals. We called it *le presbytère* because the priest brother of the Simards, Gabrielle's neighbors and good friends, used it as a vacation retreat. There was even a tiny chapel where "our brother the priest" sometimes celebrated mass when he was at home.

Before this second visit I'd become Gabrielle's "accredited translator," as it pleased her to call me. It began innocently enough when Robert Weaver asked me to translate a story of hers for broadcast on the CBC. As a tyro at translating, I simply rendered the text baldly, more or less word for word, then struggled to turn the result into something that didn't outrage too many of the rules and taboos of English. Gabrielle helped me with some of the tricky bits and approved the result so when Henry Binsse, her translator at the time, was no longer available for freelance work, she asked Jack McClelland to ask me to translate *La route d'Altamont* (*The Road Past Altamont*) of which the story I'd translated is a tiny part.

Then began our work together — work that was stimulating, instructive and at times exasperating beyond words. I'm pleased to say that when I decided after I'd completed *Enchanted Summer*, the third book of hers I translated, that I'd learned all I could from translating and was tired of turning my mind inside out for thoughts that weren't mine, we were still friends and remained friends till the end of Gabrielle's life.

So I have a double view of Gabrielle Roy — as friend and as co-worker, a co-worker who was permitted to go right to the heart of her creativity and to learn something of what she felt about her work, what she intended, and what she required of herself as well as of me. She didn't write quickly or lightly. She absorbed her material first, then and then only found the shape for it. When she was planning to write the story "Garden in the Wind," she told me, she spent hours day after day walking about in her husband's garden, a very windy spot overlooking the St. Lawrence, learning what it was like for plants and humans to struggle against wind.

If the structure of a piece of writing is weak, if even a paragraph fails to hold together when put into another language, the translator will realize this at once and sit holding some bits and pieces in her hands. Gabrielle's work is beautifully articulated, every bone, every muscle properly attached and in its place. Her stories and novels have in consequence a strong narrative push that is of tremendous help to a translator.

My difficulty was always with the style. It is so simple, always so appropriate, so unobtrusive. Yet those lovely sentences tend to go limp when turned into English. I never discovered why this was so. I simply fought and went on fighting. Translating *Enchanted Summer* was anguish because it's made up of little touches of color and intensity, each of which had to be balanced within itself and with the others, and there is no narrative push.

Gabrielle knew English, knew it well but not quite as well as she believed. (She'd even, as I think is now well-known, considered writing in English.) At the time of her schooling in Manitoba, French-speaking children were permitted only an hour a day's instruction in French. The nuns, she told me once, devoted most of these hours to prayers and the lives of the saints. This was early in our acquaintance, while she was still estranged from the Catholic church. She'd been outraged by the attitude of the priests of her childhood, their assignment of all non-Catholics to outer darkness. But when her eldest sister Anna was dying from cancer, after a life that Gabrielle felt was too limited, too drab, too lacking in challenge and satisfaction, it seemed to her that there must be more, for Anna and for all of us, that life on earth couldn't be all there was. I don't think I'm mistaken when I say that after her return to the Church not only her attitude but her memory of many things changed considerably. There is no hint in *Enchantment and Sorrow* that the nuns at her convent school so restricted their teaching in French, which was their common language. At any rate, whatever the quality of the French part of her education, her ear, a very sharp, sure and demanding ear, was a French ear. And the rhythm that ran in her thoughts and her writing was a French rhythm.

We always spent three or four days going over and over my translations. Twice I went down to Quebec, establishing myself at a hotel so I could withdraw at night to rest. Once — it was to check *Windflower*, the second book of hers I translated — she came to Toronto and we worked in my apartment. I'd suggested that it would be simpler if we went out for our meals. She agreed but, after a first lunch, we slipped into the habit of eating at my place, which was awkward because there were only a few things that Gabrielle could and would eat. (These things varied, I can't remember what was on the list at that time.) What I do remember is trying to cut up green beans with Gabrielle at my elbow, manuscript in hand, which was precisely what I'd hoped to avoid. Some people can tune out their work when it's time to occupy themselves with other things. Gabrielle could not.

This intensity of hers was only one of our difficulties. Many of them seem funny now. I didn't find them funny at the time. She was of enormous help with that pest of the translator, those French words so wide in their meaning that they swallow up a number of our nice sharp little English words, or that other pest, the words that only mean the same as their English cognate part of the time. The trouble began when we came up against the matter of Gabrielle's ear. She didn't know how an English sentence is supposed to sound. Again and again I'd read one of my sentences: "This is how we say it, Gabrielle." Sometimes I could convince her, sometimes not. Or she'd take exception to the sound of a particular word. She objected to "garbage man," I remember, because "garbage" is such an ugly word. It was no use my saying that garbage after all is ugly stuff; I had to find a circumlocution: "men gathering the refuse." This kept my mind very nimble, I may say.

Each translation I did for her brought its separate problem. With *The Road Past Altamont* it was the harmless little word "thing." She disliked our "th" sounds — it was a shock to her when I said I found the French nasal vowels hideous — and didn't consider "thing" quite up to par with *chose*. I was triumphant when I managed to remove every "thing" but two from *Windflower*, only to find that she'd now disapproved of sentences ending with "it," a structure that she stated (correctly) is never used in French and that she thought weak. "But you're not saying it properly," I pointed out again and again. "English is a verb language. We say 'I *saw* it,' not 'I saw *it*.' Poor little 'it' almost disappears." When I worked on *Enchanted Summer* I did my best to avoid such sentences but now Gabrielle had another bête noir — the word "had" and our composite verbs in general, which I had to explain and keep explaining was just one of the ways the English language went.

"Joyce is so demanding," she told someone once. "Demanding" isn't what she meant though it's one of the meanings of *exigéante*, the word I believe she had in mind. What she intended was one of the word's less flattering senses — pernickety, hard to please — because I insisted on English rhythms and syntax. The fact that I had to try to indicate what these were was of enormous help to me as a writer, a lover and student of English. Though I'm afraid it involved me in a lot of shouting: "No no no, Gabrielle, we can't say that in English," to be answered by her quiet and very determined "Why not?"

Gabrielle was intense and this made her over-anxious. She wanted the best and most exact translation possible. *The Tin Flute* had been poorly translated in New York by Hannah Josephson, who didn't know Canadian French or for that matter Canadian English — she thought we said "By jove!" and "Isn't it jolly!" — and Gabrielle had been given only twelve hours to look over the script. She was determined that such a thing should never happen again and had obtained the right to approve every word of the translation of her books. Though she respected my knowledge of English, as she often told me and others, she felt obliged to make sure — not simply in general but every time a dispute arose — that I did indeed know what I was talking about. This kept me very nimble, as I've said. And though I sometimes felt that she was rather hard on me, I was always aware that she was equally hard on herself.

I've called her intense and she was, about everything she saw and experienced as well as about her writing. She was never simply there, a quiet presence. Some people can withdraw and rest in their own minds, even in company. Gabrielle could not. She had to participate. This, I believe, was one of the reasons for her dislike of publicity. I talked her once into agreeing to be filmed for a program the CBC was making about her work and that of Marie-Clair Blais. I promised that the session would be brief, the interviewer unobtrusive. I'd be there to make sure nothing was done to trouble her. In fact, if she preferred, she need only speak a few words to me. The rest of the time she'd be photographed wandering about the garden, since that was what was wanted, a sense of where and how she lived. She consented but the next morning she was back on the phone, telling me in a choked whisper that the thought had kept her awake all night and made her ill. I never asked her to do such a thing again. And of course it wasn't in her nature to wander about the garden, now and then speaking a word or two to me. She would have been witty. She would have entertained. And she would have exhausted herself.

Though her health was never good, she could find energy when she needed it. She could be wonderfully funny, staging little scenes, imitating the voices and miming the actions of the people involved. Before she left Manitoba she was a member of an amateur theatrical group and she'd intended, when she went to Europe in 1937, to prepare for a career on the stage. (And did study acting in Paris and London till she discovered that writing was what she wanted, in fact had to do.) She could be easy and happy when there were no more than two or three friends in a room. But add just one stranger and she had to be on, on perpetually. I've seen her do it, then collapse, wishing the stranger (someone who'd been anxious to meet her) hadn't been permitted to come. It didn't seem to occur to her that a smiling semi-silent presence might have been enough.

She came from a story-telling family. As a child she was entranced by her mother's accounts of the family's journey west by ox-cart (as she described in "The Move" and other stories). When she grew up and was the only child still at home except Clémence, a mentally handicapped sister whom Gabrielle supported till the end of her life, she became in turn story-teller to her mother, embellishing and pointing up the events of her own days, practicing for her writing and, I've always felt, developing her almost excessive need to entertain.

Her mother was central to her life. A strong-minded and disappointed woman, more complex in her needs and demands than the gay adventurous

Maman Gabrielle presents to us in *Streets of Riches* and *The Road Past Altamont*, Mélina Roy clung, as such women often do, to this last of her children, the one from whom she hoped the most. It's always seemed to me that, whether or not she admitted it in quite these terms, Gabrielle came to realize that if she were to have a life of her own, if she were even to learn what this life could and ought to be, she'd have to leave home. In 1937, at the not very immature age of twenty-eight, she used her savings as a teacher to travel to Europe. She could never quite forgive herself for this desertion, which was compounded by her decision to settle in Montreal when the approach of war brought her back to Canada in 1939. *Bonheur d'occasion* is dedicated to Mélina Roy — not to her memory, though she was dead by the time the book appeared. And again and again in her writing, most explicitly in the title story of *The Road past Altamont*, Gabrielle returned to this pivotal event in her life: her abandonment of her mother and its necessity.

She was a youngest treasured child for whom everything was done. She couldn't even sew on a button when she left home, she told me. She learned to sew on buttons but all her life, wherever she went, she found mothers. When she was deathly sick on the channel ferry, as she recounts in *Enchantment and Sorrow*, the stranger who became her friend Ruby took her in charge. I was at times a sort of mother, sending messages to Jack McClelland that she was too diffident to send herself, dispatching urgent telegrams to tell her all was well. She wasn't unpleasantly selfish or egotistic. Nor did she demand service or become querulous if it was withheld. It came to her. And she gave a great deal of warmth and caring in return. Her letters to her sister, the meticulous arrangements she made for Dédette's trip to Petite-Rivière with Clémence, show this clearly. (She even sent her some tranquilizers though I doubt that they were needed. Dédette had a marvelous time, entertaining other passengers at "parties" in her compartment.) I felt her concern too, very often, especially when I was ill or depressed.

She presents herself in *Enchantment and Sorrow* as an exceedingly unhappy person — or at least as one who had an exceedingly unhappy life. It's almost as if she got caught on a single, rather dreary facet of herself; stories she told me with touches of humor or irony appear here in a more one-sided melancholy form. And certainly much of her early life was wretched, her father dismissed for political reasons from his government job as colonizer shortly before he was to obtain his pension, plunging the family into want, and the tragic histories of several of her brothers and sisters.

In her last years, it's true, though she always said she preferred living "in a French atmosphere" to her old life in the small threatened French-speaking enclave of St. Boniface, she often felt isolated, even lonely. She had few literary friends. The younger nationalistic writers snubbed her because she was not a separatist and had ceased, after *The Tin Flute* and *The Cashier*, to criticize the society in which she lived. I've seen some truly horrific reviews of her non-social books, such as one that described *The Hidden Mountain*, that parable of the artist's life, as a travelogue that might be used as publicity by the CNR. She minded this. Though she didn't want any sort of fussing, she did want to be appreciated and it was a great satisfaction to her that younger writers such as Jacques Godbout came to accept her at the last and to acknowledge publicly that they saw her as their foremother.

She always made it clear that she didn't want Quebec to separate from Canada. After de Gaulle shouted *"Vive le Québec libre!"* from the balcony of the Montreal city hall, she sent a letter to all the French-language newspapers of the province. Only two of them printed it, one with some heading as (I quote from memory): "Madame Roy supports Ottawa." When Gary Geddes invited her to contribute to *Divided We Stand*, a book of essays about Canadian unity, she wrote (and he printed):

> If I had the least hope that by my words I might be helpful to my country, I certainly would be writing all day. In a sense, most of my books have tried just that: bring more understanding between the two sides of our country which I both love. Today I don't feel that it has helped much. Still I would be willing to try again if I saw my way clearly: what to say and how to say it, and if I had all the time I need.

She was always concocting schemes for the two of us to prove we were true Canadians; our adopting bilingual names was one of them, she to become Shirley Roy, I Eglantine Marshall. She would have liked to read English-Canadian books as they came out but it was difficult to obtain these in Quebec or even to learn what books there were, so I used to send her my own copies and occasional paperbacks as gifts. I introduced her to Margaret Laurence's work, I remember, by lending her *A Jest of God*. Soon after this they began to correspond and, though they met only once, they were friends till the end of Gabrielle's life. I also lent her Ethel Wilson's books and there was at least a brief exchange of letters between them.

Gabrielle Roy and I were friends for more than twenty years. I am grateful for this friendship, which was a joy as well as a privilege, and for the fact that, reticent though she was, she let me as far into her life and thinking as she did. I described her face as tortured after our first meeting but, though the other adjectives I used still stand, it isn't as a tortured person that I remember her. What I remember is the delight she brought to us who knew her — the jokes, the laughter, her pleasure in the small oddities that escape a great many people. I miss her wonderful, often very funny letters. For years I was on the lookout always for absurdities of human bahavior and other whimsicalities that I could put into my own letters. I still watch for such things. I still find myself wanting to write to her about them.

19
Joyce Nelson

THE SAGA OF SPACE DORKS: TECHNOPHILIC FLYING BOYS FROM PLANET EARTH

IN NOVEMBER of 1989, I attended a small Toronto conference organized by members of Science For Peace to bring together people from a wide variety of disciplines. The purpose was to discuss the crisis we are in during this last gasp of the fading millennium — a crisis encompassing ecological, social, spiritual, and political dimensions. The hope was that, out of the alchemy of our combined insights, some sort of synergistic approach to solutions might arise.

During this weekend event, two eminent white male scientists rose to address the gathering as keynote speakers. Not coincidentally, each made reference to the moon landing of 1969. Until that moment, I had forgotten that, in certain circles, 1989 had been earmarked as the twentieth anniversary of the Apollo mission (or "The Boot on the Moon," as I call it), rather than any number of other events in that extraordinary year of 1969. *Chacun à son gout.*

In any case, the first scientist informed us that the moon rocks have turned out to be "no different from any other rocks" you might find in an alley in Moose Jaw but, he said, the $28 billion spent on the project was "justified" because "for the first time human beings were able to look at the earth and see it as a beautiful jewel shining in the firmament." The second scientist also waxed poetic about the Apollo mission, calling it "a turning point in the history of humanity." "For the first time in human history," he exclaimed, "we were able to see that the earth is whole, an intricate ecosystem that is our beautiful home."

By this point, my blood pressure was rising fast and I was having serious doubts about the alchemy that might arise in our gathering. I wanted to interrupt both eminent speakers and say, "Hey, guys, it's white suburbanites who were the last to know." Ancient non-patriarchal and native cultures have known for millennia that the earth is a living and intricate ecosystem, and they have certainly considered it "our beautiful home." For such pagan heresy they were killed off in droves, especially in the centuries following the Cartesian revolution in science.

While I was trying to decide which was more galling — the unconscious racism expressed in the rhetoric about "the first time in human history," or the attempt to "justify" that $28 billion price tag for putting "whitey on the moon" — an Ontario organic farmer-writer named Chris Scott stood up and reminded the eminent scientists about a member of their fraternity, Giordano Bruno, who had been burned at the stake in 1600 for coming to the same ecological insights 350 years before The Boot on the Moon.

But of course the real payoff of the Apollo Mission was ideological and psychological — summarized by that other object brought back by the astronauts that, unlike the moon rocks, has not been demystified by analysis and time. The object is the photograph of the planet that now graces the covers of "environmental" editions of many mainstream magazines, which has become the potent symbol used in every form of corporate/governmental ecobabble, and which is the numinous logo for the new Earth Flag ("Because Every Day is Earth Day") available in "full-size or child-size," screen-printed on blue polyester with brass grommets, and retailing for a mere U.S. $39.

The $28 billion photograph is also displayed on the editorial page of *Scientific American*'s 1990 special issue called "Exploring Space" — an edition sponsored entirely by Lockheed (one of the world's prime weapons suppliers), with fourteen pages of the company's ads. Under the Apollo photo of earth, editor Jonathan Piel reiterates the rhetoric about "a vision unseen and unseeable before the space age" — don't these guys read anything but science? — and calls the photograph "a symbol of the millennial human achievement in exploring space. The human eye, drawn close to the planets and their many moons, has now seen the earth in new perspective. It is a perspective that also enables us to glimpse cosmic beginnings and ends." (It's those "cosmic ends" that have me worried, especially with Lockheed and all the other military-industrial space dorks running the world. These guys get billions of dollars of government handouts and unlimited planetary resources to fire their ambitions.)

Anyway, as a mandala for our time, that $28 billion photograph of the blue-green planet is getting a lot of mileage these days. Before we examine the meaning of this photograph, however, we must delve into the murky realm of psychology: specifically, the psychology of the space-program, and even more specifically, the psychology of what the Jungians call the *puer aeternus* archetype; what American men's group leader and poet Robert Bly calls "the flying boy," and what Peter Pan apologists might refer to as the psychology of the Lost Boys.

The Latin *puer aeternus* means "eternal boy" and as an archetypal pattern of behavior and attitude, the puer has been studied extensively. The literature ranges from the wonderfully readable work of Jungian analyst Marie Louise von Franz (*Puer Aeternus*), to the less accessible prose of Jungian James Hillman (editor of *The Puer Papers*), to the pop psychology of Dan Kiley (*The Peter Pan Syndrome* and *The Wendy Dilemma*), the more personal approach of John Lee (*The Flying Boy*), and the increasingly popular (and very important) work of men's group leader Robert Bly, who focuses on various aspects of this psychological pattern.

The puer (pronounced "pooh-air") archetype is a rich one and difficult to briefly summarize, but the above experts would likely agree on this: a person who is possessed by, and thus living out this archetype has profound difficulties being a grounded adult living in the mundane, daily reality of the world. The puer is the dreamer, the romantic, the restless wanderer, the high-flying daredevil in every field (well, usually they don't go into accounting) who refuses to be "tied down" by conventional ways. Bly contrasts "the flying boy" with what he calls "the plodder" and says most North American males fit into either of these two categories, but that currently most boys and men are "flying boys."

The positive and negative qualities of the puer are expressed in such literary classics as *The Little Prince* by Antoine de Saint Exupery (analyzed by von Franz) and *Peter Pan* by J.M. Barrie (which Kiley's work addresses). A more recent example of the puer can be found in the movie made from Isak Dinesen's book, *Out Of Africa*, where the Robert Redford character is a classic puer: a flyer-pilot reluctant to commit himself to anything except the never-never land of his adventurous exploits.

Always appealing for his youthful exuberance, the puer is nevertheless likely to die young, usually by becoming ungrounded — whether from the "high" of drugs (like Jim Morrison, Jimi Hendrix, John Belushi), or by actually flying and crashing (like Saint Exupery himself and the Redford character) or some other tragedy that replicates the fate of Icarus (that mythic *puer* who ignored the advice of his father and flew too close to the sun, thereby melting his artificial wings and crashing to his death). Coming down is the hard part for a *puer*.

These examples remind us that there is a female equivalent called the *puella aeterna*, an equally rich archetype (explored in Linda Leonard's *The Wounded Woman*). But here I'll focus on the *puer*, since not that many women become space dorks. We do, however, imitate the negative Icarus pattern in the form of addictions whose high flights and crash landings can kill as surely as they killed those lovely *puellas*, Janis Joplin, Karen Carpenter, and Marilyn Monroe.

Perhaps the essence of the archetype is expressed in Saint Exupery's *Wind, Sand and Stars* where, on the one hand, "He who would travel happily must travel light," and on the other "We all yearn to escape from prison." Thus, the *puer* is usually unburdened by the conventional baggage (in every sense) and can thereby reach heights of vision, insight, or ecstasy denied to "the plodders." Not surprisingly, good artists are usually working from the "eternal youth" side of themselves, which knows how to travel light. But at the same time, there is the danger of perceiving the mundane world, daily life, earthy groundedness, and even the body itself as a prison from which one yearns to escape.

The necessity of being grounded in the body as the balance for high-flying is precisely what troubles the typical *puer*. Reconciling the highs and lows, flight and ground, "the sacred and the profane," is the challenge in this archetypal pattern. As Robert Bly says (commenting on his own career as a "flying boy" poet), "Changing the diapers brought me down" to earth. For the *puer*, the impulse is to "stay up" all the time, like the Lost Boys led by Peter Pan who don't know how to take care of daily routine (like eating and sleeping) until "the Wendy" arrives to play surrogate mother.

Turn-of-the-century author J.M. Barrie thus provides a clue to the neurotic form of the archetype as it functions in a patriarchal culture: women are stereotypically supposed to supply the earthy grounding (like Wendy) for the high-flying *puer* who, as the bumper sticker says, "would rather be hang-gliding." The work of men's groups is important in helping men to ground themselves and each other, rather than to rely on women to try to do this for them — since it rarely works.

The perennial popularity of *Peter Pan* throughout this century (the play recently finished yet another successful run in Toronto) indicates the centrality of "the flying boy" in our cultural zeitgeist. But I would argue that the *puer* is caught in those false dichotomies that characterize Western patriarchy — mind

v. body, spirit v. matter, sacred v. profane — with the first term in each "opposition" scripted in our society to triumph over the other. Although the Jungians don't say this, I will: the extreme expression of the puer archetype is the space dork — the technophilic "flying boy" (completely at home in British Columbia novelist William Gibson's cyberspace) whose dream is to soar off and colonize space.

As the predominant archetype of Western patriarchy, the neurotic puer advanced into techno-think by the turn of this century, which began with both *Peter Pan* and the success of the Wright Brothers. It went on to deify flyers like Billy Bishop, Charles Lindberg, Amelia Earhart and will likely end with a permanent lunar base for even further Dorky exploits.

On 20 July 1989, President Bush (an aging "plodder" who wishes he were a puer) voiced his support for such a project in his speech commemorating the twentieth anniversary of The Boot on the Moon. Soon afterwards, the Canadian feds expressed their space dork complicity by giving massive financial injections to the aerospace industry. By March 1990, *Scientific American* was providing details of the plans to mine the moon and also set up observatories there, for which the April 24 Shuttle "Discovery" blastoff was the next necessary step.

But the ultimate living space dork is probably Marvin Minsky, founding father of artificial intelligence (AI) at the Massachusetts Institute of Technology. Minsky has influenced many space dorks, instilling the belief not only that planet earth is passé, but that the ultimate human goal is to download the human brain into a computerized robot that will live forever and make wonderful journeys into the farthest reaches of outer space. "I think it would be a great thing to do," says Minsky. "I think people will get fed up with bodies after a while."

Thus, the problem with space dork patriarchy is that it has completely "concretized" its high-flying puer impulse: pouring trillions of dollars into a space program that is a tragically literal-minded expression of the archetype by which it is possessed. By contrast, we need only consider the fate of the earth during the same historical period: treated as a sewer, a toxic dump, mere "resources" for the greater patriarchal goal of, in *Scientific American*'s words, "embarking on more ambitious and challenging manned missions, such as those to Mars." But Robert Bly's work suggests the really challenging mission for our space dorks would be to do something simple and mundane, something respectful of embodied daily life — like changing the diapers.

Which gets us back to that planetary mandala, that ubiquitous Earth Flag logo, that $28 billion photograph said to signify "a turning point in the history of humanity." Taken from the astronautical perspective miles from earth, it shows us where we're at as a culture; spaced-out, in orbit, ungrounded, virtually disembodied, lost, and flying like that puer Peter Pan, who has a horror of growing up. Paradoxically, growing up can only be done by growing down; reconnecting to the planet, to the body, to the space-time of the divine human animal; respectful of limits and of those not-to-be-discounted but lesser flights of the embodied soul.

Thus, the photograph of planet earth illustrates the choice we're all being asked to make in our time. We can continue to soar off into never-never land (which is where the space dorks of every First World country want to go, though they may call it Mars or Venus) — a goal that is wasting the planet daily. Or we can return to earth where we started and get to know it for the first time; a pretty blue-green planet (now much the worse for wear) trying to make it through the latest round of Space Dork millennium fever.

20
David Olive

CONRAD BLACK: WRIT LARGE

I CANNOT claim as much experience in the field of journalism as Conrad Black. When Mr. Black, forty-six, made his journalistic debut as the twenty-one-year-old editor of the Eastern Townships Advertiser in Quebec, I was in the fourth grade. And yet, after only ten years or so as a journalist, I have accumulated a significant number of regrets. One of these has to do with an incident in 1987, when, at my insistent request, editors at *The Globe and Mail* reluctantly asked Conrad Black, then a columnist appearing in The Globe's *Report on Business Magazine*, to retreat from certain unflattering remarks about my work in his critique of an article I had written for the same magazine about Toronto's Reichmann family.

As a consequence, Mr. Black did reflect on my "snide and mean-spirited denigration of success," but stripped his review of its assertion that I had mounted an "almost incoherently hostile" attack on the developer family, in which "only Franz Kafka's famous charge of 'nameless crimes' was withheld." My supreme regret lingering from this episode is not the missed opportunity to have my name linked in print with Franz Kafka, but rather a belated recognition that I had failed to grasp a cardinal rule of journalism — namely, that when you dish it out, you have to be prepared to accept treatment in kind.

Three years later, Mr. Black has similarly failed to acknowledge that journalism is not a profession for the thin-skinned. He is, as he himself wrote in a letter to *The Globe*, "currently the plaintiff in seven defamation law suits against Toronto defendants" — two involving *The Globe*. In a suit launched within the last two weeks, Mr. Black seeks to have Ron Graham's book, *God's Dominion*, removed from sale. (The publisher, McClelland & Stewart, has vowed it will continue to sell the book.) Last year, Mr. Black sued author Ann Finlayson over a reference to him in her book about pensions. That suit was dropped after Ms Finlayson's publisher, Penguin Books Canada, apologized and agreed to destroy the inventory of remaining hardcover copies.

Two issues arise from this state of affairs. One is the scourge of so-called libel chill, a type of censorship in which personalities known to be litigious are simply not written about for fear of attracting the aggravation of a legal debacle. I will not deal with that issue, partly because it seems to me, despite a handful of high-profile cases, that the curse of libel chill has not taken on epidemic proportions. Mr. Black is something of a one-man phenomenon and is blessed with prodigious energies. Abraham Lincoln remarked during the Civil War that, "If I were to try to read, much less answer, all the attacks made on me, this shop might as well be closed for business." Mr. Black finds the time to read, to answer, and to attend to his other business.

My interest is limited to the journalistic principle that fair comment is a two-way street. Mr. Black should be most concerned about this prime tenet of the profession, since he has long invited us to take him seriously as a journalist.

To a degree unprecedented among major business figures, Mr. Black has obtained a variety of media platforms to disseminate his views. These views are impressive in their breadth, taking in everything from economic policy to abortion, and from constitutional reform to the performance of the Toronto Blue Jays. During the last several years, Mr. Black has rarely been off the public stage. And as a former contributor to The Globe's business magazine, to *The Financial Post* and other publications, he has asked for, and been paid, the going rate for his observations.

Notwithstanding the pressure that attends his responsibilities as an international press lord with more than 1,500 journalists in his employ, journalist Black does not absent-mindedly dash off his contributions. As befits the author of a history of Maurice Duplessis that was acclaimed for its depth of research, Mr. Black is a careful writer. He also, like many journalists who strive to be effective in conveying a point of view, writes with the intent to be provocative. And in so doing, he has often turned to the same techniques and devices he deems offensive when they are employed against him.

I find it curious, when I dip into the Black *oeuvre*, that the subjects of his commentaries have not initiated legal challenges to his credibility in making public judgments of them. Perhaps they have had a higher respect for the principle of fair comment than I did on that notable occasion. Or, they may have concluded that the attack on their character and capabilities simply "consisted of misinformed comment from a familiar source, uttered with the conviction that self-righteous ignorance alone can impart" — to borrow a description Mr. Black once applied to *The Toronto Star*'s editorial board.

Rather than single out an individual for criticism — a practice that is fraught with the potential for dangerous consequences — Mr. Black has engaged often in the technique of attacking the group. Thus, he has been able to write that much of the British Commonwealth, which has dared express shared condemnation of South Africa's system of apartheid, is itself "a ragbag of petty tyrannies and receiverships." Lest anyone think the business community is safe from his critical eye, Mr. Black asserts, without singling out any executives by name, that "gluttonous companies like Inco so abused their market dominance that they made economical the development of vast alternate sources all around the world, transforming themselves into marginal and often money-losing producers." And should anyone speculate about Mr. Black's role in the money-losing ways of the Dominion Stores grocery chain while it was under his control, he writes, again without naming names, that the firm "was run by an inbred, furtive, overconfident and, in some cases, disingenuous management."

While charitably disposed toward Ed Broadbent (a "fundamentally pleasant and intelligent man"), Mr. Black has been disappointed by the "purblindness and sclerosis of the New Democrats (whose claim to being Democratic is tenuous and who certainly should give up the pretense of being New 26 years after their party was founded)." The NDP's failings pale in comparison with the "continued dishonesty, cowardice and mediocrity of the leading liberal Democrats" in the U.S.

By now the reader may be wondering what Mr. Black can summon by way of court-worthy evidence to support any suggestion that Mario Cuomo, to pick one leading liberal Democrat, is dishonest, mediocre, and a coward; that any specific executive of Inco led the firm down the path to gluttony; or that the NDP is any less democratic than the other parties.

The reader can go on wondering, because evidence is not required. As Mr. Black knows, the rules of fair comment do not insist that a truckload of corroborating documents be kept ready to back every assertion a columnist may advance. And Mr. Black plays by the rules.

When Mr. Black directs his fire at individuals, he tends to concentrate on public figures who, journalistic tradition dictates, are fair game for the most searching observations. Often these individuals live in remote localities, where Mr. Black's *oeuvre* has not yet found widespread distribution. Thus, Muammar Gadaffi is "a deranged thug"; Julius Nyerere of Tanzania is "one of the world's most economically unsuccessful leaders"; and Lynden Pindling "has personally pillaged the Bahamas for 20 years." Closer to home, the judgments tend to soften. In a 1987 column in which he identified Michael Cassidy as one of the MPS who had heckled Ronald Reagan during the president's appearance in Parliament (Mr. Cassidy later wrote to say he had not been one of the hecklers), Mr. Black described the former Ottawa-area MP as "long among the most nauseating people in Canadian public life." And regarding a particular poem with an anti-American theme, Margaret Atwood has written "drivel," which suggests to Mr. Black that the Booker Prize nominee and her ilk "must not be allowed to speak for Canadian culture on so important an issue as [free trade]."

Just to confuse things, Mr. Black goes after one of his friends, writing that trust company owner Hal Jackman is among the "mischievous fear-mongering prophets of doom" who fret unduly about a possible collapse of the financial system. To confuse things further, Mr. Black sometimes bunches names together, like so many fellow-travellers, so that it is not clear exactly whom he intends for us to abhor, and for what: "Teddy Kennedy proved, at Chappaquiddick in 1969, to be a role model for Geraldine Ferraro, Gary Hart and Joe Biden. It is galling to see such mendacious hypocrites as Kennedy and Biden, ... etc." Finally, there are those individuals whom Mr. Black does not himself condemn, but that the People in their multitudes, Mr. Black has discovered, apparently do: "[Marc] Lalonde, in the minds of millions, was the incarnation of the arrogance, intellectual corruption, and incompetence of the late Trudeau era."

Blammo!

Intellectually corrupt! Mendacious! Pillager of countries, author of drivel! Could these accusations hold up in court?

In case you don't have a dictionary handy, mendacious behavior, while commonly taken to be synonymous with lying, is defined by Webster's ninth New Collegiate Dictionary as follows: "Given to or characterized by deception or falsehood *which often is not intended to genuinely mislead or delude*." (My italics.) Nothing about lying there. Mr. Black is, as I said, a careful writer.

I cannot quote the texts that have offended Mr. Black, for that would be to put the match to another legal round. But I can't help wondering if less scandalous words and phrases than those above have been quoted in the writs borne by Mr.

Black's process servers. And yet Mr. Black is a public figure: a global press baron; a former business colleague of the Prime Minister; and, at his annual Hollinger dinners, host to Margaret Thatcher, Elvio DelZotto, Emmett Cardinal Carter, the Reichmanns, Barbara Frum, Henry Kissinger, and the editor-in-chief of *The Globe*. (Alas, William F. Buckley Jr. was obliged last year to send his regrets.)

As for legitimacy, the argument cannot be sustained that Mr. Black, with many of his newspapers located in the U.S., was laboring under his own bias no less than was Ms Atwood, and therefore should not have been permitted to speak for the entire business community on the issue of free trade. That would have been undemocratic, as I think even the New Democrats would agree. (Although perhaps not so the potato king Harrison McCain, who vigorously campaigned against the deal.)

I have not meant to suggest that Mr. Black never veers from literary subterfuge, for sometimes he has been quite direct.

And gratuitous.

Mr. Black once conceded that Stephen Lewis's scorn for the Soviets over their occupation of Afghanistan during his tenure as Canada's ambassador to the United Nations was "uplifting," but then advanced the quaint notion that one partner in a marriage is responsible for the other's conduct: "If only [Lewis] could now persuade his columnist wife, Michele Landsberg, to moderate her pathologically anti-American ravings in *The Globe and Mail.*"

The word pathological, of course, conjures up the image of disease, and ravings suggests a form of madness. Which might lead the hurried reader, the reader who has not met the woman or read her work, to conclude that possibly Ms Landsberg is, or should be, wholly unemployable as a journalist. And, for that matter, not to be trusted with children. It would be most difficult even for Mr. Black, who is trained in the law, to make such a suggestion stick in court. But, of course, this is not his intent. He is having fun with the language, that is all. He is being provocative. Playing by the rules of fair comment.

I have noted that Mr. Black has a special interest in size, that is, in the physical proportions of the people he writes about. Thus, he wrote several years ago that the historian Ramsay Cook, who proffered a negative review of the Duplessis book, is a "slanted, supercilious little twit." The former British Columbia premier Dave Barrett he describes as "a fat silly social worker." And the journalist, Linda McQuaig, who broke the Patti Starr scandal, he labels "a weedy and not very bright leftist reporter."

It is a brave person who dares to gaze on one of Mr. Black's caricature drawings and point out an imperfectly drawn line. When former *Globe* managing editor Geoffrey Stevens, now a columnist at *The Toronto Star*, troubled to enumerate Ms McQuaig's journalistic credentials, Mr. Black hauled out his biggest guns, suggesting in the *Star*'s letters page that (a) Mr. Stevens condones defamatory journalism, and (b) that this may have had something to do with his departure from *The Globe* last year.

By the same imaginative stretch of conjecture and speculation, I might observe that Mr. Black no longer stands atop a diversified multibillion-dollar conglomerate (the Argus Corp. in a form that might be recognizable to its cofounder E.P. Taylor) because he did not know how to run one, lacked enthusiasm for doing so, or saw more financial advantage in selling off the empire piece by piece than keeping it intact. From the following passage taken from one of his 1986 columns in the *Report on Business Magazine*, I might conclude that Mr. Black has not always been entirely candid in his dealings: "I made a number of belligerent noises about rebuilding and recapitalizing [Dominion], while in fact beating the bushes for possible buyers." Adding to my impressions of Mr. Black, I can record, having met him, that he is a larger man than most. And I know also that as a student he was asked to leave Upper Canada College over a breach of discipline.

So armed, I might preface a thorough consideration of Mr. Black's views on abortion, constitutional changes, and the quality of the Blue Jays' coaching staff, with the observation that he is a fat man who was kicked out of one of the country's most prestigious prep schools, has on one notable occasion said one thing while doing another, and presided over the dismantling of one of Canada's legendary conglomerates.

I could write that, but it would probably be gratuitous, and, more to the point, irrelevant. I take Mr. Black as he is. If he advocates a tough stand against Quebec nationalists, or campaigns for progressive reforms to Ontario's social welfare system, I shall assess his argument on its merits, and not distract the reader by raising the extraneous matter of his wife's recent decision to change her name (in order, it is rumored, to somehow enhance Mr. Black's chances of obtaining a British peerage).

Some things are relevant, some not. Peter C. Newman, his biographer, thought it relevant to quote Mr. Black on his reaction to the abrupt departure from UCC, which took place after Mr. Black and two others gained access to the principal's office, reproduced copies of questions on the year's final exam, and sold these to other students. "I left Upper Canada on June 9, 1959," Mr. Black told Mr. Newman, "and as I was walking out the gates a number of students who literally twenty-four hours before had been begging for assistance — one of them on his knees — were now shaking their fists and shouting words of moralistic execration after me. I've never forgotten how cowardly and greedy people can be."

From an early age, Mr. Black has not suffered easily the occasions when his conduct has been critically appraised. This indicates that he is human. Exhibiting a tendency that is common in the general population, he might abjure introspection, and instead commence the search for external factors.

Bob Rae, when he was leader of the Ontario NDP in opposition at Queen's Park, once called Mr. Black "the most symbolic representative of bloated capitalism at its worst." If you take that sentence apart and analyze it, you find that each word in isolation offers only the most oblique character description. But, of course, the statement had its intended effect. Perhaps not by coincidence, it benefited from a rhetorical symmetry to Mr. Black's own favored style of expression.

Mr. Black did not shrink from this moment of dark celebrity. He devoted one of his columns to a spirited and convincing defence of his conduct in the controversy that had prompted Mr. Rae's remark, the deployment of Dominion Stores' pension funds. He could have left Mr. Rae out of it. Instead, Mr. Black reprinted the offending words spoken by the NDP leader — who operates outside the ambit of Mr. Black's libel team — and attempted to turn the moral tables on his accuser, complaining about "Bob Rae's abuse of his parliamentary immunity to defame me, which the press duly reported without a peep of disapprobation."

As the Duchess of Windsor held that one could never be too rich or too thin, Mr. Black is convinced that one can never protest too much.

Having made clear his own disapprobation of the press (the "swarming, grunting masses of jackals" is only his latest and most succinct dismissal of the news media), Mr. Black manages surprise when the press does not busy itself keeping his reputation in good repair. And to forget, perhaps, that *The Globe* once celebrated him as the "*Report on Business* Man of the Year: Youthful president of Argus has compiled an impressive record"; and that *Toronto Life*, which now struggles under the dead weight of a massive lawsuit brought against it by the Reichmanns, once described him as a "man of cultivation and manners, extraordinary intelligence and a subtle spirit of isolation." Of course, that was in the late 1970s. The press and Mr. Black have since made each other's more thorough acquaintance.

It is Mr. Black's peculiar misfortune to be wealthy, the proprietor of scores of newspapers and magazines and a skilled polemicist. He is mightily capable, and widely known to be capable, of providing his own best defence. That he has, so often of late, chosen to do this by placing a phone call to his lawyers rather than putting his thoughts on paper indicates that he does not understand, as I do now, how wrong it is to recoil — except in that blunt moment of reading the words for the first time — from an expression such as "almost incoherently hostile." That he can dish it out, but he cannot take it. That, finally, he no longer wishes to be taken seriously as a journalist.

Thus may Mr. Black yet drift into obscurity, not writing and not being written about. And so leave unanswered the questions we soon enough shall lose interest in — namely, is Conrad Black a man of towering accomplishment, or a conspicuous underachiever? Is he a rhetorician of the first rank, or, as Gore Vidal said of William Buckley, "a mere entertainer with a gift for mischief"?

In the course of such events does the list of the world's great unsolved mysteries grow unnecessarily longer.

21
Stephen Phelps

BE STILL, MY TEENY-BOPPER HEART: MUSINGS ON THE UNDULATING SEE OF MUSIC VIDEO

OF course, no one should be watching TV at the crack of dawn anyway. And if — out of guilt, ennui, lack of imagination, or masochism — one happens to be doing just that, it certainly shouldn't be the cable rock network, MuchMusic. Rock with dew on it is unbearable. Morning is a time for Vivaldi, for birdsong, rustling leaves and the rest of nature's primordial symphony, not power chords and wailing steel guitar licks.

Nonetheless, there I was, hunkering down to a restless day-long sprawl in front of rock's wildly successful electronic proscenium, determined to flush out the elusive romantic muse rumored to be dead or in hiding since the advent of videos.

Two bars into the opening bridge of a heavy metal video I can feel the caffeine starting to kick in. L.A. Guns is not a band that minces words. With an obvious taste for schoolgirls, the group's front-man is every father's nightmare. A picture of pale, dissipated outlawry, he waxes and wails above the shattering metallic twang: "It's seven o'clock / And time for a party / She's just a sweet little thing / But I like the way she dances / And I know what I like."

The video is intercut with peep-hole shots of an agitated coquette in front of a full-length mirror, feverishly preening for the big night. The footage is volcanic, dark and hot, swathed in sultry shadows, every frame adroitly choreographed, every pan and zoom perfectly paced to the music's undulating hard-core beat. I search in vain for signs of the amorous muse. For all its artistry and sneering eroticism, the video has a muddled message, verging on the footling vapidity of soft-core porn. What we have here is not exactly a love song, not quite sex, but a soiled daydream, a psycho-sexual fantasy in a humid vault, erotic catatonia in a detox clinic.

A live interview with the aforementioned outlaws in MuchMusic's Toronto headquarters sheds a glimmer of light on the band's goatish philosophy. I paraphrase: Life's a bitch. You are born. You die. In the meantime, there's always time to "put the moves on." It's a simple, hot-blooded creed, typical of today's heavy metal sybarite, and *de rigueur* for any mousse and mascara outsider seriously intent on cashing in on parental outrage.

A female interviewer delineates why the rakish band speaks to her more cogently than its gunslinging peers — Young Guns and Guns & Roses. As the studio camera pans the lead singer's face, the eyes, previously as opaque as limo glass, suddenly glitter and fizz. "Let's not kid ourselves, it's all about sex," he sniggers, nudging his host in a puckish come-one. The gesture leaves his interviewer breathless, her petite frame writhing momentarily in the same hormonal sea that has populated the earth since Circe came unto Ulysses. Be still, my teeny-bopper heart.

In between the video plugs, the anecdotage and the wisecracking *bonhomie* are the endless commercials tramping like an army over one's optic nerves. Camp, hype, kitsch, glamor, glitz — all of pop culture's altitudes, low to high — slide by like some kid's practice scales. Brand-name perfumes, cars, deodorants, bath salts, and beer — it's a catering caravan for the teen consumer. Swanky girls and jinking pretty boys model the latest Nike footwear and Sony headsets, invariably engaged in those all-Canadian passions — hang gliding, water skiing, and scuba diving.

Shrugging off the assault, and still pining for an honest chord in this monotonous toytown of Madison Avenue hustle, hit music and Animal House high jinks, I have to ask myself, what are the images really spelling? My first guess is that the subtext here is commodification — commodification of desire, dream, fantasy, love.

I may be stating the obvious. Wiser critics than I have lambasted the sorry state of rock since it went video. It's all corporate rock now, they say, a perfect sales culture finally coming to terms with its own bottom line. And it's some bottom line. After all, the ratings speak for themselves. Five million viewers tune into Canada's rock station every day; its American counterpart boasts a daily audience of 45 million. In the process, these networks have made truckloads of money — for themselves, the recording industry, and those artists fortunate enough to make their playlists. So, maybe I ought to get with the program?

Easier said than done.

At the risk of sounding like a spoilsport, the shame is that I hung in as long as I did. I say this because at one time I was pretty deep into music and what it had to say. It was rock that rousted me out of my adolescence. It stormed my white suburban cradle on cast-iron feet, spreading pandemonium and throwing open emotional windows at a time when convention demanded a guarded attitude in matters of the heart. It was the buttoned-down sixties, and 'cool' was still the operative word, combining as it did those virtues most highly prized at the time: sex appeal and integrity. Love, the L-word, was rarely mentioned in mixed company.

It would require a ridiculously convoluted psychoanalysis to untangle the web of motives that insisted on such a tight-lipped attitude. Suffice to say, it was the British rock invasion that blew the lid off this retentive mindset — significantly the early hurtin' songs of the Animals and the Rolling Stones. Their plaintive, soul-searching tunes were hardly original; basically, we're talking updated Muddy Waters and B.B. King. But the heartbeat was timeless, not to mention ameliorative. Songs like "Heart of Stone" and "Going Back to Walker" were tender salves for adolescent angst, cool compresses for the inevitable bruises and scratches sustained in an unending psychodrama of break-ups and brush-offs.

Identification with this music was an erotic emotional response to powerlessness, an expression of panic in the face of what lay ahead. Who knew what permutations, what hairpin curves, what torments, lay in store — jealousy, nastiness, pain, rejection. Enough of my friends had come from broken homes to be impressed by the despairing odds. You bet one number — security, warmth, affection, trust, rapport — and one time in a thousand it turned up.

Living under such a cloud, the record room was your sanctum and your asylum. Solace was automatic, summoned by the simple act of slapping an LP on the turntable. The lyrics were sacramental, instantly responsive, a blank slate for every fantasy you could muster. The images that interposed themselves into this communion were invariably your own. The record jacket told you all you wanted to know about the artist. Listener loyalty was not sustained by telegenic appeal. Influences rose and fell, depending on the degree of cosmic sympathy or coincidence the songwriter's message exerted on your being or mood that particular week. Whenever a new release was on the turntable, that platter was on trial. Genial despots, we listened, passed judgment. Failure to deliver the requisite soul resulted in that record's being ripped from the turntable and traded in. No laurels could be rested on. Shifts in the pantheon were volatile. I was witness to the day the Stones's entire *oeuvre* was banished from a friend's collection, for no other reason than the band had strayed into commercially hot acid rock. Other bands too would be culled from his collection for pandering to showbiz.

If my friend has stayed true to his manic standards, I'd hazard he's no longer buying records today. It's just as well. After all, it's finally all about packaging. I expect he would not be able to relate to today's rock fan. Consider that rock's new consumers have grown up in front of a twenty-one-inch screen, wearing headphones, and having their attention spans compromised by thirty-second spots. Feelings and thinking are now a priori abstract, something to be fast forwarded or reduced to snappy, digestible bites.

I'm not suggesting that the marriage of rock and TV hasn't been an exciting alliance, just a barren one. Granted, video technology has given rock something it never had before: a caring and altruistic face. Superstar concerts for the homeless and the starving are now routinely bounced around the globe via satellite, with the proceeds going to needy organizations the world over. But it must be noted that those same humanitarian headliners inevitably head back to their mansions, home to their sultan perks, in limos whose interior appointments would probably pay for the medical relief of entire villages in Guatemala.

And if the same technology has made possible a kind of musical ecumenicism, an unprecedented infusion of Third World influences from Africa, South America, and Asia, the coupling of rock and television has also made thin gruel of a potentially rich stew. The reason is simple enough. There is no fame today without having first passed muster on the tube. And though television's reach is immense, scheduling constraints and bottom-line considerations have stacked the deck against experimentation. I have no doubt Hendrix, Morrison, and

Joplin are turning in their graves at the tube's growing hegemony over musical expression.

Still, rock TV's ascendency over the charts has not exactly gone unchallenged by the old guard. My favorite confrontation, recorded by an interviewer with *Rolling Stone* magazine, has Gene Simmons, formerly of Kiss, storming the offices of the American rock network, MTV. Wearing a pair of knee pads, heavy metal's oldest bad boy reportedly accosted a senior network honcho and demanded, "Who do I have to blow to get my video played?" A priceless piece of theater, but only a footnote. Alas, in a lost cause.

TV's chokehold on the record industry continues unabated, with obvious ramifications for the record industry and the consumer. Competition among record labels is fiercer than ever and, as a result of this competition and the profits that go with exposure, labels won't sign an act that is not video friendly. For the same reason, record producers, heeding television's prudish vetoes and provisos, tend to look coolly on controversial or problematic material. Record executives are told at the outset to mind their Ps and Qs. American MTV, for example, now requires record companies to include a copy of lyrics with every video submitted for consideration — a cautionary measure, say network honchos, that serves to head off potentially offensive references to drugs and sex.

The latter is an especially sensitive area these days, thanks to the ambiance of AIDS. After a twenty-year wallow in pill-protected, no-fault lubricity, sex is once again being associated with sin, danger, and consciousness of death. Today's rock fare bears bald testimony to this apocalyptic mindset. Suitably demonized, sex is something most recording artists now approach with a ten-foot pole. Fear has also polarized the subject of romance, squeezing out of the picture both the rueful and the rhapsodic while leaving the field almost exclusively to confection and smut. Thus, on the one hand, you have the extraordinary success of those marvels of cadence and crudity, 2-Live Crew, four rappers whose nasty couplets are currently at the center of an obscenity witch hunt. Likewise you have the voodoo sex of Satanic heavy metal — another legacy of the emergent puritanism presently mired in court battles. At the other extreme, you have the candy rock fluff chart-busters like New Kids on the Block and Milli Vanilli — artists who have a lot to say about puppy love, but nothing about adult love's formidable terrors, travails and joys.

Now, I realize that bitching about the state of contemporary rock and its lack of range and honesty, and railing against the consumer product it has become, sounds like the last stand of a curmudgeonly aesthete. But putting in a full day in front of the flickering circus called MuchMusic, I am reminded just how alienated I've become from rock since it went video. I came away from the experience a little worse for wear, with nary a glimpse of the romantic muse, and only these truths to show: For all its flash and eclecticism, video rock has a tin ear for poignancy. Anyone looking to be rocketed to new heights of romantic awareness might as well break out their old LPs and settle for a dusty cab ride down memory lane.

22
Jane Rule

DECEPTION IN SEARCH OF THE TRUTH

EARLY in my writing life, I wrote a story called "A Walk by Himself" about a boy in his first year at college, recorded it on tape and sent it to CBC's *Anthology*. The story was rejected because the editors admitted a frank bias against autobiographical material. I was very angry at both such a bias and their assumption that the piece was autobiographical. I should probably have been flattered that the story was convincing enough to a staff of male editors for them to make that mistake. At the time, having the story accepted would have done more for my confidence.

Their error was also encouraged by the depth of my voice, a property I did not gain as boys do at puberty but have had since I began to speak. I am always mistaken for a man on the phone, an embarrassment I have learned to turn to my advantage when I can. I have discovered that when I need advice, I should pitch my voice unnaturally high, or my ignorance will be treated with impatience and even contempt. When I want to lodge a complaint, give advice or an order, I speak in my normal voice and receive a prompt, "Yes sir." But I still feel uncomfortably split when I am, say, making plane reservations for myself and get the question, "And where can she be reached?" I feel like my own doting father managing the hard details of the public world for me.

Over the years, by this means, I have learned a lot about socially constructed expectations of gender, how little they really have to do with who people are, what they are capable of and what they need. As a writer of fiction, my job is to understand as much as I can of social constructions of all sorts, the ways they inhibit, distort, and to varying degrees shape the much more complex and individual creatures who try to lead their own lives.

For women writers gender has been an issue not only inside our texts but on their covers. Even today in genres like the murder mystery women write under male pseudonyms in order to reach a male audience. A bookseller I know delights in offering men who ask specifically for male authors of mysteries women authors in that disguise. We still suffer from a large group of readers who automatically take us less seriously because of our gender. Fewer of us now go the route of George Eliot, and most of us no longer take satirical swipes at our own craft, Jane Austen's defense. We are learning to take ourselves seriously, which is by definition a gender disturbance in women.

The issues of gender inside our texts seems to me both less important and more complex than recent debates about authenticity of voice might suggest. The vast majority of us have been marginalized by gender, class and/or race. Our first attempts to break our silence are bound to include defensive strategies. Most of my earliest stories were written from a male point of view because I wanted my characters to be taken seriously. They are not very convincing stories, not because I was incapable of writing from a male point of view but because I chose that point of view for the wrong reason. James Baldwin made his main character in *Giovanni's Room* self-consciously white as well as homosexual. The difficulty here is not Baldwin's inability to present the view of a white man but his need to assert that whiteness against the reader's assumption that Baldwin's characters will be Black because he is. His choice of whiteness may also have come from defensiveness about his own homosexuality.

The choice of point of view should be dictated by the needs of the narrative, not by the assumptions of the audience or the defensiveness of the writer. Good writing does not serve cultural biases though it may often illuminate them. Good writing does not protect anyone, not even the writer.

There is no woman's point of view instantly recognized as automatically female. In *My Name Is Mary Donne*, Brian Moore's main female character seems to me self-consciously preoccupied with her menstrual periods. I'm sure there are some women who are, but that is not Moore's point. He simply wants to be sure she sounds like a woman. Both men and women have written about women convincingly without concern for their menstrual cycles. On the far side of adolescence most people take their primary and secondary sexual characteristics for granted. Authenticity is about a thousand other things, all chosen for the insight they bring to a character.

It is a peculiarity of contemporary Canadian women writers that the vast majority are mothers. Our foremothers were mainly not mothers and therefore probably in the eyes of their society not successful examples of their sex. Even mothers don't automatically qualify. Most of ours are divorced. I myself am a lesbian. How can any one of us claim to speak for women, unless we are taken in by the deception of gender?

As writers, it is not our job to represent our sex, though in the course of our careers we will probably be called upon to create a number of female characters. If any one of them can be judged "typically female," we'll know in that instance we have failed to serve our own humanity unless, of course, we're writing farce.

The ability to create a range of characters is one of the requirements for a writer of fiction. Each of us draws on our own experience, sometimes quite directly, much more often by such circuitous and subterranean ways, neither reader nor writer could uncover the connection. Authenticity cannot, therefore, be judged by the identity or experience of the writer. It can only be tested in the work itself.

I have been asked how I can write realistically about children when I have none of my own. I was a child. I have also spent more time with children than many people do because I like having them around me for what they teach me not only about childhood but about language and politics.

I have been asked how I can write about old people when I'm not yet sixty myself. Like children, the old are not segregated in my mind or my life. My grandparents and even my great-grandparents were very real to me. I have always had close friends much older than I. I have also had arthritis since I was in my early forties and have had to come to terms early with physical limitation.

I have been asked how I could possibly write from the point of view of a heterosexual man. I grew up with a father and brother. I have worked with men in my professional life and have close male friends. I am, like them, attracted to women.

In the course of writing a dozen books, I have included all kinds of characters, male and female, gay and straight, American, Canadian, English, Japanese, Black and white, one-armed, working class, upper middle class, and they've had a wide variety of jobs and a great range of personal experiences. In each instance, if I am asked how I can write about being a Black draft dodger or an electronic music composer or a father, there are explanations within my own experience, connections and affinities.

Offering personal credentials, however, doesn't really explain why characters seem believable. A character has to have a magnetic core which attracts detail of all kinds, and out of that rich rubble comes the material by which a writer shapes and moves the character. Only some of those details can be traced. Many of them have been attracted from the subconscious or magpie consciousness of the writer.

Characters in fiction are not real people any more than photographs are real people. A believable or authentic character is a plausible composition made out of words. A writer doesn't have to become a character in the sense that an actor does, whose body is as important as the dialogue for creating the image. But even with the enormous limitations of one's own body, a good actor can present a surprising range of characters, even, in the skin of one, age twenty years in an hour. We know it's not really happening, and perhaps the distinction between reality and art is clearer on the stage than in a novel. We know that asking an actor to play no one but herself would be denying her the basic point of her craft.

Deception is so much a part of acting that it is underlined to the delight of the audience. Gender deception, for instance, is the stuff of comedy. Long after boys were required to play women's parts on the Elizabethan stage, which invited ironic unmaskings of gender itself, actors have been challenged to play roles of the opposite sex. But rarely is deception the only point. There is something to be learned, a new insight to be gained.

Because in fiction a writer is usually invisible, it may be easier to confuse art with reality, to form suspicions about authenticity that have nothing to do with art.

By a willing suspension of disbelief, we allow ourselves to experience another's idea of reality. We must always be willing to risk that if we are to gain insight into who we are as individuals in our own culture. Misogynists are not necessarily telling lies about women when they express their genuine dislike. The same is true of racists and snobs. We'll not cure them of biases we don't approve of by silencing them, but we can help to cure the world of their power by expressing world views that are different from theirs. We must, however, claim the world as our own to do so, not be inhibited by any narrow view of what our authentic voices are. The first essay I ever wrote was the assignment, "I am part of all that I have met." I wrote for days and days. There was no end to it, nor should there be. It's an assignment I won't have completed even when I've written my last word.

Robertson Davies may write all he wants about lesbians as long as I may write all I want about men like Robertson Davies. We are both concerned, in our own ways, about gender disturbance. On the whole, I think it's a good thing. My characters, clothed in whatever gender, are deceptions in search of the truth.

23
Rick Salutin

BRIAN AND THE BOYS

*FUNCTIONALISM: a way of explaining behavior that pays no atten-
tion to what people say they are doing, or even what they think they
are doing, and concentrates instead on what they actually do. In functionalism, as in politics, motives don't matter; what count are effects.*

IT IS possible to discern, for the first
time since the Second World War, the existence of a Canadian ministry of propaganda. It's not surprising that the new ministry is not officially known by this
name. During the Second World War, Canada's ministry of propaganda was
called the Wartime Information Board. How much use would propaganda be if
everyone it was directed at realized it was propaganda?

The ministry was created through the common-law merger of *The Globe and
Mail* with the CBC, a process that has been gradual and consensual. A harbinger
was the weekly gum-flap on CBC's "Sunday Report," convened by Peter Mansbridge along with David Halton, CBC's "national correspondent," and *The
Globe*'s Ottawa columnist, Jeffrey Simpson. From the start in 1985, there was
something irritating and portentous about those sessions, as if these boys had
seen the future.

When CBC's "Newsworld" went on the air, *The Globe and Mail* provided
business reports. Together they have created a national polling system, a serious
sign of commitment in relationships of this sort. But what really cements the
connection and makes it a matter of propaganda is the main project on which
they have collaborated: support for the federal government's agenda.

It's unlikely any Liberal government, no matter how servile to business interests, could have moved *The Globe and Mail* to run lead editorials that read as if they'd been faxed from the latest cabinet meeting. For that to happen, the government actually had to change to suit *The Globe*. The CBC, on the other hand, had to change to suit the government.

This is less odd than it might seem. A lesson of the 1980s is that under conservative governments, public broadcasters can become even more pliant than private ones. For example, in the United States, PBS, once targeted by Nixonites, is now rated by the right-wing lobby, Accuracy In Media, as the most "balanced" — read grovelling — of the networks. The BBC has also ... *adjusted* under Thatcher. Since 1984 and the Tories, so has the CBC. It bore savage, disproportionate cuts with barely a whimper. It started the cheery business show "Venture." It hired a "business specialist," Der Hoi-Yin, who did respectful interviews with termites like Adnan Khashoggi. It found a "journalistic policy" in a reliquary somewhere, which it used to harass subversives like Dale Goldhawk, Roy Bonisteel, and David Suzuki.

For a long time, it looked like unappreciated submissiveness. As late as the spring of 1988, cabinet vetoed a CRTC decision granting the CBC an all-news channel, and the prime minister said, "Why? So they can hammer us twenty-four hours a day instead of two?" Now one never hears Tories snipe at the CBC. It makes you nostalgic; it's one of the few public agencies *not* on the block. Only Michael Walker of the Fraser Institute, like John the Baptist crying alone in the wilderness, still wails about privatizing the CBC.

It's important to understand the separate roles of the two bodies working together. In the heat of any political moment, the CBC may seem central, because it is immediate, visual, and extensive. But *The Globe* is essential. For *The Globe* is the source consulted by all other sources, including the CBC. Especially the CBC. CBC news and current-affairs staff troop to their posts across Canada each morning bearing copies of *The Globe* like government-issued weapons they have been trained to clean, load, and fire. Without their *Globe*s, they are nothing.

There has also been a spiritual symbiosis. Once, both *The Globe* and the CBC projected smug self-images, but they were also competing elites. Now it's hard to differentiate either the personnel of the institutions or the views they hold. They are as tough to distinguish as union and management reps on a typical labor-relations-board panel. Shuffle them and you'd never know who really works for whom.

The free-trade issue is a good case study, since the government had an explicit propaganda goal, leaked in a "communications strategy": the less information Canadians had, the better, since the more people knew, the more they'd oppose free trade. "Benign neglect" was the objective of the day.

The head of CBC English radio programming, Donna Logan, warned her staff to beware of manipulation by *opponents* of free trade, since they were "far better organized and more articulate" than its supporters, among whom were the federal government, much of the civil service, and most of the business world of Canada and the U.S. She demanded a computerized record proving "balance." Reporters and producers of sound mind tended simply to avoid the subject. CBC-TV even declined to attend a meeting about a national debate on free trade; at least Global and CTV showed up.

The CBC did cover the final weekend of free-trade negotiations in breathless style, a sort of warm-up for the week of Meech. "The Journal" ran a psychodrama masquerading as history, which seemed to ask the question, "Will a queasy character called Canada find the confidence to enter into a free-trade relationship with the United States?" During the election, correspondent Halton managed to ask the opening question of the candidates' debate on something *other* than free trade in a campaign in which free trade was the only issue.

But free trade was an odd case because the government's propaganda strategy carried a negative mandate: *avoid* this topic. And *The Globe*-CBC relationship hadn't been truly consummated. What's needed is a test with positive content. I propose the final phase of Meech:

THE MISSION: The government's down-the-stretch "communications strategy" for Meech amounted to selling the sizzle, not the steak. Polls showed a clear majority of Canadians opposed the accord, a genuine fact rarely mentioned in public. Pressure would have to come from somewhere else: fear of the consequences of rejecting the deal, never mind what's in it — and make it *really* scary. On June 1, the Prime Minister said, "What is really at stake is Canada." That day's *Globe* had a full-page ad sponsored by business, in letters even bigger than Jeffrey Simpson's byline: "CANADA'S FUTURE IS IN PERIL.... GET THE MEECH ACCORD IN PLACE.... YOU MUST NOT FAIL."

National Unity was hauled out of the closet where Pierre Trudeau had left it — though National Sovereignty continued to gather dust. (It was a neat way for a government that had free-traded away most of Canada to look as though they did so give a damn.) Enough panic and the hold-out premiers might collapse. But with Brian Mulroney's credibility, this kind of psychological terrorism needed more goosing than he could give it by himself.

THE BUILD: On May 23, one month to the deadline, CBC-TV ran three hours of anxiety on the subject. Barbara Frum eased in, "It's as if the fuse has been lit on a time bomb." Beside her stood Peter Mansbridge. "There's a widespread feeling that this is a decisive time, that the days ahead could be the most important we've ever lived through as a nation. Canada has endured for one hundred and twenty years but all of that is now on the line.... Can Canada work, or is Canada drifting apart?" It had the sonority of Walter Cronkite in his heyday ("All things are as they were then except — You Are There").

There was a grim segment called The Road to Deadlock ("The time of decision grows steadily closer") and lots of interviews with suits, mostly male. But the key was the questions put and context framed by the CBC; the guests and experts were furniture. "How much damage have we [sic] done to the future of this country?" said Frum. "Was there a dragon there sleeping?" Their assumptions were those of the government: the accord was about Quebec's demands and nothing else ("It *was* the Quebec round ...," said Frum); opposition was based solely on rejection of Quebec. There was no hint that Meech might not have been just a "Quebec round"; that Mulroney cut his deal by giving *every* province what Quebec requested, thereby undermining national institutions; or that antagonism towards Quebec surfaced only late in the debate. A segment near the end by reporter Kevin Newman posed some of these issues and vaguely contradicted the earlier assumptions. It must have confused viewers, if any were still thinking rationally.

"The National" followed, with more Meech crisis: men in suits going in and out of meetings with the prime minister. This was followed by At The Lodge on "The Journal," a documentary about seven ordinary Canadians brought together for a weekend. It was a welcome change: forty minutes of real people, no suits, and no intrusive interviewer or reporter. But the Newfoundlander referred to June 23 as "a doomsday machine that's gonna go off," in case we'd forgotten. And the show closed with the tears of a woman from Alberta, convinced that the separation of Quebec would follow from the failure of Meech, and the takeover of the rest of Canada by the U.S. would follow *that*. "Hell, we can't exist without you," she sobbed. "Don't force us to do what we don't want to do.... I don't want to be an American, I don't give a shit what anybody says." The others were crying too — anyone would. You could almost hear the producers say,

"Okay. Got it. That's a wrap."

As propaganda, it was soft-core. A week later came the hard-core follow-up: two complete "Journals" called In Search of Ourselves. The shows were ostensibly built around "conversations with eleven noted Canadians" — i.e., our betters — who, said host Brian Stewart, "believe their national may be in peril." But everything important was communicated through the host himself, his commentary, the photography, the editing, and above all the music.

Stewart, who prepped for this job by covering the Ethiopian famine, was perfect casting: gaunt, anxious, stressed-out. "Can you give us you own, very calm" appraisal, he asked the editor of *Le Devoir*, as though he were interviewing a hijacker on crack. Guests were shot against darkness, with perhaps a single source of light. The many bridging shots were haunting landscapes of a stagnant river, a wave-beaten coast, a lonely lighthouse, a city in fog, all photographed through filters to give the impression of perpetual twilight, plus repeated images of Canadians walking slow motion, perplexed and ghostly, through their cities' streets. The music was orchestral and mournful — lots of woodwinds and strings. In reaction shots, Stewart was fiddling with a pencil fretfully, or reinforcing negative comments ("There's a lot of cynicism" — cut to Stewart nodding).

His commentaries and summations were relentless: "A brooding sense of national doubt ... we are talking about the end of Canada as we know it ... a huge fatigue ... the nation is drifting out of control ... the ground always seems to be shifting ... Too much change can be numbing, it can depress and it can sour ... the mood is very bleak ... a people rudderless and uncertain, bobbing away none too happily on these national currents ... bitterness and self-doubt ... prone to easy despair" — all threaded among the filtered shots of twilit rivers and slo-mo crowds. The only figure presented as upbeat was Newfoundland painter Mary Pratt. ("In the arts everything is blossoming.... It's simply wonderful.") Stewart wouldn't even let Pratt's optimism sink under its own weightlessness. Over a shot of her working, he keened, "But after a decade of great stress, the canvas of Canada is so very much more complicated than ever before." In the days after these shows, I found a kind of surly, sour mood among those I ran into and I came to believe it was related to the inexorable gloom laid on by Stewart and his producers. People said so.

"We could lose it all," moaned Stewart at the end, ticking ominously like the crocodile who swallowed the clock in Peter Pan. "The land is coldly indifferent to our survival."

Allen Booth, who did the music, said he looked at the style of photography and thought immediately: "Twin Peaks." That's what we got. Who Killed Laura Canada? A figure, when you started to investigate, who turned out not so sweet and innocent as we'd thought. ("Maybe it's the real Canada beginning to show itself for the 1990s," said token left-winger Stephen Lewis in his interview. "Maybe this isn't a very nice country.")

Canada's first director of propaganda — whoops, wartime information — was John Grierson, a Scot who coined the term "documentary." He fought a long fight for the use of the word "propaganda" to describe his work, but late in life he admitted it had been a losing battle. Grierson's picture hangs prominently in the reception area of "The Journal" in Toronto.

MEECHWEEK: From June 3 to 9, the first ministers met in secret in Ottawa. There was no real news, so government leaks became a sort of news substitute. The government leaked in torrents — to *The Globe* and the CBC. The phrase "CBC news has managed to learn" became equivalent to "The government would like us to say."

They showed the premiers going into the room in the morning, to a martial air (*Dumdadum* — "The talks go on," said Mansbridge), and when they emerged at night, subjecting an already morbid nation to those mediocrities twice a day. It was like a walk into The Club: CBC's Don Newman acting as head waiter, showing them to choice tables, while Wendy Mesley took their dinner orders. Left leakless, the other networks tended to provide some real comment. "We have a form of executive federalism here," said Global's Doug Small. "Eleven white males meeting in secret deciding Canada's future." Meanwhile Mansbridge and Halton were dissecting "what the premiers have to do to make Meech work" or grimly muttering the week's password, FAILURE.

In the beginning, the premiers were supposed to have Sunday supper in private, then go to "public sessions" or simply give up. Monday came and they were still closeted. Word leaked that they would "go public" only if they had an agreement; in other words, the "public sessions" would be at most a press conference. Simpson of *The Globe* explained on CBC's "Midday" that open talks wouldn't work any better than the Treaty of Versailles did. Meanwhile, they also served who read the local news. "While politicians in Ottawa are working to save the Meech Lake accord," said CBC Toronto's Hilary Brown, "ordinary Canadians are working to save the country." You might have heard it on the Moscow evening news — in the old days.

Barbara Frum of "The Journal," for all her professionalism, has never developed the ability, or perhaps desire, to hide her biases. When she interviewed the week's designated villains — Premiers Filmon and Wells — she struck a tone rather different from the one she took with pro-deal premiers or, later, the PM. To Filmon: "I wish you'd help me understand what you just said. I heard you say it when you came out of the afternoon session. I don't know what it means." Filmon, who'd been clear if not profound, stumbled, unsure whether to repeat himself. "Go on," interrupted Frum. "Go on." To Wells: "Premier Wells, I guess if I sat and pumped the well, I wouldn't get very much with you."

Polls that week proved propaganda works. An Angus Reid/Southam News poll found only eleven percent of the population actually liked the accord, but fifty-five percent were ready to pass it to save the country. The strongest testimony came from Clyde Wells. Making the grand entry on Saturday, he said, "I felt so uncomfortable all week. I've been reluctantly agreeing to compromise against my stated principles ... and what's worse, I have great difficulty understanding how I could allow myself to be taken in and kept on that vortex without being able to get out of it." He sounded as disoriented as the woman from Alberta who broke down and wept At The Lodge. She and he were the two most plausible outcomes of *the build*.

THE BREAKDOWN: The "Sunday Report" on the day after the conference was a full-court smear of Clyde Wells, apparently the only obstacle left facing Meech. The recap of events the CBC had "managed to construct" was a tale of one bad boy ready to sabotage his country out of pique. "Premier Wells complained endlessly.... Premier Wells is enraged.... Wells's sense of grievance has not subsided." The Prime Minister came on to say a few conciliatory words. All Wells's buds among the premes were down on him. They felt "consternation" (Halton), "extremely annoyed" (Simpson), and "aghast" (Mesley). Was this, ahem, "inconsistent person" growing unhinged? "Some premiers" — unnamed — "worry that protracted talks and lack of sleep have left Wells emotionally distraught." (When criticized for this phrase, the Ottawa bureau chief for CBC television said, "Emotionally distraught does not convey emotionally unbalanced or insane." Tell it to the judge.) A *Globe* editorial the next day referred to Wells's — ahem — "public ambiguity." For an hour that night there wasn't much — except the Bulgarian election — besides Wells-baiting. Over on CTV, Pamela Wallin was comparatively serene. "There's a feeling in Newfoundland that the debate is only beginning," she said calmly.

CBC news also squeezed in a rare mention of doubts held by women, natives, and multicultural groups — relegated to "social-affairs specialist" Karen Webb. The next day's *Globe* also had a teensy story on the minor players. "Opposition politicians and businessmen like the weekend agreement on the Meech Lake accord," it read, "but interest groups, especially those representing women and natives, are highly critical of it." Note that businessmen are not an interest group but women are. Interest-group coverage changed notably when Manitoba native MLA Elijah Harper, backed by native organizations, blocked the accord in the Manitoba legislature.

The Globe editorialized that "Native groups should see Meech Lake as an ally" and that "Natives would gain nothing from Meech Lake's end." In other words they may not know what's good for them but we do. The tone was forbearing. "Yes" — you could almost hear the sigh — "more has to be done." Meanwhile, on "The Journal," Barbara Frum was suggesting to Nelson Mandela that the sanctions he was calling for would hurt black South Africans most.

It was a relief, after weeks of suits, to see native leaders interviewed without ties, in polo shirts, talking deliberately and clearly. Or workers and fishermen in Newfoundland. My God, they can *think*. (CBC executive Trina McQueen explained later that the CBC had covered the vast opposition to Meech among "the people" by interviewing Clyde Wells sixty-nine times.) By June 17, on "Sunday Report," Simpson was bilious. Elijah Harper was "getting advice from sharp minds in Winnipeg.... He's getting advice from New Democrats who don't even live in Manitoba.... There are some Tories who are privately delighted ... some trendy Liberals in Winnipeg who are very keen." In *The Globe*, he named "Jack London and Deborah Coyne" as two of the manipulators. He was especially hard on Coyne, whose career he summarized as "worked unhappily ... felt unappreciated ... kicked around ... had dim prospects." The suggestion that Indians couldn't act without white legal advice was noted. "Well, I'm a lawyer," said one native leader.

In an exclusive interview with *The Globe* on June 12, Brian Mulroney had congratulated himself for "rolling the dice" on Meech with brilliant results. In the transcript, he used the term "the boys" often: "the boys" who made the original Confederation deal in Charlottetown; "the boys" who drank while they dickered. It was his view of politics. And you got a strong sense as he spoke — calling "Sunday Report" "your program" and flattering Jeffrey Simpson ("I guess that's a better way of putting it") — that he felt he was still with the boys, he was among friends. That's why he said things so damaging to the Meech accord that, said one crony, any decent press secretary would have thrown his body across the tape recorder.

As the deadline approached there wasn't much left, except to crank the tension machine tighter. Mulroney went to Newfoundland and threatened every plague except boils if Meech didn't pass. Premier McKenna said Quebeckers were ready to "vote with their blood" if it failed. Simpson loosed his jeremiads. "We all wish there was a better way," said a Newfoundlander. "But there is no other way," said the CBC reporter wrapping up. On June 23, when it went under, they all scrambled for cover. It turned out the sun would rise again. "Canada needs gentle tending," said *The Globe*. "Canada is still going to go on," said the country's leading business spokesman. Canada has the strength to survive, said the PM.

DAMAGE CONTROL IN THE AFTERMATH: This was their finest hour.

1. *Laying the Blame*. A culprit was needed to distract attention from the government's botch. Natives were too sympathetic. Manitoba's leaders were candidates: they *had* refused to ram Meech through. But in the end Wells won again. Senator Lowell Murray signalled this subtly on national television by waving a copy of the agreement Wells had signed. In a "Journal" interview the next Friday, Brian Mulroney contributed one of TV's tackiest moments when he too thrust Wells's signature under Barbara Frum's startled gaze. "This is his signature. This is the Meech Lake accord.... He cancelled the most fundamental and noble dimension of a democracy." (Minutes later, Mulroney said, "I haven't a word of criticism of him." Frum didn't even twitch.)

A day after Meech died, native leader Georges Erasmus was already complaining about these and other attempts to write his people out of the history that led to the accord's defeat. They were perfectly happy to take the rap.

2. *Rejection of Quebec, That's All*. On "Sunday Report" the same day, *chansonnier* Gilles Vigneault said, "We know what Canada wants. Canada wants we disappear." In an interview, Premier Bourassa had roughly the same explanation. Days later, Quebec City cancelled its Canada Day celebrations because, according to the mayor, Canada had slammed its door on Quebec's fingers. No reporter challenged this view, or mentioned the many other objections to Meech; before long it became commonplace. After the Houston economic summit, Mulroney said blandly that his fellow leaders were "baffled" by Meech's failure. It had become an irrational act of hatred and self-destruction.

3. *We Told You So*. This was difficult, since life did go on. The Canadian

dollar actually rose. "It will be weeks till Canadians feel the international reaction," said a CBC report hopefully. And one could still look forward to the disintegration of the country. Jeffrey Simpson wrote columns headed "The illusions of those Canadians who still think Quebec is bluffing" and "Just when you think things can't get any worse, they can get worse." He didn't so much predict disaster as demand it. He took to reading the souls of those who had failed, like that of McKenna, who "made a ghastly mistake ... that will torment him" as he watches "the demons of disunity running loose." Shortly after, Simpson went on holiday.

We Told You So, Part Two: Vive le Québec libre. The Globe's Montreal arts reporter, Stephen Godfrey, described "the province's increasingly serene and confident nationalism" at a St-Jean Baptiste Day concert. A week earlier he had written of his envy for Quebec's *vedette*/fanzines and a week later, after Canada Day, another *Globe* writer, Mark Miller, wrote about two Montreal musicians "who don't shy away from injecting politics into their music" under a headline reading "Quebeckers and proud of it." This wasn't exactly new in Quebec. But the artists protesting the War Measures Act back in 1970, or marking René Lévesque's death, or attending countless language demonstrations didn't get quite the same play in *The Globe*. Then, Quebec nationalism was an upstart, fought by federal and provincial governments and the business world. Supported now by the prime minister, his government, their own government, the *conseil du patronat*, and an opinion elite with a single voice — opposed apparently only by Indians and Newfoundlanders — the sentiments were hailed. (English-Canadian artists had been equally assertive against free trade, but I don't recall a single *Globe* article commenting on, much less admiring, them. Marcel Masse, however, was shocked that they didn't speak up for Meech. A *Globe* editorial and Jeffrey Simpson agreed.)

4. *Go Easy on the Boss.* When "The Journal" got *its* exclusive interview with Mulroney, Frum sounded like his therapist. "I think a lot of Canadians would like to hear you speak about this from a totally personal perspective.... This must be terribly frustrating." She set up his attacks on Wells ("I think Clyde Wells gave you supper at his house. Is that right?") and failed to challenge even his most preposterous statements ("You had some two percent of the population doing it in"). She let him ramble without interruption — in contrast to her style with, say, Wells on June 22, whom she "stopped just short of calling a liar," according to a TV critic. She handed Mulroney cues ("Was it just an indigestible amount of change for Canadians facing a world of too much change?"), which

he picked up ("Well, if you believe in a little Canada ... a timorous nation ... that can be protected against the winds of change that are now swirling ..."). She flattered ("You have been sensitive throughout to where Quebec is and where it's heading"). She ended with a word of care. "You really suffered throughout this. But people saw your face and you looked pretty grim, pretty dispirited.... What did that do to you?" Near the end, she asked what blame he accepted. He ducked easily. "One final note," said Frum. "Starting Monday I'm on holiday for the summer."

On "Sunday Report" of July 8, Peter Mansbridge announced the new *Globe and Mail*-CBC News poll. "Do Canadians think national unity is an important issue?" he asked. "They sure do." By forty-one percent, versus a mere twenty-three percent for the economy and a feeble seven percent for the environment, last February's winner. The effort had not been in vain.

If there is an emblem of the new dispensation, it is Peter Mansbridge. Last May, *Frank*, the disrespectful Ottawa biweekly, reported that Mansbridge and his wife, Wendy Mesley, were "frequent private dinner guests" of Brian and Mila, followed next issue by a dubious cover photo of the two couples in bed together. Mansbridge denied having intimate dinners with the Mulroneys, and *Frank* backed off — though they found evidence that Mansbridge wasn't quite accurate either.

Mansbridge is a true fit for the times. He treats the news like a new acquisition, a 4WD maybe. He starts broadcasts as if he's about to host a great party ("It's been a significant day for Canada"), and he ends by thanking us for coming (watching). In between he keeps moving things along ("Now ... Now ..."). He's a cooler version of the frenzied hosts on Global's "Sportsline." Maybe "The National" should change its name to "Newsline."

For years I've tried to figure out what irks me about the Mansbridge manner — for example, when he introduced the 1988 election debate saying, "So sit back and enjoy it. This is what the election is all about." I think I know. He tries to turn citizens into spectators. An election debate is not there for entertainment. It's there to help you decide how to participate in your society's decisions. When he says "Thanks for watching" — it's not up to him! People aren't doing him a favor. They're staying informed as an act of citizenship, a responsibility. Thanking them is a smarmy way to disarm them as citizens and transform them into mere viewers. As has happened in the U.S., where most people have given up on the political realm as anything but entertainment: a *bare* majority now vote and those who do often vote for the candidate who makes them feel good or puts on the best show. Maybe that was the underlying theme of the Meech coverage: the transformation of our politics into spectacle, so you stay glued to the drama, but it's not about anything that you can affect or is likely to affect you. Politics as culture. Wondering what'll happen next — like "Twin Peaks."

The July/August issue of *The Globe*'s *Toronto* magazine had Mansbridge on the cover, in a suit, in a lawn chair, posing as relaxed. Inside, Peter and Wendy tell what they like to do in the summer. Wendy, "national-affairs correspondent" of the people's network, says to readers of Canada's National Newspaper, "I like to go to Riverdale Park and watch the ducks on the pond. First I go to the ice-cream store on the corner and buy an ice-cream cone." At last, at long last — a moment when words fail.

Certainly, there are people working at the CBC and *The Globe and Mail* who are conscientious and give the government occasional fits. Perhaps even those in the upper reaches — the ones we know about when they go on holiday — don't think they're part of a ministry of propaganda. Maybe they could pass a lie-detector test on whether they're there to serve the government. In a functional analysis it doesn't really matter. It may even work better that way. After all, the propaganda agencies of Eastern Europe were totally ineffective — because everybody *knew* they were doing government PR. In fact, the only effective propaganda agencies are probably the ones that officially don't even exist.

24
Audrey Thomas
PERIL BY THE LAKE

$\mathbf{A}$S A general rule the English don't like the French very much ("Wogs begin at Calais"), but they don't hesitate to borrow a word or two of the French language if they think it will add a touch of class. (You won't find much *cake*, for example, in even the most modest of English tearooms, but there's bound to be a selection of *gâteaux*.) Thus it was that, when I found myself in the comfortable seat of a *Rapide* coach, I was not off on an adventure in the French countryside but heading out of London's Victoria Coach Station on the National Express bus bound for the English Lakes. I had just seen my youngest daughter off on her first great solo adventure (she was to be an *au pair* for a year in Toulouse) and as I stood there watching her boat train pull out I thought, "From now on, she will only come home as a visitor," and I felt a little blue. Not indigo, mind you — all my daughters are great letter writers and telephoners — but a bit wistful, the pale blue of the smoke from a solitary cigarette, perhaps. My solution for this feeling is always to get moving, and as I didn't have to be in Edinburgh for another ten days I decided to make a little walking tour of the Lake District, a place I'd never been. As almost everything I needed for the coming year had already been sent ahead to Scotland I had only to pick up my pack, buy an ordnance-survey map of the district, splurge on a good pair of boots, and be on my way.

A hostess checked our tickets as we boarded: blue skirt, white blouse, red jacket. (The bus was white with a red and blue logo.) Later she changed into a red "pinny," or apron, as she made sandwiches on request and served coffee, tea, and juice. ("Hello, me name's Angela. If you need anything just give me a shout.") She came from Whitehaven, quite near Cockermouth, where Wordsworth was born, and I wondered if William and Dorothy had sounded like this; if Dorothy had called him to supper with "Tea oop, Wil-yum." After all, Keats spoke with a Cockney accent, something our high-school English teachers forgot to mention when pointing out the beauties of his written English.

I was extremely lucky to be sitting next to a woman who actually came from Cockermouth, although she had travelled widely and had what I always think of as a Third Program accent, which dates me — "Radio 4 accent" I suppose they say these days. She gave me all sorts of advice (be sure to go to Wast Water, the deepest and most dismal lake in England, make Keswick your base for a few days, see Grasmere at all costs — lovely in spite of the tourists). I was also lucky in that the video was broken: Angie was sorry but we wouldn't be able to watch *The Prince and the Showgirl.* This meant my seatmate and I could actually talk to one another without shouting. We hurled up the motorways, past the exit to Birmingham, where I had taught school and had married many years ago, did a quick whip around Lancaster, and were soon into the Lakes themselves. Hills were "fells," said my companion (from the Old Norse word *fjall*), brooks were "becks," and valleys, "dales." A small mountain lake was a "tarn." From a distance the fells (which can rise in sharp crags, or "pikes," to over three thousand feet) looked like enormous lichen-covered rocks. I later saw that this was the bracken, turning brown. We skirted lakes, including one, Thirlmere, where an entire village was drowned in 1894 in order to build a dam and raise the water level fifty feet for a reservoir. (Long after Wordsworth's and Coleridge's time, or think of the poems we might have had about that!) In 1984, the driest English summer on record, the water level was so low that you could see the village. How strange it must have been to look down into that clear water and see what might have been a reflection, except that there was nothing on the banks to be reflected.

The green of the dales was a very acidic green, because of all the rain in 1985. The bus, large as it was, negotiated the narrow mountainous roads with ease. I had an impression of stone fences and black-faced sheep. The woman on the bus said that the Victorians, in their pictures and descriptions, used to exaggerate the heights of the fells and the depths of the lakes to make them appear more romantic, but it all seemed very romantic to me, face pressed against the window of the moving bus. Although I'd had no particular destination (I'd bought a ticket through to Whitehaven, the last stop), I decided to get down at Keswick and find a bed and breakfast place before dusk. Because these express buses have a hostess and a toilet on board, there are no "rest stops" and they halt only to pick up or let down passengers. When I stepped off the *Rapide* I could barely walk; I'd been on the bus for nearly six hours.

Keswick ("Kessick") is one of the three top holiday resorts in the Lake District and the base for serious walkers and rock climbers. I use "serious" in the English sense, as in "serious money." We're talking serious walking here. I am not a serious walker in any sense and at first, as I walked through the town after finding a bed and breakfast on a quiet street, I was awed and a little put off by the *real* walkers with their great muscular thighs and well-worn boots. Ordnance-survey maps hung in large plastic wallets around their necks and their eyes seemed to be fixed on distant hills. I felt like Gulliver among the Brobdingnagians and remembered a friend of mine, who is a real walker and climber, and a guidebook about which he wrote me. I couldn't remember where the walks were located, but he said he enjoyed reading of one called "An Easy Day for a Lady." The tourist information office was closed, but I decided that first thing the next morning I would go there and get some advice. I suppose I had had, in my mind's eye, the lakes without the hills that surrounded them, or without *these* hills. "Fell" now seemed to me an ominous word, as in "she fell."

After a walk around the stone-built town (Southey lived here at one point, as did Coleridge, his brother-in-law; and the Wordsworths often came to visit), I had dinner in a vegetarian restaurant full of the proud walkers and went back to the place where I was staying. The landlord, who turned out to be an expert on old theater organs, offered me tea and biscuits and told me there were not only fell walkers but fell runners as well and great races every year to see who could run up and down in the least time. There were more mountain rescues in the Lake District than anywhere else in Britain. However, I would be fine if I stayed off the fells themselves.

He was right — or ninety percent right. At the tourist office the next morning I bought some small local maps and decided to do a circular walk around Derwent Water. All the footpaths were clearly marked, as well as bridges, farm tracks, and stiles. I've walked in England before and one of the lovely things is the great number of public rights of way. Some of these date back hundreds of years and the right to use them is fiercely defended, although some farmers, naturally enough, resent it. Because most of the Lake District is a vast national park, it turned out that there were endless walks from easy to hard that one could take without risk of breaking one's leg or neck on the fells. The walk around Derwent Water would take about five-and-a-half hours. If it started to pour or if

I got tired I only had to head out of the woods to one of the small jetties where a regular boat made request stops.

Until very near the end of the walk — say four-fifths of the way through — the day was everything I had hoped it would be. I bought a blue rain jacket in the town, one with a hood and long enough to come down to the backs of my knees so I could, if I chose, sit on walls or logs without getting a wet behind. Into the large pockets of the jacket I stuffed maps large and small, my small cartons of juice, a Granny Smith apple, a poetry anthology, my notebook, and my pen. *Fol de re, fol de rol*, off I went.

Although the ground was extremely wet and the footpaths were stony and slippery in places, when I climbed up Friar's Crag with the high blue hills to the west, the crag walk to the east, and the Jaws of Borrowdale ahead, any last traces of my blue mood disappeared and I knew I was getting what I came for. There was hardly anyone about (presumably they were all out rock climbing or fell running) and at what I judged to be lunch time I sat on a mossy stump, eating an apple and reading *The Prelude*:

Fair seed-time had my soul, and I grew up
Fostered alike by beauty and by fear:
Much favoured in my birth-place, and no less
In that belovèd Vale to which erelong
We were transplanted.

I began to understand about the fear as well as the beauty — would understand it even more after I'd been to the dreadful Wast Water and up over Hardknott Pass: this was not a countryside you could simply take for granted. When the young Wordsworth steals the little boat and rows out into a lake on a summer evening, all of a sudden "a huge peak, black and huge ... upreared its head." It seemed to stride after him and in a state of fear and trembling he quickly makes his way back to shore. We tend to forget that stuff and remember instead the dancing daffodils.

And then, in the late afternoon, I had my own small and ridiculous encounter with fear. I came to a bit of the path that had been completely flooded out by the recent rains and I couldn't quite see how to get across. I went farther inland, away from the lake, but the situation was the same. On the other side of this boggy bit three black-faced sheep stood and stared at me. "Go on," they seemed to say, "it's quite narrow right here. Just jump across. Nothing to it." I jumped

— and sank into a bog up to and beyond my knees. Then I found I couldn't pull myself out. No matter how hard I tried the bog kept its tight grip on my legs, like some powerful dog with no teeth but terrible gums. I was now somewhat off the beaten track and nobody came along. Because I was not fell walking, I had with me neither flashlight nor whistle, both mandatory on the hills. Besides, if I blew the correct signal, would the rescue team proceed to an area which really was an easy day out? I had recently seen the fellow the natural-history experts had jokingly named Pete Marsh. There he was in the museum, in his glass case, perfectly preserved and stained the color of a cured tobacco leaf. I had no desire to be known as "The Bog Lady" to generations to come. I told myself not to be silly: this wasn't a real bog, simply a boggy area. Help would eventually arrive.

And then I heard a dog bark and soon saw a large collie bounding towards me. He was followed by a fast-striding woman in a green mac and a man's old felt hat. "Hello, hello," I called out, "can you give me a hand, I'm stuck!" Startled, she looked over in my direction, thought for a few seconds, then whistled the collie back to her and resumed her stride. "The boat's just comin' in," she called over her shoulder, "there'll be others along no doubt." I couldn't believe it; she was going to leave me there. To my right, out of sight, I could hear the faint putt-putt of the little launch pulling up to Hawes End Pier. The woman had managed to skirt the boggy bit and so had her collie. She probably thought I had got what I deserved. (I told myself to remember that the reason why the parable of the Good Samaritan is so important is that there were Bad Samaritans as well.)

Fifteen minutes later I was rescued — by a farmer and his son. They were both wearing enormous Wellington boots. Each extended a brawny right arm — "Hold on, lass, we'll get you out" — and out I came. The bog let me go with a dreadful sucking sound and I completed the rest of my journey with my cold, evil-smelling trousers clinging to my legs.

The landlord and his wife were all concern. I sat in a blanket and listened to Wurlitzer music while he cleaned my boots and she washed my trousers and hung them in the back passage to drip. They didn't laugh and I told myself, as I often do in situations like this, "It's all material." That evening I put on my only other outfit and my runners and, for revenge, had a grand meal of local lamb chops at a good restaurant.

That was my only big adventure in my ten days in the Lakes. I did a lot of walking and some riding: on local buses, Royal Main vans, and, for a day, on "the mountain goat," a minivan that took me and five others over Hardknott Pass (where, in the middle of nowhere, we saw two white high-heeled shoes side by side at the edge of a mountain stream) and to Hardknott Roman Fort. The soldiers who inhabited the fort had marched all the way from what is now Yugoslavia. I stood among the ruins on an eight-hundred-foot plateau looking up at the fell above and wondered, surveying the desolate scene, what those soldiers had done to amuse themselves once they had arrived. There was a parade ground above, so presumably they marched up and down, cleaned their weapons, and told each other stories of their villages back in Dalmatia. Hardknott was not a peaceful place and in winter it must be dreadful.

Before I went to Kendal to catch a bus north to Edinburgh, I made a personal pilgrimage to Grasmere, in the very center of the Lake District. This is where William and Dorothy Wordsworth lived from 1799 to 1813. The rain was pouring down the morning I arrived, and I decided the first thing I would look for would be a good cup of tea. But then, as the wind changed direction slightly, I smelled fresh-baked gingerbread. I have a weakness for gingerbread of any kind — our North American variety is more a dark cake than the true gingerbread of Europe — so I followed my nose and came to a little shop, Sarah Nelson's Shop, at the north entrance of the very churchyard where the Wordsworths are buried. The woman behind the counter told me that in Wordsworth's day the building had been a little school and Wordsworth himself had taught there briefly. Although she did not serve tea, she offered me a mug from her own pot, and, armed with gingerbread-for-now and a packet of gingerbread-for-later safe in my waterproof pocket, I went into the churchyard and stood for a minute or two, eating gingerbread and looking at the simple graves. William lies here, and his wife Mary, their two children who died as children, and his sister Dorothy. I had been reading the journals of Dorothy Wordsworth and was more and more convinced that, without her, William, and perhaps even Coleridge, would not have been half the poets they were. As a feminist I'm always interested in just who is baking the bread and pies and doing the washing up while the poets are busy with the muse. Dorothy did an enormous amount of baking of bread and pies. But she was also passionately in love with the countryside around here, a great walker, and most generous with her observations. (It was she who first described the "dancing" daffodils.) I suspect that she was also, like Coleridge, a heavy user of laudanum and the end of her life was sad.

I stood in the churchyard eating my gingerbread, the rain streaming down, and said a little prayer for all of them. They wouldn't have minded about the gingerbread; the Wordsworths were partial to it themselves: "Sunday the 16th January [1803]. Intensely cold. Wm. had a fancy for some gingerbread I put on Molly's Cloak and my Spenser and we walked towards Matthew Newton's ... they took their little stock of gingerbread out of the cubboard and I bought 6 pennyworth."

From that morning on whenever I think of Wordsworth I think not of the shades of the prison house or leech gatherers or even daffodils but of St. Oswald's churchyard, of gingerbread in the rain, and a kind of unexpected communion with those sleepers under the brown Cumbrian soil. But that is what travel is all about, is it not? Finding the unexpected links with those who have been this way before.

25
William Thorsell
LET US COMPARE
MYTHOLOGIES

E ARLY in March 1990, Paul Martin Jr., who was for some reason seeking the leadership of the Liberal party, said this about Canada: "We have declared war on ourselves. We are engaged in a civil war of monumental proportions that simply staggers the mind. East versus West, western alienation against the center, English versus French — whatever can divide us, we build a monument to it."

Civil war overstates it, but Canada is experiencing doubts about its future that are unparalleled in history. Unparalleled because, unlike the period of the Quebec referendum 10 years ago, the doubts are spread across a broad swath of Canadians, in all sectors of society and all regions of the country. They are unparalleled because, in some particulars, it is difficult to imagine a way to escape them.

How can we explain such angst at a time when Canada's economy is still strong on its feet after seven years of healthy growth and the national government is secure with a second working majority? Does it all come down to our conflict over constitutional negotiations with Quebec — known as the Meech Lake accord? I think not, for while that conflict is serious, the distress of the Canadian people runs too wide and deep to be explained by one variable alone, no matter how important. In many ways, our constitutional conflict is a symptom, not a cause, of our problems.

Instead of focusing on specific issues, I want to explore what you might call the atmospherics of Canada's sour mood today — the context. I will argue that

Canada's distress in 1990 cannot be understood without appreciating how much the basic moorings of Canada have been loosened by a series of largely unrelated events. We Canadians have experienced the collapse of several major ideals or mythologies that, until recently, helped to sustain Canada's sense of nationhood. The collapse of these ideals signals the death of Canada as we *knew* it, which is obviously very unsettling to many people. I do not think that Canada as we *know* it is therefore dead or doomed, but the question is certainly in the air.

Somewhere in the world today, there may be a country that is not profoundly changing, or that is not at least confused in a sea of change around it. I might have cited such an example of stolidity in Mongolia, until February when *The Globe and Mail*'s China correspondent visited that vague and forgotten land only to report that it, too, is riding a crest of social change — from green-sequined dancers on local TV to a multiparty system in Ulan Bator.

I am forced therefore, to cling to Albania, Cuba, and the Shining Path guerrillas of Peru as islands of stability in a stream of change — and they are only small islands, surely destined to erode under the insistent pressure that humans feel for individual freedom, the pressure of a global information network, and the seductive power of world consumer culture.

Canada, then, is not alone as it grapples with the suddenly shifting foundations of its nationhood and identity. The same forces of globalization that disorient so many other countries are playing themselves out in Canada to the general consternation of its people, most of whom would prefer that the future get back where it belongs. But Canada adds its own disturbances.

Let me march quickly through the main traditional myths of Canadian nationhood — myths well rooted in fact once upon a time, but now detached, more obviously every day, from the realities of life as we experience it. These are dead or dying myths, some more important than others, but few of them publicly recognized by our national leaders as having run their course. I will start with a small and simple one.

MYTH NUMBER ONE says that Canada is a constitutional monarchy in which the head of state is a king or queen.

Like it or not, this is simply a fiction in the minds of most Canadians who do not conceive of their country as a monarchy, or Elizabeth II as Canada's head of state, or Prince Charles as its king-in-waiting. The deep monarchist sentiments of some Canadians aside — and I fully respect them — this point hardly needs expansion it is so obvious a fact in our national life.

I would go as far as to say that, in the unconscious minds of most Canadians, Canada no longer *has* a head of state. There is only a governor-general representing an anachronism — a shadow symbolizing a memory at the pinnacle of the nation. No leading Canadian politician is willing to say it, but the myth of the monarchy is essentially dead, and our failure to admit it leaves our country headless.

MYTH NUMBER TWO says that Canada is a duality — the product of two founding peoples, English and French, who came together in 1867 to form Confederation "from sea unto shining sea."

This is the core, binding myth of Canadian nationhood taught in every school (insofar as schools teach history any more). Precisely because this mythology is so fundamental, very few of Canada's leaders, including its academics, artists, and journalists, dare to suggest that this ideal has also seen its best day. (I must observe here that academics and journalists are among the most powerful agents of the status quo in any free society, so their conservative role in this case is entirely predictable.) One need only walk awake through the streets and fields of our country to know that the myth of duality, too, is cracking and breaking under the weight of our daily experience.

It is not that duality is untrue, but that it is hopelessly incomplete. Our aboriginal peoples — Inuit, Indian, and Métis — challenge the model of two founding peoples that excludes them. They were, after all, here first and there is no logical or moral ground to oppose them on this point. (Members of the government of the Northwest Territories recently dared to ask why English and French were the official languages in the North to the exclusion of native ones.) Less obvious, but just as tenacious, is the historic and growing presence within Canada of other national backgrounds and races who also see themselves as "founding" peoples.

The prairie West was largely settled by the ancestors of its current population, a whole generation *after* the original Confederation of 1867. The West was settled, not as a compact between the two founding peoples, but as a compact among many peoples, notably from continental and central Europe. Western Canadians have never been satisfied to see themselves as late arrivals at someone else's party, and who can blame them? The same can be said of hundreds of thousands of recent immigrants from all over the world who are still coming to Canada's major urban centers. More than 50% of our immigrants now arrive from Asia, Africa, and the Caribbean.

Canada is not four original provinces frozen in time that can project one moment of their history onto the rest of the land. Canada is 10 provinces, two territories, at least five regions, three city states, many new generations of citizens, and continuing immigration from increasingly exotic places in a bewildering flux of time. Canada is alive, and unless we see it as alive, we will not keep it alive.

Still, hardly anyone in a position of national influence dares to acknowledge fully that duality is too narrow and dated a concept to contain the reality of Canada as we actually live it. We have invested too much since the 1960s in the historically limited concept of duality to raise common-sense questions about this without scaring ourselves half to death.

As in the case of the monarchy, the collapse of this myth happens in private hearts long before its public funeral. People in the streets are beginning to recognize that the concept of Canada as a duality is essentially academic in most areas of the country — the word "official" in the phrase "official bilingualism" says it all — but we have not yet created another workable concept to take its place. At the heart of our national mythology, then, we are stuck in the purgatory of pretense that we are something considerably simpler than we actually are. The duality of Canada — which is a truth, but far from the whole truth — is an ideal that is dying on the vine. It leaves our country — which is already headless — drifting without a functioning sense of its own history.

MYTH NUMBER THREE says that, unlike the United States, Canada has a mixed economy split between large, state-owned enterprises and private firms. It is habitually said that, without the state-owned firms, there would be no Canada. *L'état, c'est le Crown corporation.*

This myth was quite well founded in history. It grew out of the railroads that were built as a condition of union in 1867 to bind together a far-flung country. It does not matter that the railroads were mostly private undertakings in their beginnings that had to be bailed out of bankruptcy through enormous public subsidies, or nationalized to be saved. The railroads emerged as important symbols of successful national action to build one Canada that could stand independent of the United States in North America.

This symbolism became so powerful that it was imposed on airlines when the time came for a national air system in the 1930s. Despite the intense desire by private entrepreneurs to establish national airlines themselves, Canada's government insisted on a publicly owned air monopoly in the 1930s as another tie to bind the nation.

Electric utilities, telephone systems, hotels, aircraft manufacturing firms, oil companies and, of course, a national broadcasting corporation, were added to the stable of public companies meant to serve as bulwarks of Canadian nation-hood in North America. Crown corporations were the flesh on the bones of the state, and in their time, some of these undertakings served their purpose quite well. Now this national security blanket has also been pulled off the bed. For better or worse, the days of economic nationalism appear to be gone.

Privatization of public companies is just one part of a rushing stream of glob-al change that is *de*-nationalizing economics. You can take the cue from the very word "multinational," which describes the main economic engines of the modern world — stateless corporations whose homes are where they find their fat. Throw in the computer revolution that integrates world financial markets, freer trade through the GATT, common markets, multinational passports in Europe, international TV and the vast mobility of modern man and woman in the age of the 747, and the denationalization of economics knocks a giant prop out from beneath all countries that have counted on economic nationalism to define themselves.

Think of Mexico, Argentina, Brazil, central Europe, China, and the Soviet Union, and the Canadian experience is just a side show in a much bigger play. But, of course, it is *our* side show, so it matters.

Our 1988 election debate over free trade with the United States forced us to face up to the myths of economic nationalism much more squarely than those of the monarchy or two founding peoples. We are now trying to articulate new economic ideals calling for excellence, innovation, and global competitiveness for Canadian individuals and firms. But the death of the mixed economy in fact, and the acceptance of economic continentalism through free trade by treaty, are still causing a crisis of identity among many Canadians and nostalgia for a Canada we thought we knew just ten years ago. Headless, and without a func-tioning sense of history, many Canadians are also feeling a distinct lack of meat on their economic bones.

Now I must turn to our fluttering hearts. Other traditional mythologies are also fading at visible cost to our sense of Canadian identity and pride. They include the myth of the helpful fixer in international affairs, where Canadians saw them-selves as good-guy mediators serving the interests of peace and justice among bigger powers. We often think of Lester Pearson in the 1950s, but this is the

1990s. Too many new players have arrived on the world scene for Canada to play convincingly its role as Mother Teresa any more.

There is also the myth of Canada, the kinder, gentler nation — to borrow a phrase — than the United States, embodying peace, order and good government, humanized by universal medicare, unemployment insurance, old age security, children's allowances and regional development programs. Canadians' hearts are still in the right places here, but their national treasury is empty.

As debts and deficits continue to grow, even universal social programs erode before the need for solvency and the public's resistance to higher taxes. One of the strongest arguments made for universal social programs is the sense of common interest and citizenship they give to everyone in the country. Now this is under pressure, and many Canadians worry that we may be losing our heart in the financial crush.

A troubled heart, no head, a poorly functioning history, meat melting from the bones — you can begin to understand the extent of Canada's angst.

And if that is not enough, I would say that democracy itself must be added to the list of ideals in doubt in certain parts of Canada. In the western and Atlantic provinces particularly, many people feel that democracy does not function at all well at the national level. Unlike most federations, we have representation by population in the House of Commons in Ottawa, unbalanced by a legitimate Senate speaking up for regional interests. It is shocking but true to say that the ideal of democracy — which lies at the heart of our body politic — is now questioned by many thoughtful Canadians. That's how deep the malaise has gone.

All this adds up to a volatile, destabilizing mood in Canada, which would be difficult enough to manage without the additional crisis of the Meech Lake accord. This set of constitutional amendments was unanimously endorsed three years ago by the Prime Minister and ten provincial Premiers. It was a kind of "second marriage" ceremony between Quebec and the rest of Canada, seen by many as a necessary outcome of the 1980 Quebec referendum on sovereignty-association. Under Canada's constitutional amending formula, Meech Lake must be ratified by everyone by June 23. Now it looks as though it will not be ratified by three provinces that have changed governments since 1987 — Manitoba, New Brunswick, and Newfoundland.

If Meech Lake fails, an unprecedented consensus will exist within the leadership of Quebec — including even the business community — that something else must be done to establish a modern relationship between Quebec and Canada. Most of the talk revolves around some version of the European Community, and the talk is very public, involving everyone from the Premier of Quebec to artists and bankers. Time will tell how long it lasts and how far it extends into the public, but a recent poll in Quebec says that 58% of the population — a historic high— favors sovereignty.

We are also seeing a significant change in mood among English-speaking Canadians outside Quebec. In 1980, English-speaking Canadians everywhere fought hard and passionately to keep Quebec within the country. These positive feelings are eroding.

The goodwill of many English-Canadian nationalists towards Quebec has been drained by Quebec's strong embrace of free trade with the United States in the 1988 federal election. This is seen as a betrayal of Canada by those who equate free trade with political submission to the United States. Many economic nationalists feel that Quebec is no longer on Canada's side.

The goodwill of other anglophones has been drained by Quebec's vigorous policies in defence of the French language in that province, including a ban on English on outdoor commercial signs. These English-speaking Canadians had accepted the ideal of official bilingualism in their own provinces, and sent their children to French immersion schools as a personal act of nation building. Now they, too, feel betrayed by what they see as Quebec's unforgivable attack on the individual rights of its anglophones. Many of these people feel that Quebec has made them look like fools.

Finally, the goodwill of many Canadians outside Quebec has been drained by a perception that the Meech Lake accord gives Quebec favored legal status among the provinces — a status many anglophones feel Quebec already exploits in the economic sphere through excessive claims on Ottawa's purse strings. Many people feel that Quebec is picking their pockets.

Never in our postwar history has English-speaking Canada felt cooler to Quebec as a partner in nationhood. And never in our postwar history have Quebec's political, intellectual, and economic elites felt more *common* cause in testing the rest of Canada's desire for continued union. Canada as we knew it assumed that a clear majority of Canadians ultimately preferred partnership within one country to partnership between sovereign states. This assumption has prevailed over many tests and challenges, including that of René Lévesque and the Parti Québécois in 1980. Remove this assumption — and for the first time, it is eroding on *both* sides of the cultural divide — and Canada as we knew it could die in more than myth and emotion.

What are our political leaders doing in this increasingly chippy game? For the most part, they are sticking to a rigid strategy of defence. The more Canadians are buffeted by change, the more fervently their leaders exhort them to cling to old verities. Day after day in Parliament, we hear calls from the various political parties to resurrect the mythologies of economic nationalism, Crown corporations, the duality of Canada and official bilingualism as the saviors of Canadian nationhood. An occasional voice even suggests we rally around the Queen, but a rally requires more than a dozen people. None of this addresses what really needs to be done. Indeed, it exacerbates the sense of unreality that already has the nation so much on edge.

A particularly depressing example of this occurred in February when Prime Minister Brian Mulroney threw everything he had into one small drawer of the status quo. He said — and I quote — "Simply put, Canada is the coming together of English and French-speaking Canadians, and our future lies in the continuing will to live together.... This country will rise or fall on the bilingual nature of its character. What is Canada without it? There's no country; it's like an adjunct of the United States. If you dispose of bilingualism, if you dispose of the protection of minority language rights, then you have dealt a lethal blow to the fundamental tenet of our nationhood."

I believe this is a gross overstatement, indeed, a dangerous gross overstatement. The bilingual nature of Canada is an attractive and important asset, but I don't think most Canadians believe it's the *sine qua non* of our national identity. I don't think most Canadians believe, to quote the Prime Minister, that "there's no country" without official bilingualism. There was a country called Canada long before bilingualism appeared as a policy in 1969, and this country is rooted in much broader ground than that. I firmly support official bilingualism at the federal level, but little in our experience over the last 25 years indicates that it is an essential force for keeping Canada together, within Quebec or elsewhere. It's a good and natural policy at the federal level, and a good policy in some provincial arenas, but it simply cannot bear the weight of our nationhood from sea to sea.

Mulroney is just as silly in saying that our Constitution is "not worth the paper it is written on" because one clause allows legal exemption from the Charter of Rights and Freedoms under certain conditions. Such hyperbole does not serve the nation well in a time of confusion when Canadians desperately need a ring of truth.

Like Argentina, Canada is a richly endowed country sparsely populated by intelligent and cultured people. But we know from observing Argentina that, even with such advantages, things can go terribly wrong. Some observers feel Canadians have developed a bad habit of hectoring and bitchiness akin to masochism. We nurture the chips on our shoulders until they become humps on our backs. Yes, we have bad habits, but I am suggesting that more rational explanations exist for our current malaise. We are clinging too loyally to Canada as we knew it, and too cautiously to Canada as we were told to know it.

Canada as it actually is need not be an inferior place. On the contrary: Canada is a fully independent, multicultural society, comprising distinctive regions — dare I say, a community of communities — where two major language groups predominate in certain geographic areas, which should be confident enough of their majority rights to value the various minorities among them.

In this context, I firmly support the Meech Lake accord, whose contents have been carelessly distorted and whose ratification is justified in history and in law. The great preponderance of evidence shows that Quebec, when secure in its identity, will be comfortable within Canada and at least as fair as any other province to its minorities. Quebec sees Meech Lake as a test of Canada's political maturity, and I share Quebec's judgment on that. Let's not lose our country in a fit of pique.

Accepting the distinctive cultural histories of regions outside Quebec would also make it easier for the rest of the country to live in a more generous national spirit. And it would make it easier to fight the racism stimulated by immigration and the growing presence of visible minorities across the land. People who are secure in their own sense of history tend to be less suspicious of social change. In any case, the history of much of Canada is one of multiculturalism in the first place. Acceptance of diversity is bred in our bone.

At the same time, our leadership groups — including artists, intellectuals, and even journalists — must stop being so much part of the problem in refusing to face up to change. Whether it be economic nationalism, the nature of social programs, the state of Canada's democracy or the monarchy, the truth will out. Leaders do not deny truth: they work to give it meaning. It is their responsibility to articulate new national ideals that can ease our passage to the future and broaden the consensus needed to reform our federal institutions.

I said at the outset that the death of Canada as we *knew* it need not mean the death of Canada as we *know* it. The fundamental threat to Canada is not intolerance — though awful intolerance there be — but hypocrisy. We have nothing to fear from the truth about our national situation and character, but our leaders keep telling us tales. If we stop lying about ourselves, I believe we can get away from warring among ourselves, and go back to our more familiar national wrestling matches. Wrestling matches give us much better odds on settling our problems. And we have reasons to be optimistic about Canada if we have the wits to be frank. Like Sigmund Freud, I believe the truth can set you free.

NOTES ON THE AUTHORS

MARGARET ATWOOD is the author of such acclaimed works of fiction as *The Edible Woman* and *Cat's Eye* as well as *Survival: A Thematic Guide to Canadian Literature* and *Second Words: Selected Critical Prose*.

PETER BEHRENS is the author of *Night Driving*, a collection of stories. He was born in Montreal and now lives in California.

CLARK BLAISE is the author of several books of fiction, notably *Lunar Attractions* and *Resident Alien*. Born in the United States, he has lived in Canada for long periods of time.

ROSE BORRIS was born in New Brunswick. Paulette Jiles is the author of several books of fiction and poetry, including *Celestial Navigation* and *Sitting in the Club Car Drinking Rum and Karma-Kola*.

SHARON BUTALA is the author of the novels *Luna*, *The Gates of the Sun*, and *Country of the Heart*. She was born in northern Saskatchewan and now lives on a ranch in southwest Saskatchewan.

DALTON CAMP is a former president of the national Progressive Conservative Party who appears regularly on radio and television as a political commentator. He lives in New Brunswick.

DENISE CHONG lives in London, England. She is at work on a book based on her essay "The Concubine's Children."

ANN DIAMOND lives in Montreal. Her publications include *Snakebite*, a collection of stories, and *Mona's Dance*, a novel.

MOIRA FARR is a freelance writer and editor whose work has appeared in *Toronto Life*, *This Magazine*, *Canadian Business*, and *Registered Nurse*. She lives in Toronto.

DON GILLMOR is the author of *I Swear by Apollo: Dr. Ewen Cameron and the CIA Brainwashing Experiments*. A regular contributor to *Saturday Night*, he has also written for *Rolling Stone* and *Reader's Digest*. He lives in Montreal.

HUGH GRAHAM is a freelance writer who lives in Toronto.

ERNEST HILLEN was born in Indonesia and was interned in a Japanese prison camp during World War II. He lives in Toronto and works as an editor for *Saturday Night*.

MICHAEL IGNATIEFF is the author of *The Needs of Strangers* and *The Russian Album*, which won the Governor General's Award for Nonfiction in 1987. He lives in London, England, where he works for the BBC and *The Observer*.

MARNI JACKSON lives in Toronto. Her writing appears regularly in *Saturday Night* and *This Magazine*.

M.T. KELLY is the author of *Breath Dances Between Them* and *A Dream Like Mine*, which received the Governor General's Award for Fiction in 1987 and has been made into the movie *Clearcut*. He lives in Toronto.

MYRNA KOTASH is the author of *All of Baba's Children* and *No Kidding*. She lives in Edmonton.

DAVID MACFARLANE is a former associate editor of *Saturday Night* and the author of *The Danger Tree*.

JOYCE MARSHALL is the author of two novels, *Presently Tomorrow* and *Lovers and Strangers*, as well as the collection of stories *A Private Place*. She received the Governor General's Award for her translation of Gabrielle Roy's *Enchanted Summer*.

JOYCE NELSON is the author of five non-fiction books including *The Perfect Eye: TV in the Nuclear Age* and *Sultans of Sleaze: Public Relations and the Media*. She lives in Victoria.

DAVID OLIVE is the editor of *The Report on Business* magazine published by *The Globe and Mail*.

STEPHEN PHELPS is a contributing editor of *Border Crossings* and the founding director of Main/Access Gallery in Winnipeg.

JANE RULE is the author of such novels as *Memory Board, Outlander*, and *A Hot-Eyed Moderate* as well as the collection of stories *Inland*. She lives on Galiano Island.

RICK SALUTIN is a playwright, novelist, and critic whose works include *1837: The Farmer's Revolt, Les Canadiens*, and *Marginal Notes*. He lives in Toronto.

AUDREY THOMAS is the author of such critically acclaimed works of fiction as *Real Mothers* and *Intertidal Life*. She lives on Galiano Island.

WILLIAM THORSELL is editor-in-chief of *The Globe and Mail*.

ACKNOWLEDGEMENTS

"If You Can't Say Something Nice, Don't Say Anything At All" by Margaret Atwood is reprinted from *Language in Her Eye* (Coach House Press) by permission of the author.

"Refugee Dreams" by Peter Behrens is reprinted from *Saturday Night* by permission of the author.

"The Border as Fiction" by Clark Blaise is reprinted from Borderlands Monograph Series #4, Borderlands Project, University of Maine (1990), by permission of the author.

"At a Loss for Words" by Rose Borris with Paulette Jiles is reprinted from *Saturday Night* by permission of the authors.

"Field of Broken Dreams" by Sharon Butala is reprinted from *West* by permission of the author.

"The Plot to Kill Canada" by Dalton Camp is reprinted from *Saturday Night* by permission of the author.

"The Concubine's Children" by Denise Chong is reprinted from *Saturday Night* by permission of the author.

"Zen in America" by Ann Diamond is reprinted from the *Macmillan Anthology III* by permission of the author.

"Women and Wanderlust" by Moira Farr is reprinted from *This Magazine* by permission of the author.

"Clues" by Don Gillmor is reprinted from *Saturday Night* by permission of the author.

"Life and Death in Ontario County" by Hugh Graham is reprinted from *The Idler* by permission of the author.

"Back on Java" by Ernest Hillen is reprinted from *Saturday Night* by permission of the author.

"August in My Father's House" by Michael Ignatieff is reprinted from *Granta* by permission of the author.

"Gals and Dolls: The Moral Value of 'Bad' Toys" by Marni Jackson is reprinted from *This Magazine* by permission of the author.